LEAVING

THE SURFACE

Also by
Sydney J. Harris

Strictly Personal
Majority of One
Last Things First
On the Contrary

LEAVING
THE SURFACE

By Sydney J. Harris

HOUGHTON MIFFLIN COMPANY

BOSTON

1968

To my mother
and the memory of my father

"We . . . live this mean life we do because our vision does not penetrate the surface of things . . . Let us settle ourselves, and work and wedge our feet downward through the mud and slush of opinion, and prejudice, and tradition . . . till we come to a hard bottom and rocks in place, which we can call *reality* . . . Most have not delved six feet beneath the surface . . . yet we esteem ourselves wise, and have an established order on the surface."

— THOREAU

CONTENTS

LEAVING
THE SURFACE

I

OF THE LIFE
OF THE SPIRIT

How the Authentic Self Is Hidden

THE PERSONALITY of man is not an apple that has to be polished, but a banana that has to be peeled. And the reason we remain so far from one another, the reason we neither communicate nor interact in any real way, is that most of us spend our lives in polishing rather than peeling.

Man's lifelong task is simply one, but it is not simple: to remove the discrepancy between his outer self and his inner self, to get rid of the "persona" that divides his authentic self from the world. This persona is like the peeling on a banana: it is something built up to protect from bruises and injury. It is not the real person, but sometimes (if the fear of injury remains too great) it becomes a lifelong substitute for the person.

The "authentic personality" knows that he is like a banana, and knows that only as he peels himself down to his individuated self can he reach out and make contact with his fellows by what Father Goldbrunner calls "the sheer maturity of his humanity." Only when he himself is detached from his defensive armorings can he then awaken a true response in his dialog with others.

Most of us, however, think in terms of the apple, not the banana. We spend our lives in shining the surface, in making it rosy and gleaming, in perfecting the "image." But the image is not the apple, which may be wormy and rotten to the taste.

Almost everything in modern life is devoted to the polishing process, and little to the peeling process. It is the surface personality that we work on — the appearance, the clothes, the manners, the geniality. In short, the salesmanship: we are selling the package, not the product.

There is a vast disparity between our outer and inner selves; in many of us, the real person never comes to life at all, never reveals itself, never knows itself. It lives through its functions, it lives as a type, a response to an environment, and dies without ever having found its true existence. This, and not unhappiness, is the tragedy of life; this, and not "selfishness," is what causes human misery.

So long as we live behind the peeling, we can have no genuine encounter with the world. So long as we go on polishing, we sacrifice the substance for the image — until, at last, there is no substance left. What is all the good of our "individualism," if it means merely the freedom to be like everybody else, the liberty to remain secure within the peeling?

Spurring Our Better Selves

IT AMUSES and embarrasses me that so many readers apparently think I am able to direct and control my life by my "thoughts" or my "philosophy." And they want to know how they can do likewise.

Actually, a "philosophy of life" is meaningless unless it reflects one's deepest feelings and attitudes — and then it is unnecessary. Some of the world's worst men have had the noblest philosophies, which they failed utterly to put into practice. It is not what one consciously believes that counts; it is what one feels at the marrow of existence. Millions of people call themselves Christians, and believe every item in the Apostles' Creed, who in their daily lives are as far removed from the gospel of Jesus as if they had never heard of Him.

We cannot direct or control our lives by such inanimate things as a body of thought or philosophy, but only by following an example of a person. I have long had such a person in my life; and in times of stress, I try to imagine what he would do in similar circumstances. Most of the time, I know exactly what he would do — but I am not always good enough to do likewise.

It is no accident that the two greatest teachers of the Western world, Jesus and Socrates, wrote not a word. They taught by questioning, by parable, and most of all, by example. They were not so much concerned with how we think, or what we think, as with how we behave toward one another.

Not a single thought or piece of philosophy is able to help me when I am confronted with a moral decision — for one can find all sorts of reasons to justify any sort of conduct. The crimes committed over the centuries in the name of "religion" by well-meaning men have been far greater than those committed by evil and irreligious men, as all church historians will unhappily admit.

We can draw strength and righteousness only from another person, from someone we perceive to be better than we are, to be more of what a person was meant to be. When we find such a person — and he or she can always be found if we look hard enough — we must use him as a touchstone for testing the truth of our own behavior.

For truth cannot be found in ideas, in institutions, in books, in philosophies or theologies — but only in the living person as he confronts us in the fullness of his existence. When Jesus said, "Follow me," He did not mean in creed, but in love, in sacrifice, in suffering. How much easier it is to follow Him only in prayer, only once a week.

Learning to Accept Ourselves

"MOST OF THE ADVICE we get is so confusing," said the college boy. "On the one hand, we are told to accept ourselves as we are; on the other hand, we are told to be dissatisfied with ourselves. Which is right?"

The trouble with so much advice is not that it is untrue, but that it stresses one part of the truth at the expense of another part. And education consists in learning how to fit together different aspects of the truth. What is hardest in one's continual journey toward self-knowledge is "separating and combining" — which St. Thomas called nearly the whole art of intelligence. We need to separate those things which seem similar, and to combine those things which seem different.

There is a right way and a wrong way to "accept ourselves." There is a right way and a wrong way to be "dissatisfied with ourselves." The wrong way of accepting ourselves leads to smugness and complacency. The wrong way of being dissatisfied with ourselves leads to despair and defeatism.

One's life is a matter of *becoming what you are*. This rather simpleminded statement is both more subtle and more complex than it seems. "Becoming what you are" means two things at once: accepting one's basic nature and limitations, and at the same time struggling to realize one's full potentialities. A creative and developing life is a continual "tension" between these two.

The kind of "self-acceptance" we require is acceptance of what we have inherited, physically, spiritually, culturally, temperamentally. The kind of "self-dissatisfaction" we require is dissatisfaction with the perversions and encrustations of the self. Many people, if not most, do exactly the opposite: they are satisfied with the perversions and encrustations, those prickly defenses behind which the true self resides while, at a deeper level, they resent the limitations which their nature has placed upon them.

To be dissatisfied with oneself is a good thing, if the dissatisfaction is aimed at the proper target: not at the inner self, but at the modes of thinking and feeling and acting that prevent the inner self from becoming what it is. This is why philosophic advice is so sentencious and shallow. No one can tell you what should be accepted or rejected within yourself. Socrates did not make any man better by his teaching; only by his example of a man who had come to terms with himself by accepting who he was and rejecting all that was alien to his nature.

Rituals versus True Religion

THE GIVING UP by the Catholic Church of its ban against eating meat on Fridays marks not so much a religious change of attitude as a psychological change. And one all to the good.

Contrary to the belief of most people, the prohibition against eating meat on Fridays was never a religious dogma. It was simply a church rule, to remind communicants of their faith and its meaning.

Yet, this is the paradox of so many rules and rituals: rather than being reminders, or symbols, of something deeper and more important, they become in themselves more important than the things they symbolize.

Not long before he died, Albert Cardinal Meyer, Archbishop of Chicago, reminded his flock, as most clergymen of all faiths should remind theirs, when he spoke out and said: "It is a mystery to me why Catholics seem to think that men go to hell only for sins of impurity, for missing Holy Mass or for eating meat on Friday. They do not remember that defrauding the poor man of his wages is a sin that cries out to heaven, or that dishonesty in business or professional life, or the corrupt exploitation of public office, are *even more serious* than private sin because they directly injure the common good of all."

A religious practice or ritual begins as a *symbol* of some spiritual truth, and too often ends as a *substitute* for it. Many people identify their religion with its forms, rather than with its substance; and if they satisfy the forms, they often delude themselves that they are fulfilling the substance.

This is the psychological trap in all rituals, and it is precisely what Jesus opposed in the Pharisees — their emphasis on procedures and taboos and the outward signs of religiosity, while neglectful of the spirit of justice and love. Legalism is always the enemy of love.

The church's new stress on individual liberty, on freedom of conscience, on mature responsibility rather than fear of mortal sin, is both an awakening and a return that should gladden the hearts of all men. It is an awakening to the recognition that "systems" and "methods" and "laws" weaken, rather than strengthen, the individual's religious conscience; and a return to the deepest, most ancient, roots of Christianity — which began as a "revolt of love" against legalism and parochialism. For the greatest blasphemer is not the atheist, but the so-called "religious" man who worships the forms of his creed while smugly and comfortably and respectably violating their spirit.

Bolstering Our Attitudes

ONE OF THE MOST distressing and depressing habits of the human mind is a process we might call "selection and rejection." We select whatever buttresses our beliefs and prejudices, and reject whatever confounds them — even if it is from the same source.

I received a letter recently from a reader objecting to a piece of mine about "extremists." He pointed out that Jesus was an "extremist" when he violently drove the money changers from the temple.

People do this all the time, and the Bible is one of their favorite devices for selection and rejection. Jesus' whole message was one of love and nonviolence; yet this person picked out the one line in the Gospels to justify his own beliefs. If the rich man wants to vindicate his indifference to the social problem of poverty, he quotes Jesus' line that "The poor ye have always with you." If the radical reformer wants to prove the opposite, he quotes Jesus' remark that "It is easier for a camel to go through the eye of a needle than for a rich man to enter Heaven." The pacifist quotes from Jesus; so does the nationalist. The optimist takes what he wants; so does the pessimist. The moralist finds his own quotes; so does the libertarian.

"Christianity has not been tried and failed," said Chesterton, a half century ago. "It has never been tried." And it has never been tried, of course, because of this tendency to draw out of it that one element that most appeals to our fancies and prejudices, and to make that one element the principal creed.

And this is not necessarily because the Bible is a "mass of contradictions." It is because life itself is a paradoxical affair, and learning how to live the good life calls for much more than simply a warm heart: it calls for *accepting and understanding the opposites.*

This we cannot and will not do. "The opposite of a small truth is a lie," said a famous scientist, "but the opposite of a great truth is often equally true." Such statements make us uncomfortable; they confuse our categories of thought. But unless we can grasp the fact that the whole art of life consists in *holding contradictions in balance*, we shall perpetually veer from one extreme to the other, never doing justice to the contraries.

If the problem were easy, we should have solved it by now. If just following the Golden Rule were the answer, it might be done. We fail partly because our feelings are not good enough, but also because we select and reject, and fail to see that the part we reject contains an essential truth in the structure of existence.

Learning to Stretch Our Minds

THE DAY AFTER I wrote a recent column on the way in which all people "select and reject," I received a letter from a man in San Francisco who said, "After reading you for a long time, I am convinced that you are a Buddhist." (Quite right, I am.)

A few weeks earlier, I lectured at a Lutheran college in Iowa, and the dean remarked, "It's obvious from your column that you are a Lutheran." (Quite right, I am.)

Taking part in a seminar for a Catholic group, I was told by the Monsignor who was moderator, "I can tell from your philosophy that you accept most of St. Thomas Aquinas. You're a Thomist, aren't you?" (Quite right, I am.)

Speaking to the National Council of Jewish Women, I heard from an attending rabbi that I "share the convictions of the Old Testament Prophets and must be devoted to the Hebrew faith." (Quite right, I am.)

Following a symposium on mind-and-body, in which I thought I had presented a Freudian view, a distinguished Christian Scientist in the group said to me, "You may not know it, but at heart you're a Christian Scientist." (Quite right, I am.)

The Jehovah's Witnesses claim me for their own. So do the Seventh Day Adventists, and the Quakers, and the Disciples of Christ, and the Rational Humanists, and the two-and-seventy jarring sects that Omar wrote of.

What does this make me? Some kind of intellectual chameleon, all things to all men, a weak and vacillating creature? I think not, and hope not. What I prefer to think is, rather, that each doctrinal group (unconsciously) selects what is congenial to its views, and rejects whatever does not fit in.

As Nehru remarked in an interview in the *India News* a half-dozen years ago: "Grownups have a strange way of putting themselves in compartments and groups. They build up barriers . . . of religion, of caste, of color, of party, of nation, of province, of language, of custom, and of wealth and poverty. Thus they live in prisons of their own making."

The truth, said Aristotle, is like a barn door — nobody who throws at it can miss it entirely, but nobody can hit it all at once. Yet the truth becomes fragmented: each group tries to stretch its portion to fit across the whole barn door, but it cannot be done; whereupon the group simply decrees that what it does not cover cannot be the truth.

This principle of selection and rejection is mankind's worst and most perpetual enemy. The first "ecumenical movement" must start in the mind, which has to learn to stretch itself, and not the truth.

Human "Progress" — and Murder

WHAT is human "progress"? We have heard many definitions, ranging from technical development to economic affluence. Some even question whether the word "progress" has any objective and permanent meaning.

Perhaps the best definition I have ever heard comes from Margaret Mead, the world-famous anthropologist. After studying primitive tribes, and many different cultures, for more than 40 years, she said this: "There is progress when the group in which the fact of killing a man is considered murder grows larger."

In earliest days, it was not considered murder to kill a man outside one's immediate family. Then it became murder to kill a man only within one's clan. Then the concept spread to the tribe, the town, the medieval duchy, and now the modern nation-state.

The ultimate goal of "progress," by this standard, is for the human community to recognize it as murder when we kill anyone belonging to the human race. "If we look back at the factors which made us first human beings and then civilized beings," Dr. Mead says, "the most striking of all is man's capacity to recognize as members of his own group an ever-growing number of individuals separated by ever-increasing distances from his clan, his tribe, his nation, his religion, his hemisphere."

This has been a steady trend in the history of humanity. Almost all primitive societies are characterized by exclusiveness — the clan across the river, the tribe across the woods, are "strangers," "aliens," to be feared, despised, and conquered. We still find remnants of this feeling in backward areas of the United States, where someone from the next town or county is considered a "foreigner," neither to be trusted nor dealt with as benevolently as one would deal with one's immediate neighbors.

But the slow and irresistible movement of human history goes against this primitive tendency. Century after century, we are involved in larger areas of loyalty; it must not be forgotten that the "patriotism" of the modern nation-state is a relatively new phenomenon, only a few hundred years old. Before then, only regionalism commanded our loyalty.

"Now, nuclear weapons," Dr. Mead goes on to say in a statement to the French magazine, *Réalités*, "have placed us before an ultimate problem: we can no longer fight a war with the enemy. In order to protect 'our' children, we must protect 'his' children, too." We have not yet risen to this recognition. It is still "murder" if we kill a fellow-American, but only a "casualty" if we kill a fellow human in warfare. We can only hope that our area of loyalty spreads faster than our capacity to kill each other off; if not, "progress" will indeed be robbed of all meaning.

Our Hypocrisy on Violence

IT IS EQUALLY AMUSING and depressing that we are so "shocked" when natives in the Congo imitate on a small scale what civilized nations have done on a massive scale throughout history.

A U.S. foreign service official recently observed that the rebel rioters in the Congo are just out for loot, for "personal

gain and theft." I wonder what in the world he imagines most
wars have been fought for, since the first Assyrian dynasty.
Wars are begun for gain, and for nothing else, in almost all
cases. Invasion of foreign soil is nothing but theft, "legal-
ized" by the judges of the invading nations, and "sanctified"
by the preachers of the invading nation.

When a rioting bunch of natives slaughters women and
children in Stanleyville, it is a "massacre." When a U. S. air-
plane drops the first atomic bomb that slaughters women
and children in Hiroshima, it is — what? Justice? Retribution? Charity? Strategical necessity?

Our capacity for wrongous indignation is nearly limitless.
What happened in the Congo was barbarous behavior, but a
good case could be made out that the most "civilized" nations in the world have been the most barbarous, in the 20th
Century and before. The bloodiest and most devastating wars
in history have been fought not by "savages" in Africa but by
presumably Christian countries against one another. The
most appalling instruments of warfare have been devised and
used not by "primitive" peoples but by highly sophisticated,
intelligent, educated peoples against one another. It is precisely the "advanced" countries that have looted, pillaged, exploited and enslaved the "backward" countries, and not the
other way around. We have used our superior knowledge for
the most inferior motives; and our "education" has enabled
us to camouflage these motives as grand and noble ones.

Our indignation at events in the Congo is what psychiatrists
would call a "displacement" of feeling. It is easy, it makes us
feel good, to be angry at the native rabble who are butcher-
ing innocent civilians. Meanwhile, we are creating more and
more bombs whose ultimate purpose is to assure that nobody
on earth will be an innocent civilian.

Everybody is against other people's wars, other people's

atrocities, other people's massacres. But, in truth, there are no "other people." Not only are we all of one flesh, but of one spirit. And the next war will teach us that lesson — for if we cannot all live together, we shall surely all die together, in the agonized embrace of involuntary brotherhood.

We Are All on One Spaceship

WHILE IN THE COUNTRY this summer, we watched, like most other American families, the week-long space orbiting of our astronauts. We marveled, we applauded, we sighed in relief as they came down safely.

"I wonder what it would be like to be on a spaceship," mused my ten-year-old boy. "You're on one," I told him. "And you have been all your life."

The earth itself is a very small spaceship, by astronomical standards. It is only 8,000 miles in diameter, which makes it just a tiny speck in our galaxy. And our galaxy is only one of millions. Yet this tiny speck has sustained billions of human passengers for more than two million years as it has orbited around the solar system. It shows no signs of running down for millions of years more, and all it needs is radiation from the sun to keep it going and to regenerate life "on board."

If we could implant in our children, at an early age, this concept of a global spaceship, they might possibly be more prepared, in attitude and action, to treat one another as crew members should, when they grow up.

It may be too late — psychologically speaking — for most adults to adopt this approach. We see the world in narrow, sublunary terms: in terms of racial divisions and national territories, of ancient rivalries and provincial fears, of airtight compartments separating one portion of the crew from another.

But to see the world as the astronauts saw it — this fragile yet sturdy sphere revolving in the immensity of space, carrying its millions of passengers locked together for a lifetime — is the only way to make it viable in the future. When two men can circle the globe in less time than it takes us to mow a good-sized lawn, then anything less than a global viewpoint is dangerously inadequate.

Nature has provided us with a magnificently self-renewing space ship, containing everything it needs for perpetual flight, for nourishment, for comfort — and even for beauty. If the Gemini astronauts had quarrelled and fought, or sulked and sneered, even a week's flight would have been imperiled.

Everybody is an involuntary crew member on Earth I. The compartments we create are artificial and destructive. Until now, however, we only had the power to injure other members of the crew. Today we can easily blow up the whole ship and everybody on it.

The only hope is to think of ourselves as astronauts.

Man Finished or Finished Off

FROM ARISTOTLE to the moderns, man has been variously defined as many kinds of animal — as a "rational" animal, as a "problem-solving" animal, as a "self-conscious" animal, an animal with "tools" and "language" and "history." But perhaps the most satisfactory definition I have ever heard is the one that calls man the "unfinished" animal. Alone of all the species, man seems to have been assigned the task of *completing himself*.

Every other species is complete, and has been so for countless years. The tiger, the rabbit, the dog, the eagle, the earthworm, are (so to speak) finished products. There is nothing more for them to be or do; no further possibilities, for good or evil, are open to them.

We, on the other hand, seem to have been conferred the dreadful freedom to finish shaping ourselves in whatever way we will. We can become more like Socrates, or more like the men who put him to death. We — alone of all living creatures — can elevate ourselves, or degrade ourselves, or totally destroy ourselves.

Other animals have a *nature*; we, as Ortega suggested, have a *history*. This means that we are not "given," as they are — we have an infinite number of moves, and combinations, on that chessboard called "human nature."

The only important question facing mankind today is "How shall we complete ourselves?" For the first time, we have the technology, the energy, the knowledge and the resources, to unify the human race, to feed everyone, to protect all from want, to lift the living level of the have-nots without lowering the level of the haves.

Yet, while all this is happening on the intellectual and physical and technical fronts, precisely the opposite is happening on the political, the social, and the emotional fronts. We are more divisive, more hostile, more suspicious, more chauvinistic, more irrational than at any time in the present century.

Every thinking person knows that the smallest possible unit of survival today is the human race. This has been forced upon us by atomic fission; neither philosophy nor religion, but the stark demands of science call for an ultimate decision on our part — co-operation or catastrophe.

Man is still evolving, by his own hands, with his own mind and feelings. We have the power to finish ourselves or to *finish ourselves off*. This is the frightful burden of our freedom, a burden not carried by any other creature. If we cannot rise to this responsibility, will we not perish, to be replaced with some other species more fitted for the task? For one thing is sure — we cannot continue to survive in this uncompleted state, an animal so bitterly divided against itself.

We Beg to Be Despised

I HAVE BEEN BROWSING through the new revised edition of Walter Sullivan's book *We Are Not Alone,* in which the science editor of the *New York Times* examines "the search for intelligent life on other worlds." At the same time, I heard another man on a television interview discuss the "flying saucers" that have been reported around the country for many years. He, too, is writing a book to document these cases. Most speculation and science fiction on the subject is based on the theory that highly intelligent creatures, living in distant space, are either trying to communicate with us, or are actually investigating life on earth, with a view toward attacking or conquering us.

I cannot believe this. If there are creatures intelligent enough to spy on us through vast galactic distances, then they must also be intelligent enough to let us alone after they learn what we are like. For the human race on earth, it seems plain to me, must rank quite low in the order of conscious intelligence. We seem to have just enough brains to make trouble for ourselves, and not enough to learn how to live together amicably. Just enough brains to create a huge technology that could turn the earth into an Eden, and not enough to prevent us from using this technology to blow ourselves up.

Creatures from another planet, if they have observed us for any length of time, are more likely to be perplexed and disgusted with our irrational behavior than tempted to conquer us. What could they get from us but grief? They may study us, but only as we study bacteria.

Civilization after civilization has toppled in the ten thousand years of history. Wars between people have become more ferocious and fatal as the art of weaponry has developed; and the future holds grim promise of chemical and bacteriological warfare even more sinister than the threat of the hydrogen bomb.

We have made tremendous advances in living conditions — but they have been more than matched by our ominous advances in dying conditions. Prejudice and passion, hate and rivalry, are more intense today than in the pastoral environment of Biblical times. People may *be* no worse, but we have increased by a millionfold our capacity to *do* worse.

Any truly intelligent beings from another galaxy would not touch us with a ten light-year pole. We are quite capable of attacking and destroying ourselves without their help. And not because we are "bad" in any grand and classic sense of the word — but because we are weak and petty and more concerned with our immediate advantages (delusive as they are) than with pledging our allegiance to the survival of the human race.

When We Go Beyond Reason

SOME MONTHS AGO, I was invited to take part in a television forum on the subject of "The Unreasonable Man." The program's point of departure was Bernard Shaw's famous aphorism: "The reasonable man adapts himself to the world; the unreasonable one persists in trying to adapt the world to himself. Therefore all progress depends on the unreasonable man." Illness prevented me from appearing on the program, or even watching it, but I had been thinking about Shaw's quotation and wondering what was right and what was wrong with it.

8 LEAVING THE SURFACE

It seems to me that the catch lies in the phrase "the unreasonable man." There are two distinct ways of being "unreasonable" — we might call them the *irrational* way and the
suprarational way.

The irrational way is a perversion of reason; the suprarational way is a going beyond reason. There is a world of
difference between the man who twists the facts to fit his
preconceptions, and the man who is dissatisfied with the facts
and looks for new and different ones to support and validate
his views. The irrational way is the way of tyrants and
bigots; the suprarational way is the way of prophets and inventors and creative geniuses.

As someone has pointed out, Hitler was "unreasonable,"
but so was Pasteur. Hitler tried to change the world to fit his
paranoid version of reality; Pasteur, who was derided by all
the "reasonable" scientists of his time, plowed ahead to find
justification in reality for his revolutionary view of the germ
theory of disease.

It is true that reasonable men do not accomplish very much;
they are content to accept the world as they find it, to rub
along, to make the best of things, to adjust themselves to conditions, to limit their vision, curb their imagination, and repress their zeal. It would be wrong, however, to agree with
Shaw that "all progress depends on the unreasonable man."
Most evil depends on him, too, if he is merely irrational and
not suprarational, if his intuitions and drives are for destruction, division and despotism. An enormous gulf separates the
fanatic who has not yet risen to reason, and the one who has
gone beyond it.

Was Jesus "reasonable" or "unreasonable"? In one sense,
he was profoundly unreasonable in making demands on human beings that are nearly impossible to fulfill. On the other
hand, we might say that he exemplified the essence of reason-

ableness, for, as Shaw said elsewhere, "nobody has ever been
sane enough to try his way."

Science Can't Give Us Everything

THERE is no way of deciding the running argument between the people who believe in a liberal arts education and
those who believe in a technical education until we ask and
answer one prior question. This question is: what kind of persons do we want our colleges to turn out? Is it enough to
"train" students, or do they somehow have to be changed in
outlook and attitude? If we decide it is not enough just to
"train" students, then we must look to the humanities and
social sciences for means of changing them.

Literature, history, sociology, philosophy, anthropology —
these differ in much more than subject matter from physics,
chemistry, engineering, mathematics. They differ in that *the
knowledge we have of them affects both the future of the
subject and of ourselves.*

Our knowledge of the table of atomic weights does not
change the atomic system. Our knowledge of algebra or calculus does not affect those mathematical concepts. Our
knowledge of metal fatigue and structural stress does not alter
those physical laws. But our knowledge of the humanities and
social sciences is an essential part of those systems. In sociology, for instance, once we truly understand the nature
of group pressure and the influence of prejudice, both we and
the subject have been modified.

If we know what Shakespeare was getting at in *King
Lear*, if we can grasp what was wrong with the Treaty of
Versailles, if we see what the existentialists are trying to ex-
press — then we are able to utilize this knowledge to reshape

our own views of life and to exert influence on those we live with and work with.

The humanities are not "superior" to the technical studies because they are more ancient or more "cultural" or more intellectual; these would be poor, and snobbish, reasons for granting them any sort of priority. They are superior because they expand the imagination, enlarge the personality, enable us to become something different and better than what we were before. Learning a chemical formula does not make a man different; reading Donne's sermons can change his whole life drastically.

Our great need today is not so much for better-trained technicians as it is for well-rounded persons who know how their subject fits into other subjects, and who can relate their experience to some general framework of human experience. Without this, we will breed only a generation of technical barbarians, who do brilliantly what they have been taught to do, but who are blind to the consequences of their actions. This may be an admirable quality in a soldier; it is a disastrous one in a free citizen.

Creativity's Complex Sources

WHAT MAKES highly creative people different from others? This is a question that has perplexed, and preoccupied, researchers for several decades. It used to be an academic question; now, business and industry, which desperately need innovations, are joining in the search.

Some University of California researchers have turned up with answers that make more sense than most. They suggest that the qualities *all* creative people have in common, whether artists or scientists, are these: "A general openness to experience from both without and within; a tolerance for ambiguity, confusion and disorder; strong disposition to be independent rather than conforming; and the tendency to perceive through intuition rather than through the senses." It was found, for instance, that 100 percent of creative people are intuitive, as compared to only 25 percent of the general population. They are more easily able to express the opposite sides of their nature, to reconcile the conscious with the unconscious, the rational and the irrational, the scientific and the artistic aspects.

As an interesting sidelight, it was found that in the matter of interests, *all* the creative people studied in the tests, no matter what their own calling, scored high on interests "which might lead them to become psychologists, architects, or author-journalists." And all, without exception, scored low on scales for office workers, bankers, farmers and policemen.

Some of the mystery and contradiction in the creative personality was explained by Frank Barron, of the university's Institute of Personality Assessment, as springing from the fact that "The creative person is both more primitive and more cultivated, more destructive and more constructive, a lot madder and a lot saner, than the average person." One reason that business and industry have had such a hard time in harnessing and keeping creative people even after they have been discovered, was expressed by Barron: "Almost everything we know about highly creative people suggests that neither they nor their creativity may be used as a mere means to an end, but that both will flourish when respected as ends in themselves."

The real problem for organizations that want to become more creative as well as more productive is to learn to respect intuition as well as facts, to tolerate ambiguity and a certain amount of disorder — and to realize that someone a lot madder than the rest of us may be a lot saner, too.

Love Is the Key to Survival

I TOOK PART in a college seminar recently, at which one of the participants was a nun. She was attacking some public figure with a great deal of asperity.

"Sister," the chairman gently chided her, "I thought you're supposed to love your enemies." The nun smiled thinly. "I love him, all right," she returned. "But I just don't like him one bit!"

Her answer was neither flip nor hypocritical. She knew that the verb "to love" is not an intensive of the verb "to like." Most people think it is, and that is why they often confuse the two.

We cannot help what we like, but we *can* help what we love. Liking is a matter of taste and inclination, background and temperament. The food we like, the music we like, the kinds of people we like are not subject to commandment or moral law. But we are commanded to love our neighbors and our enemies — who are so often the same people. How could the Bible be so psychologically stupid as to *command* us to love, if love were merely a matter of personal preference, like choosing vanilla ice cream over chocolate?

Anybody can learn to love what he already likes; there is no trick in that. But the love spoken of by the scribes and prophets is *love of what we do not especially like, or even actively dislike.* This is the only kind that has any particular merit. Liking is a *feeling*, and love is an *act of the will.* The nun may have intensely disliked the public figure she attacked, but nevertheless at some deeper stratum of her being she had trained herself to love him — which means to regard him as a human being coessential with herself, as worthy of the same treatment, as sharing the same mark of creation. And only this kind of love can save the world from chaos and self-destruction. Without this absolute commandment — which is also a commandment for self-preservation of the human race — we embrace what we like and destroy what we do not like, and there is no end to killing.

Modern man looks with suspicion upon "moral laws" and absolute commandments of any kind, because in the past they have so often been perverted for evil ends. We must learn, however, to look upon them as *psychological laws*, which are true for the character and destiny of man. For if a moral law does not express a deep psychological truth, it is useless and ultimately false.

"Love thine enemy" is not a piece of "spiritual" sentiment; it is a rule as imperative for our human survival as our need for air and water.

Nobody Sees "What Is There"

WE USED TO THINK, in our naive way, that the act of perception consisted of two independent things: the perceiver and the thing perceived. The act of perception simply meant "seeing what was there."

Perhaps the most important advance in the behavioral sciences in our time has been the growing recognition that the perceiver is not just a passive camera taking a picture, but *takes an active part* in perception. He sees what experience has conditioned him to see. We enter a restaurant, and six persons are sitting there. What do we "see" beyond the mere fact that these are six human beings? Do we all see the same picture, either individually or collectively?

A European will note that these are six Americans, by their dress and attitudes. A woman entering the room will probably note that the six consist of two married couples, an older woman, and a single man. A Southerner will see one man who could possibly be a light-skinned Negro. A homosexual will single out one of the men as a fellow deviate. An anti-Semite will immediately label one of the couples as "Jewish." A salesman will divide the group into "prospects" and "duds." And the waiter, of course, does not see people at all, but a "station" and "food" and "drinks."

What perceiver, then, "sees what is there"? Nobody, of course. Each of us perceives what our past has prepared us to perceive: we select and distinguish, we focus on some objects and relationships, and we blur others, we distort objective reality to make it conform to our needs or hopes or fears or hates or envies or affections.

In the physical sciences, we have long been aware that the very act of examining and measuring some physical phenomenon changes the phenomenon itself: what the scientist sees during his experiment is not the same object that it would be if not under scrutiny.

Now we have begun to learn that the behavioral sciences contain this same subjective element: that our eyes and brains do not merely register some objective portrait of other persons or groups, but that our very act of seeing is warped by what we have been *taught* to believe, by what we *want* to believe, by what (in a deeper sense) we *need* to believe.

And this is the main reason that communication is so difficult: we are not disagreeing about the same thing, but about different things. We are not looking at the same people in the dining room, or on the picket line, or around the conference table. How to correct this built-in warp may very well be the basic, and ultimate, problem of mankind's survival.

Alien Saints and Heroes

DURING a college commencement address last month, I happened to mention that eight signers of the Declaration of

Independence had been "foreigners." Afterward, some of the students came up to me in astonishment and disbelief; in all their civics and history classes, they had never been informed that some of the most illustrious signers of our Declaration were "immigrants" who had been born in Europe.

Actually, as if to symbolize the relatedness and interdependence of peoples, it is an historical fact that many leaders, heroes and even patron saints have sprung from alien soil — which we too easily forget. It is widely known by now that St. Patrick's original name was Succat, and that he was born in Britain, not in Ireland. Less known, however, is the fact that St. George, the patron saint of England, was born in France, on the coast of Brittany.

Abraham, the progenitor of the Hebrew people, was a Babylonian, born in Ur. According to the Old Testament, his name was changed by the Lord when he was selected to be the "seed" of the Hebrew people. (Incidentally, Freud, in his *Moses and Monotheism*, insisted that Moses himself was not a Jew, but an Egyptian. His evidence seems persuasive to some scholars, and flimsy to others; at any rate, it is undeniable that Moses chose a Midianite, and not an Israelite, maiden to be his wife.)

The original Buddha, Siddhartha, who has been revered for centuries in China and Japan, was neither a Chinese nor a Japanese, but an Indian, born in Nepal. And of course, Jesus the Man was born a Jew, lived a Jew, and died a Jew. He had no knowledge of a new religion called Christianity, and sought to reform the old church rather than found a new one.

If one detects any kind of thread running through human history, it must seem more than a remarkable coincidence that the Irish have enshrined a Briton, the English a Frenchman, the Hebrews a Babylonian, the Chinese and Japanese an Indian, the Christians a Jew — and, doubtless, research could bring more such examples to our notice.

We too readily forget that America was begun wholly by "foreigners"; that our great folk-hero of the Revolution, Paul Revere, was of French Huguenot descent, whose father had changed his name from "Revoire." When Providence seems to have chosen so many "aliens" to do noble deeds for their adopted lands and peoples, the bigots still among us must be condemned for ignorance as well as for malice.

To the Brink of Fear

WITHOUT A DOUBT, the most interesting play I saw during ten days of theater-going in New York recently was the off-Broadway production of *A Slight Ache*, by Harold Pinter, the gifted British playwright. Not only was it beautifully written and impeccably acted, but the theme itself illustrates a deep and universal tendency in human relations. It takes an ordinary situation and projects it to the very brink of our unconscious fears and needs, and the fantasies they instill in us.

The story concerns a husband and wife who invite a ragged matchseller into their country house to find out more about him and why he has stood motionless near their rear gate for many days. First the husband speaks to him at great length, and then the wife. The matchseller never says a word throughout the whole play; he simply stands there, hunched over, holding his tray, and we do not know whether he can even hear what they are saying to him. He seems to have suffered a stroke, and scarcely moves at all, like some wounded animal.

The husband, who, at the play's beginning seems prissy and smug and supremely self-confident, slowly turns fearful in the man's presence. He imagines him to be a spy, or someone seeking vengeance for an evil deed that the husband committed long ago.

The wife, who, at the play's beginning seems blandly passive and conventional, slowly turns amorous in the man's presence. She overlooks his foul odor, his repulsive rags, his utter unresponsiveness, and caresses him as the answer to her unspoken prayers for romantic relief from her grim marriage.

Here, Pinter is merely pushing to a menacing extreme the kind of behavior we all indulge in, only we usually do it more prudently and less dramatically. We project our own feelings into others; we reshape them, as it were, into an image that has preexisted in our own minds; we use them as sounding boards for our most deep-seated fears and frustrations and infantile hopes.

We do not see the Other as a "Thou" in Buber's terms; we see him or her as an "It" — as an object, as an instrument, as a projection of what we would like the world to become or what we are afraid it might be. The Other is not a true person, in his own right, but a Thing, like the blind, deaf, paralyzed matchseller, who becomes Retribution to the husband and Romance to the wife.

This paranoid projection, which everyone engages in to some degree, is perhaps mankind's most persistent and implacable enemy, both on the personal and on the social scale. For we do it not only with individuals, but also with classes, races, nations, and sexes. We turn a Someone into a Something, and then wonder why we cannot live together happily.

The Tragic Yearning for Youth

How can we blame the youth of America for taking themselves so importantly when we ourselves have made a national cult out of the idea of youth? No other country in history has worshipped so fervently at this shrine, or with more disastrous results.

Currently, the government and some of the airlines are engaged in a dispute about the proper age limits for retiring stewardesses. Some of the airlines set age limits as low as 32 or 35 for their stewardesses. If these limits are set because the physical condition and dexterity of the stewardess disable her from arduous duties at those ages, it is one thing. If, on the other hand, such limits are set because the attractiveness of youth itself is the determining factor, then the airlines are simply encouraging and perpetuating this great American myth.

The French, who understand such matters better than we do, quite sensibly value the more mature woman above the younger one. The French recognize that she reaches her fullness of womanhood in the thirties, and is at her absolute peak at 40. Most other European nations have the same realistic attitude.

Our absurd adulation of female youthfulness has caught most of our women in an agonizing trap. Instead of learning to grow, and to take pride in the assets of maturity, they are engaged in a desperate race to keep young — and nothing ages a woman faster than trying to look younger than she should.

It is one thing to want to look sleek and attractive; it is quite another thing to become neurotic and discontented about the fact of growing older, and to regard time as an enemy instead of an ally. What a woman loses in freshness, she should make up in other qualities equally as appealing — but if she is obsessed with freshness, she merely loses the charms of youth without gaining the depth and serenity of middle age. And even on the physical level, an older woman whose face has earned character through living and suffering and expanding can be more attractive than the unformed, unlined, trivial and narcissistic face of a young girl who (like most young people) wants only to be given and not to give. This, of course, is why so many young marriages utterly fail.

Being one's self, and becoming one's self, is the prime task in life to which we are all directed; but this is impossible, if one is perpetually trying to be someone else, someone younger, some stereotype based on the cosmetics ads. For self-rejection ends only in self-contempt, and the idolatry of youthfulness is a religion that devours its worshippers.

What God "Gives" To Us

SEVERAL READERS have asked me to explain a recent paragraph, in which I said that "to 'thank God' for having spared your family in a tornado, when families across the street have been blown up, is a blasphemy against the true God."

The God they give thanks to, in cases like these, is the one who has been proclaimed "dead." This is what the new theologians mean by the phrase. They mean that being blown up, or not blown up, in a tornado, is a natural phenomenon, having nothing to do with God. He does not arbitrarily spare some and sentence others.

The phrase "God is dead," so widely misunderstood, is not a slogan of atheism; it is simply a different way of looking at the creative purpose behind the universe. It is an attack on what the new theologians conceive as idolatry, superstition, and infantile fantasies. The God they proclaim "dead" was always a kind of Santa Claus, beard and all, rewarding the "good" people and punishing the "bad" ones. To thank God because we were spared in a catastrophe, while those around us perished, is indeed a kind of blasphemy. It assumes that God shoots dice with human lives, that He has decided to be particularly good to us, for reasons we are unaware of.

And this is the kind of God that many modern people have

refused to believe in — a capricious deity, dispensing favors and punishments, protecting "our" soldiers in a war, and giving us prosperity and contentment if we obey His rules and regulations.

And belief in that kind of God has permitted so-called "religious" people for centuries to ignore their social and moral obligations, to think of religion as totally irrelevant to contemporary problems, to imagine that following dogmas and rituals assures them a place in heaven, or at least a partial remission for their sins.

The new theologians stress that God is the one who gives us freedom, gives us love, gives us reason, gives us moral choice, and gives us personhood. Whether we accept these or not, is up to us. The new demand is that we become mature — and the first step is giving up the child's concept of God, which has only succeeded in turning into atheists some of the finest, kindest, most loving, reasonable persons ever created.

Each Day Could Be the Last

On Tuesday night, Feb. 7, 1967 I was sitting on a rooftop cafe on the 11th floor of a hotel, when a boy brought in the papers. The headline read: INFERNO ON 11TH FLOOR; ROOFTOP CAFE FIRE KILLS 26.

It was the most startling coincidence I have ever known; although the fire was in Alabama, and I was in Iowa, it was the exact identical situation: a hotel, a rooftop cafe, the eleventh floor, and the same evening.

I finished my sarsaparilla hastily and descended to my room. It gave one, as the French say, furiously to think. But for the grace of God, all of us sitting in the rooftop cafe in Iowa could have been burned to cinders as quickly as those in Alabama. And, from my boyhood, there came back the dim memory of a psalm I once used to recite: "Lord, make me to know mine end, and the measure of my days, what it is; that I may know how frail I am."

We push into the deepest recesses of our mind the knowledge of how frail we are, how like a ripple on the waters of time, how in the midst of life death is hovering above our heads. If we did not, we would be paralyzed into inaction, all boldness gone, all foresight abandoned. In some sense, we must live as though we were immortal.

And yet — this being perhaps the prime metaphysical paradox of human existence — we must also at the same time keep in mind our frailty, our impermanence, our moment-by-moment vulnerability to sudden tragedy or disaster. For, in some other, and equally important, sense, we must live as though we were going to die tomorrow. Keeping a balance between the sense of immortality and the knowledge of sudden oblivion is the only attitude that can give us proportion and perspective, and is finally what humanizes us: For those who deny and repress the imminence of death turn into brutes, and those who cringe from it turn into vegetables. Neither is a human being.

If most of us, more of the time, could maintain an awareness that the flash fire, the split-second auto crash, the unwarning heart attack, were just as likely to happen to us right now as to anyone we read about in Alabama, we might go through each day with a more sympathetic and humane attitude toward our fellow mortals, trapped in the same web of time.

Deathbed contrition has always seemed a little cheap to me — a form of taking out additional God-insurance just as the policy is about to lapse. Every day we live, a little bit more of us is on the deathbed. A calm acceptance of this might make us act as if each day might be our last — not hoarding our penitence until the fatal hour, but lavishing our love before the tolling of the bell we will not hear.

Just What Is Self-Interest?

THE MAN who thinks of himself as a "realist" laughs at the man he calls an "idealist." He looks upon the idealist as someone with a distorted and inflated view of human nature.

It is my suggestion that the so-called realist's view of human nature is just as distorted — in the opposite direction. The idealist often makes the mistake of believing that men are better than they are; but the realist makes the contrary mistake of believing that men are worse than they are. The realist is fond of pointing out that "people act in their self-interest." But he is incapable of seeing how fuzzy and even tautological this statement is: it says so much that it really says very little. For "self-interest" is not as clear and unified as he thinks it is.

First of all, what is the "self"? When I am confronted with a tax raise on my property, do I respond as a property owner, as a parent who wants better schools, as a Democrat or a Republican, as an urban dweller who knows the city needs more money to render better services, or as an absentee landlord who merely wants more profit from his property?

Secondly, the maxim that "people act in their self-interest" implies that people know what their self-interest truly is. But history is replete with the tragic instances of people acting *against* their real self-interest under the illusion that they were favoring it.

Moreover, the interests of people are numerous and complex, often contradictory. Hardly anybody has an obvious, unequivocal and singlefaced interest in any important issue. Each of us is a "multiple" person — wage-earner, homeowner, citizen, parent, and many other functions. And to suggest that our immediate economic gain is always the overriding motive is to fall into the Marxist trap of economic determinism.

The maxim that "people act in their self-interest" is true only in the most blurred and broadest sense. We might say that the martyr who willingly goes to his death for a cause is acting in his self-interest, because he belives that his deepest self is best served by sacrificing himself for an idea and ideal he cherishes beyond life. This is why "self-interest" is a useless tautology as an explanation of men's motives and behavior. Nobody is only one self, and nobody has only one interest. We are a mixture of impulses — and the idealist merely suggests that we can change the mix to favor our long-range and benevolent interests rather than our short-range and greedy ones. This is nothing for the so-called realist to laugh at.

Doomed by Our Own Power?

MAN can no longer live with the power he has created. It is as simple — and as complicated — as that. The human race has turned ino a collective Frankenstein, increasingly menaced by the monster of its own making.

This is why all partial schemes to save us must fail; why merely shifting and transferring and reallocating resources will not accomplish their purpose; why social or economic or political systems (of whatever type) cannot do more than ease our symptoms of malaise for a few years. As Professor Robert Theobald acutely observes in a recent issue of "New University Thought," mankind has moved out of the industrial age and into an utterly new era. In this new cybernetic era, *our means control our ends*, our technology shapes our values, and our environment more and more threatens our well-being.

In the 19th Century, Marx conceived that the task of man was to change the nature of society; this done, he believed,

man could live justly and harmoniously, with the profit motive subordinated to the service motive. This was an enormously appealing — but basically defective — view of the human situation.

We can now clearly see, in the 20th Century, that unless the
nature of man is somehow modified, it matters little how society is changed. For what happened to Marxism was not a
perversion, not a historical accident, but an inevitable degen-
eration when so much power is given to so few men.

The core problem of our time, indeed, has little to do with
capitalism or communism or any other ideology — although
politicians wave such banners in order to confuse the issues
and solidify their own positions. The core problem has to do
with the progressive *dehumanization* of human beings everywhere in the world, on all sides of every curtain.

In the cybernetic era we are entering, this dehumanization
will become even more widespread and severe, as nation after
nation learns to use this new power of technology. Whether
we live under American "individualism" or Russian "collectivism," *the system will take precedence over the person*, because this is the nature of the technological monster. It is a
runaway machine, and we all are inside it. And the only way
to control it is not to improve it — as the technicians think
— or to smash it — as the romantics think — but to change
ourselves so that *our personal values become paramount ends
for society*. Today, alas, only the teen-agers seem to see this
clearly.

The Fallacy of Abstractions

THREE HEADLINES on the foreign news page today read: RED
PLANES SHOT DOWN NEAR FLEET, SHAKY GREEK COALITION FALLS,
and WEST GERMANY MAY LET FRENCH TROOPS REMAIN.

Almost all headlines are abstractions, because they must of necessity compress a lot of meaning into a little space. But the danger is that we begin to *think* in headlines, too — that is, we transform the living world into a set of abstractions.

There is really no such thing as a "Red plane." It is a plane flown by a human being and owned by the Soviet government. There is really no such thing as a "Greek coalition." There are only human beings who live in Greece, and have differing political opinions. And so on.

What Gabriel Marcel, the French Catholic existentialist, has called "the spirit of abstraction" is responsible for much of our woe in the world. As long as we think of our enemy as the "Vietcong," we can pursue our war, for we are just killing a hated abstraction. And they, in turn, are just killing "Yankee imperialism." But the lads who fight for us are no more "imperialists" than the lads who fight for North Vietnam are "Reds." They are all mothers' sons, doing what they are told to do, fighting because they have to, hoping to God they get out alive and return to their families.

When we hear that "the French" are doing this, or "the Germans" are doing that, we forget that these are unreal entities, like "the 31st Ward" or "the upper Mohawk Valley." And the philosophy called *existentialism* has taken hold so firmly these days precisely because many thinkers have at last rebelled against the tyranny of abstraction.

It is people who fight, not countries. It is human beings who bleed and die, not ideologies or political units. As long as we continue to think in abstractions, we will find it easy to fight and to kill; once we begin to think (and to feel) in terms of living entities, we can no longer lie to ourselves about what we are doing.

Abstraction is necessary for some mental processes, but it is dangerous and fatal when we apply it to the concrete human condition. Yet this is what all governments want us to do — to regard our own citizens as "people," but to regard the citizens of other places as "the Vietcong" or "the French" or "the enemy." As long as we can be persuaded to substitute the abstraction for the reality, we can be persuaded to commit any crime in the name of "patriotism."

On Disturbing Nature's Fine Balances

THE DOMINANT WORD in the world's dictionary today is "conquest": We speak of "the conquest of space," or "the conquest of disease," or "the conquest of nature."

I happen to believe it is a wrong word, a dangerous word, an illusory word. The proper word we ought to use is "co-operation." Only if man co-operates with the external elements in the world can we survive and flourish; if we try to "conquer" them, we shall fall victim to our own ill-considered efforts. As Dr. Bodo Manstein warned, in a scientific forum held at Stuttgart last spring, man has injected himself into the natural order as a dominant factor — without considering our tolerance toward these rapid changes, and without sufficiently understanding the long-range effects of technology. We have rushed ahead too fast with antibiotics in our "conquest of disease." In our relentless campaign for the "conquest of nature," we have ignored the *balance* of nature, and one ominous result is the worldwide change in the bacterial flora. We are spending billions in our "conquest of space" to deliver a man to that sterile slag-heap called "the moon," before we are ready to handle so massive a project. In his own practice of gynecology, Dr. Manstein reported that the number of malformations is increasing slowly but steadily. As a conclusion, according to the SSRS Newsletter, he "urged that we should

stop pushing ahead in all areas without limit; we should con-
fine our attention to essentials."

The whole realm of nature is something to work *with*, not
against. Man is not an alien invader but an inextricable part
of the pattern of nature. Until we better understand our own
stresses, our own tolerances, our own capacities and limitations, our mad rush into technological "progress" could well
land us in a serious, if not permanent, regression.

It is one thing to advance our *theoretical* knowledge —
which should be pushed to the absolute frontier — but quite
another thing to tamper with the ecology of the earth and to
disrupt the delicate homeostasis of the human organism. All
change is not progress, as the political conservatives quite
properly remind us; and too-rapid changes in our physical
environment can be as damaging and unsettling as a revolution
in the body politic.

A shrewd doctor of my acquaintance recently said to me,
"I'm very wary about taking any kind of drug myself — because I suspect that any drug strong enough to do me good is
also strong enough to do me harm." This is a lesson we all still
have to learn.

We're Not at All Civilized

MAN is still living in the primitive world. The division we
make between "barbarism" and "civilization" is compounded
out of vanity and illusion. Viewed a thousand years from
now, our century will seem as much a part of the "dark ages"
as the eighth century now seems to us.

What fools us, and sustains us in our illusion, is our growth
in technology. Our mechanistic world view makes us think
that because of electricity, airplanes, conveyor belts and

skyscrapers, we are somehow superior to the Hittites, the Babylonians and the Goths.

But the true mark of "civilization" is *civility* — that is, good manners at the deepest level of behavior. And our manners are no better than they were a thousand years ago; indeed, given our awesome instruments of technology, our bad manners are now infinitely more dangerous than ever in the past. We are now able to hate more effectively, but we do not know how to love any better. We are now able to conduct massive and mutually suicidal wars between whole continents, whereas in the past, wars were limited to small city-states or duchies at the most. We are now able to poison the air everywhere, pollute all the waters, and make every crop radioactive — even among people with whom we have no quarrel. We have been able to despoil the countryside and make the city increasingly uninhabitable, so that we retain neither the consolations of rusticity nor the advantages of urbanization. Whichever environment we opt for, the discomforts are beginning to outweigh the benefits; and there is no place to live that combines the beauty of the country with the culture of the city — which is what civilization *ought* to mean.

I was born during one Great War, lived through another, and perhaps will see the third (and final) one before I die. I cannot believe this represents a significant advance in human affairs since "barbarian" times. We are able to keep many more people alive on a retail basis, through progress in science, medicine and sanitation — only to be able to kill many more on a wholesale basis, through battleships, bombs and gas chambers. The 20th Century is the most murderous era of mankind.

Let me not conclude on a bleakly pessimistic note. It need not remain this way; there is nothing inevitable about our fate. But, just as the first step to becoming better is to know you are bad, and the first step to becoming well is to know you are ill, the first step to becoming civilized is to know you are still barbarous. When we stop thinking of ourselves as "civilized," and begin to inquire what the word truly means, we may begin to cross the threshold of humanhood.

Changing Human Nature

THE ONE CLICHÉ I cannot bear above all others is that "human nature doesn't change." I am sure that is what one cannibal said to the other cannibal, when some daring soul proposed that they stop eating people.

We use this cliché as an excuse for not making ourselves better, and the world better. But we don't really believe it. As Professor John Platt points out in his book, *The Step to Man*, all our vast educational activities would be absurd if we actually thought there was no possibility of changing human nature.

This thing called "human nature," as I conceive it, is like a musical instrument — say, an organ. Now, it cannot be changed, in the sense that the range of notes is given, and we cannot play the instrument outside that range. But the range of possibilities is large enough so that we can play a nearly infinite number of melodies. We can play harmonies, and we can play dissonances. We can soothe or deafen. We can play war marches and love songs and lullabies and hymns. *How* we use the instrument depends largely upon social conditioning, upon the kind of culture we grow up in. It is not necessary to "change" human nature in order to get sweeter melodies out of the organ. It is only necessary to change the social order so that more people will have an incentive to press the keys and push the pedals that make melody, rather than discord.

We have within us an enormous range of possibilities for behavior, unlike all other animals, which can only behave one way in any given situation. Education is the way in which society selects the kinds of possibilities it wants to encourage in young people — but education, to be effective, cannot be limited to the schools. It must be the whole example society gives to its young people.

Human nature will always contain badness and goodness, enmity and love, destruction and production. In this sense, we cannot change, we cannot eliminate, the possibilities of evil. But we *can* place a premium on the constructive, the creative, and productive impulses of man — by rewarding these impulses, and penalizing the sour notes.

It is a difficult task, and it will never be wholly successful, but we must not blame our failure so far on the fact that "human nature doesn't change." We know we can change it for the worse — as some societies have done — and so we can change it for the better. Our first step is to agree upon what kind of people we want to have; and, as in most things, the first step is half the distance.

The Real Spirit of Christmas

EVERYONE SAYS that what is wrong with Christmas is that it is "too commercial" — but that is not the trouble. What is wrong with Christmas is that it is "too spiritual" — in the wrong way. The commercial aspect of Christmas can easily be ignored or repudiated by anyone who wants to take this holiday seriously. But the false "spiritual" aspect is harder to separate from the true message.

The three wise men, and the star of Bethlehem, and the

babe in the manger, and the mystery and the miracle — all these make it tempting and easy for us to forget what the whole story is about. And the whole story — the whole message of the whole messiahship — can be summed up in two sentences from Jesus' own lips:

"*If anyone says 'I love God,' and hates his brother, he is a liar.*" (I John 4:20).

"*Inasmuch as you did it to one of the least of my brethren, you did it unto Me.*" (Matthew 25:40).

This is what Christmas — the mass of Christ — must mean, if it is to mean anything. If it does not mean this to us, then what we worship is superstition and idolatry. You cannot love God without loving every fellow creature He made; and an act of contempt or rejection or injustice or neglect toward the least — the lowest, the poorest, the weakest, the dumbest — is an act against Him. If Christianity does not mean this, it means nothing. If this central fact is ignored or slurred or rationalized away, the whole structure of Christianity falls apart, and we are left with nothing but another primitive "magic" religion.

And it is not the impious, the pagans and unbelievers, who must be most on guard against forgetting this message. It is the believers, the "spiritual" people, who mistake form for substance, prayers for performance, worship for practice. For Christianity is not a "spiritual" religion, like some religions of the East. It is an intensely "practical" religion, having its moral roots in the practicality of Judaism. It was not designed to change the way men *think* or believe as much as to change the way they *act*.

It is easy to *think* Christmas, and easy to *believe* Christmas; but it is hard — sometimes intolerably hard — to *act* Christmas. It is not our false commercialism that prevents it, but our false spirituality. Not the clang of the cash register, but the jingle of bells, calling us to sentimentality, and seducing us from the grim, patient, year-around task of brotherhood.

Worst "Sins" Aren't Physical

ONE REASON that the so-called moral reformers fail to interest me is that they pay far too much attention to the lusts of the flesh, and not enough to the lusts of the spirit.

Drunkenness and lechery and the stultification of the senses by fast living are usually foolish and pathetic endeavors — but the real evils in this world come not from these appetites but from the lusts of the spirit.

Alexander the Great was proud of his chastity — proud that, contrary to the custom of his times, he refused to violate the wives and daughters of his captives. Yet Alexander's over-vaulting ambition to conquer the world was a much greater and deeper flaw than incontinence. Hitler was a model citizen, so far as the reformers are concerned. He was sober, continent, a vegetarian, and lived a Spartan personal life. But no more sick and evil man has existed in history, for the mortal sins of the spirit were his.

Men with a lust for power, with an insensate desire for fame and glory, with a desperate need to manipulate and humiliate and harm others who get in their way, are the ones who cause all the trouble. The weak men — those who easily succumb to their physical appetites — are scarcely worth bothering about.

One reason the reformers — and so many religious leaders — have failed to alter the scheme of things is that their conception of "vice" is so narrow. They fritter away their energies in fighting alcohol and tobacco and gambling and pornography — while the real evildoers sit in the front pews of the congregation and applaud their harangues.

In his topography of Hell, Dante (who really understood the essence of religion and morality) placed the lechers and the topers in the milder circles of punishment, reserving the hottest places for those who sinned against the spirit — hypocrites, traitors, exploiters, the hard of heart and narrow of mind.

It is no accident that Jesus was accused by the "respectable" citizens of his day of "consorting with publicans and harlots." He was pointing out by His action that such people are often more worthy and savable than those who called Him "Master" and secretly violated most of the basic tenets of Christ.

Physical sin merely proves that we are partly animal in origin; but spiritual sin is a repudiation and perversion of our distinctively human nature. It is this perversion that has brought mankind to the edge of catastrophe time and time again; not a thousand drunkards, wastrels or libertines can do as much damage as one bigot, one sadist — or one misguided reformer.

Such Things Youth Should Know

WHAT I WISH I Had Known at Eighteen:

— That a "free offer" is usually the most expensive kind.

— That a man isn't judged by what he knows, but by how he wears it.

— That it's useless to get into a spraying contest with a skunk.

— That when a man's position in life depends upon his having a certain opinion, that's the opinion he will have.

— That friends who break fast at the wire often fade in the stretch.

— That the best person to borrow from is one who doesn't have much.

— That women who seem the most "feminine" turn into the most feline and most feral.

— That the cynic is good-hearted beneath his facade, whereas the sentimentalist is flint-hearted beneath his.

— That the worst sins are committed by indifference, not by vice.

— That the people who are suspicious of certain things are the very ones who are the most capable of doing that of which they are suspicious.

— That nobody can misunderstand a child as much as his own parents.

— That the more neurotic partner in a marriage is the one who is *not* seeing a psychiatrist.

— That ends never justify means, but, quite the contrary, means tend to corrupt ends.

— That being able to do exactly as one pleases is the surest way to remain perpetually unpleased.

— That human nature doesn't need to change: it just needs to ask itself continually what is meant by "human," and to give itself an honest answer.

— That the way in which we say something is often more important than what we say.

— That the "liberal" who gets power can be violently il-liberal, just as the "conservative" who gets power can be greedily unconserving.

— That it can take less courage to face death than to face life.

— That the atheist who believes in man and scorns God can be closer to holiness than the religionist who believes in God and scorns man.

— That nobody has the power to hurt us or help us as much

as we fancy; and mortal hurts are almost always self-inflicted.

— That it is impossible to have a good opinion of one's self and a low opinion of others; the down-grader is projecting his self-contempt.

— That "pleasure" and "joy" are not synonyms, but may be as profoundly different as Heaven and Hell.

Conscience No Built-in Thing

ONE OF THE most fascinating discoveries I made during the 17 years I was leading Great Books was that perhaps the most widespread misconception among people consists in their idea of what "conscience" is. Most of them really believe that conscience is "something inside you" that permits you to distinguish right from wrong; a kind of built-in traffic signal, automatically lighting up "Stop" or "Go," for moral acts.

Of course, it is nothing of the kind. What is built-in is the human *capacity for conscience*, which no other animal has; it is like an empty vessel that can be filled with nearly any kind of social content.

What does the "conscience" of the cannibal tell him? That it is wrong and immoral *not* to eat your enemies after conquering them in battle, that to bury them under the ground is dreadfully impious and sickeningly indecent.

In one of the most moving passages of *Huckleberry Finn*, Twain makes Huck express shame at himself for helping Nigger Jim escape. Huck was violating his "conscience," and was afraid he would to to hell for doing so. His socially-conditioned sense of right and wrong warned him that he was committing a sin in violating the canons of slavery.

It is precisely *because* conscience is an empty vessel waiting to be filled that education becomes so important — not mere book learning, but education in its broadest sense of training the mind and shaping the character. If we were born with infallible detectors for good and evil, then conscience would be a reliable guide; but it is not, and cannot be. And, once we grasp this fact, we can possibly comprehend the adamance of the white Southerners today in the civil rights struggle. Whatever other social and economic and psychic pressures may also be at work, the white Southerners are obeying their "conscience." A deep, deep voice within them tells them that integration is wrong; and no amount of reasoning on the conscious level can still that voice.

Our conscience is shaped by the society we live in; but the whole imperative of religion demands that we rise above and beyond the society we live in. And this is almost impossibly hard for most people to do, white or black, North or South. Humanity is trapped in partial loyalties, and mistakes them for ultimate loyalties. This is the basic idolatry of mankind, and the thing that separates us from God and from one another.

"Christianity has not failed," said Chesterton many years ago. "It has simply never been tried." Nor will it be tried until we manage to achieve a universal conscience that takes precedence over the conscience of class, or color, of section, of all the little gods who murder God.

We Need Heart and Mind

SINCE there are more people in the world with good characters than with good minds, the world makes a lopsided judgment of its leaders. We are perfectly aware of the danger in a man with a spacious mind and a small character; but we are not aware of equal, if different, dangers in a man with a lofty character and a small mind.

The brilliance of an Iago or a Richard III cannot conceal their lamentable deficiencies of character; but if we study

history, instead of literature, we shall find that more troubles
have been visited upon humanity by the well-meaning, up-
right man with a deplorable deficiency of mind. For every
war that has been started by an unscrupulous genius, a dozen
have been started by honorable men whose narrow and rigid
mentality made it impossible for them to see beyond the ends
of their noses.

The tragic mistakes of the British Empire in the 18th and
19th Centuries were not the result of intellectual cunning,
but the stupidity of men who were not broad enough to foresee the evil consequences of colonialism and imperialism. And,
in Germany, the men who paved the way for Hitler were honorable, patriotic dullards like Hindenburg, whose moral rectitude covered an abyss of ignorance and befuddlement.

We appreciate good character because we know that it
means well toward us; and we suspect brilliance of mind because we know that, unless checked by a high ethical sense, it
can be fatally used against us. We feel more comfortable with
amiable simplicity than we do with the complex personality
of a first-rate mind. This is only natural, but it would be prudent for us to be as aware of the perils on the one side as on
the other. The ideal answer, of course, is a man who has both
character and brains; but a Lincoln or a Lee arises with pathetic
rareness in the history of mankind.

According to the Buddhists, there are only three sins: ill-
will, sensuality, and stupidity. We may not look upon stupidity as a sin, for it is not a voluntary act — but the consequences
of a limited mind can be as damaging as the consequences of
ill-will or unbridled appetites.

But as long as the world lives in fear, we shall respond to
people emotionally, not rationally. The man of character
soothes our fears and gives us the faith that somehow we shall
muddle through together.

In the highly organized, not to say explosive, society of the

20th Century, this is scarcely a sensible or farsighted attitude to have.

Knowledge without character is wicked, and character without knowledge is wasteful. We tell the man of mind, "It is not enough"; we should tell the man of character the same.

Few Leave Giant Footprints

How MUCH has any individual personally affected history, either for good or for bad? In his fascinating new book, *The Step to Man*, Dr. John R. Platt mentions what he calls the "Streetcar Test" for making such a measurement.

His test consists of asking this: Would world history have been appreciably different if such-and-such a man had been run over by a streetcar at, say, age ten? For most kings and presidents — and most scientists, too, Dr. Platt suggests — the answer is no.

"If they had not lived," he writes, "their places would have been taken by others with substantially similar opinions and policies and discoveries. But for some men — in our time, Lenin, Gandhi, Hitler, Churchill — the answer is obviously yes."

In considering American presidents since the turn of the century, only Franklin D. Roosevelt surely passes the test. The others — even Wilson and the first Roosevelt — could have been replaced by different men without substantially altering the course of American history. But without Lenin there would most likely have been no Russian Revolution; without Gandhi no independent India and the subsequent dissolution of the British Empire in our time; without Hitler no personality with enough pathological power to mobilize the German people into mass irrationality; without Churchill nobody to symbolize and concretize British resistance to the Nazi invasion. And this, of course, is where Marx's whole theory of "economic determinism" breaks down. The forces of history are not as implacable or as inevitable as he thought; one strong personality, for good or for evil, can deflect the whole apparent course of events.

Who could have predicted in 1932 that the conservative and patrician governor of New York State, Franklin Roosevelt, would have set the country on an entirely new course — a course it is still pursuing 30 years later, and which was not reversed even an inch during two Republican administrations? Whether one agrees or disagrees with the general drift of these policies, they demonstrate the strength of one personality to alter dramatically the social landscape of his time.

Indeed, the whole Russian Revolution itself is an ironic refutation of Marx's theory that men are largely motivated by their economic status and possessions — for Marx himself is a looming exception to that rule, the son of middle-class parents, who repudiated the bourgeois society of his age and almost single-handed changed the face of the earth.

Such men are exceedingly rare, but when they arrive on the scene, the script is thrown away, and historical predictability goes by the boards. Today, caught up by vast impersonal forces that seem too complex and overwhelming for the average man to cope with, it is heartening to remember that, somewhere in our land, a ten-year-old who is not being run over by a streetcar may shape the future in some utterly unimaginable — and perhaps quite wonderful — way.

The Power of Our Non-self

AFTER ATTENDING the services for Paul Tillich — a fine man as well as one of the most influential religious thinkers of our time — I returned home and began rereading one of his books, *Love, Power, and Justice*. I couldn't think of a better way to honor his memory.

In one of the early chapters, he speaks of the power of life as "self-affirmation." Life is divided between the self and the non-self; what makes a life truly powerful is the ability of the self to include the non-self in it, without being destroyed by it. The neurotic, he pointed out, can include only a little non-self in his self-affirmation; the average man, a limited amount; the creative genius, a large amount.

What does this mean in specific terms? Shakespeare immediately comes to mind. In what does his great power of life lie, his immortality, his tremendous appeal, his overcoming the barriers of translation and different cultures?

It was not merely his literary genius as such. His poetry is great, of course, but language alone cannot account for his transcendent popularity among all people everywhere who have come in touch with his works. There is something more basic in his plays, beyond poetry, beyond literature, beyond all intellectual and esthetic categories. It is, indeed, his capacity to include a superlatively large amount of non-self in his self-affirmation. While there are some characters in the plays that he obviously prefers to others, there are none that he does not in some way sympathize with, that he cannot absorb into his own nature and understanding.

What we loosely call "the power of empathy" was stronger in him than in any other literary figure. Like Terence (only with more justification), he could say, "I am a man, and therefore nothing human is alien to me." He was not censorious, did not judge men as we judge them, did not assume that even the darkest villain was a creature different in *kind* from himself.

Shakespeare had his own standards of rectitude and morality, of course; but while he abhorred certain qualities and deplored certain weaknesses, he was not willing to indict a total personality. How easy it would have been, for instance, to depict Shylock as the stock figure of fun in the 16th Century; and how impossible for Shakespeare not to turn the stage Jew into a man who bleeds just like anyone else.

The more non-self we are able to include in our self-affirmation, the more power of life we have; for all life is a striving toward reunion with the separated. Beyond theology, this was Tillich's most profound reminder to our generation of coldly separated egos.

Rising Above Our Desires

MOST PEOPLE, if asked to give you a capsule version of their ultimate belief, will tell you that although they don't know much about religion or philosophy or such matters, they agree with Polonius when he said "to thine own self be true and . . . thou canst not then be false to any man."

This statement, shrewdly placed by Shakespeare in the mouth of one of his most windy, vapid and self-seeking characters, has assumed almost Scriptural status in modern society; and scarcely anyone has bothered to examine what it really means.

What does it mean to be true to one's own self? Hitler, as a psychopath, was fanatically true to himself; Jesse James, as a reckless adventurer, was gloriously true to himself; and the new Soviet leaders are now excoriating Khrushchev because he was truer to himself than he was to Marx, to Lenin and to the Russian state.

A man has both private needs and public responsibilities. While it is important that he satisfy some of these private needs, it is equally important that he carry out his public responsibilities. And what does he do when these two come into conflict?

How then does Polonius' advice help us? What is this "self" to which we should be true? The self that whispers "satisfy your desires" or the self that sternly urges "do your duty"? The self that says "you only live once" or the self that says "this is not right"?

The men we revere and honor are those who trained themselves to be true to ideas that were greater than, and outside, themselves. They were men who subdued greed, or lust, or envy, or sloth, and were willing to live and die for an ideal which could never be realized in their own time.

Man is not, and by nature can never be, his own frame of reference. Man cannot be true to himself, because the self is hopelessly divided, is in continual conflict.

We can only be true to a core of beliefs, and a code of conduct, which we think is *right*, even when it goes against the grain of our desires and appetites.

"Trueness" consists in the willingness to sacrifice one's private satisfactions and benefits, in the willingness to postpone present pleasures for the sake of future goals. These goals — whether we call them Blessedness, or Justice, or Maturity — make us more of what men ought to be; and without them, we can be true only to a grasping and self-deceiving ego, as was Polonius.

2

OF MEN, WOMEN,

AND CHILDREN

School Can Curb Initiative

IF EDISON had not dropped out of school at the early age he did, it is likely that he would not have turned out to be the prolific inventor he was. Great inventors and innovators, on the whole, have been more hindered than helped by formal schooling. The chief reason for this, it seems to me, is the intense and perpetual "fear of failure" that the school instills in the pupil. The pupil is more than anything afraid to fail — but the truly creative mind is prepared to fail and fail again in order to succeed once in a new and different way.

My children attend a school that gives no grades, and no competitive rankings, for the first half-dozen years; at first I was dubious about the advantages of this system, but I quickly came to see that it does encourage curiosity and creativeness, rather than forcing the children to be "right" at first, even at the expense of understanding what they are "right" about.

Much of the cheating that is currently worrying parents and teachers in the colleges springs from this hysterical "fear of

failure" and the absolute need to come up with the right answer in exams, rather than mastering the subject and learning
how it relates to other subjects.

In this connection, it is interesting to note that in the course
of a seven-year-long study at the University of California,
testing part-time inventors, it was found that the *most inventive* of the inventors got a shockingly low score of only *six*
on the Terman Concept Mastery Test. He got this low score
because, as the researchers pointed out, "he was more than
willing to impart any information he had in his head, including wrong information or hunches." It was his willingness to
try anything, his lack of fear of being wrong, that made him
so productive an inventor.

And it is a known fact that the brightest and most creative
of pupils often get a worse score on some tests than less bright
pupils — because the creative ones detect subtleties and
nuances in the questions that the less bright ones are not even
aware of. The average pupil is soon conditioned to answer
"Right" or "Wrong"; the superior pupil sees the shades of
gray in between, and his answers are more qualified.

Emotionally, too, the inventive minds are able to tolerate
disorder and ambiguity, while the average mind becomes upset
if things are not neatly pigeonholed. The school values rigidity within a closed system; but all innovation comes from people who are open to newness, who question all closed systems, and who don't mind ambiguous answers. One wonders
how many dropouts have been simply "too good" for their
schools.

Why Vice Raids Mean Nothing

PERIODICALLY, my city, like all big cities, features "vice raids"
by flying squadrons of police. In these raids, a few saloons
are closed down, a handful of prostitutes and panderers fined,

a bartender sent to the County jailhouse for a minimal term. When the heat is off, in a few days, new places open up for the same old business — girls soliciting at bars, phony champagne at $30 a bottle, and cabdrivers carting conventioneers to "where the action is." It is a futile, farcical, and hypocritical affair. All seasoned newspapermen know it, the police know it, and the denizens of *le milieu* know it; this is what makes them so cynical about "crusades."

There is one simple and efficient way to stop it, or at least to reduce the business to a minimum; but few officials in any city would care to invoke it. And that is to stop applying the double standard to prostitution.

The so-called "respectable" patrons of these joints are never fined or arrested; it is always the disreputable elements who take the rap, such as it is. Since they make their living out of this, they shrug it off stoically and charge it up to "business expenses," as a kind of insurance premium they must pay to stay in business.

They provide the supply. The demand is generated by respectable and responsible members of society: by conventioneers from small towns, by suburban paragons of virtue sneaking into the city for a night of fun, by companies subsidizing the expense accounts of salesmen "entertaining" customers. It is not riffraff who patronize these girls and these places. It is the small-town vestryman, the suburban dentist, the loving husband and father who oversubscribes to the Girl Scout Cookie Drive back home. Ninety-nine percent of the customers are what the *milieu* contemptuously refer to as "square Johns."

What if these square Johns were arrested in raids, fined or jailed for taking part in an illegal transaction? What if their names and addresses were publicized in the newspapers? How long do you imagine the business would continue to thrive under such conditions?

Naturally, this will not be done. We maintain the fiction that the prostitutes are culpable, while the men are innocent victims. But, of course, that is nonsense. The men know exactly what they are looking for, and what they are paying for. Thirty bucks for a bottle of champagne isn't for the bubbles, John.

I am not suggesting that we should engage in this painful exposure of middle-class hypocrisy; merely that until we do, the raids are silly.

We Can't All Bloom Early

A HALF-DOZEN years ago, on his 70th birthday, the late T. S. Eliot remarked in an interview: "I am just beginning to grow up, to get maturity. In the last few years, everything I'd done up to 60 or so has seemed very childish."

He recognized, as few of us do about ourselves, that the emotional rate of growth bears little relation to one's age or even to one's intellectual capacities. Some personalities bloom early, some bloom late, and some never bloom at all, but pass from adolescence into senility. I have known farm girls of 16 who were already more mature than Eliot thinks he was at 60 — who knew their identity, their responsibility, and their limitations; who knew, in short, what it is to be grown up, in the way in which one accepts oneself and handles other people.

This ability is much rarer than we think, and is partly a matter of inborn constitution and partly a matter of early environment. Both together are needed to bring about the full flowering of the personality at the proper age. Nor is it a matter of consciously "knowing oneself." Many a genius has known himself thoroughly, but "knowing" is not "being" or "doing" — and all his knowledge does not change what he is or does.

William James spoke of the "once-born" and the "twice-born." The former are those, endowed with a mysterious grace, who recognize themselves the moment they are thrown into the world, who fit snugly into their skins and grow all of a piece as the years progress. The numerous twice-born are those, like Housman, who described himself as "a stranger, and afraid, in a world I never made." It is necessary for such to shed their skins, like a snake, in later years, and become born again, after many mistakes and suffering.

Some of the most rewarding people in the world are the twice-born; but millions never succeed in shedding the first skin, merely spending the years in adding layers of defense to it.

Modern man is particularly vulnerable to this "crisis of identity." Psychoanalysts have noted, for instance, that the type of patient has been changing over the past several decades: they no longer see the kind of illness Freud began working with, but a different kind. It is not a person with a particular symptom or complaint, but the "lost personality" who cannot relate to himself or to others, creatively or lovingly. These are, somehow, physically "displaced persons."

The pressures of modern times have made it more imperative than ever that we become mature as soon as possible, and yet these same pressures have made it harder to do so. This is the contemporary "bind."

Semi-Literates Clog Colleges

WHAT if the nation's high schools simply refused to graduate most of their students next June? What if the whole educational process were backed up a year or so?

Apart from overcrowding, this radical suggestion might be the only solution to the growing problem of illiteracy in the nation's schools. If pupils can't read, write and spell, should they get a diploma and go on to college or to work?

And they can't read, write or spell — even at the highest

levels. The University of California, for instance, takes only the *top one-eighth* of the state's high school graduates, and gives them a three-hour English test before admission. This year, as in past years, about half of these "top one-eighth" incoming college freshmen flunked the English test. Of the 9,000 admitted to the University of California, nearly 5,000 have to be given "bonehead" remedial English courses, at a great loss of time, expense and energy.

You can well imagine what the other seven-eighths are like, in terms of having a command of their mother tongue. Yet, they are being turned out of high schools by the millions, to clog up college classrooms, to hold back the efforts of the minority of serious students.

If pupils, however, absolutely knew that they could not get out of high school until they had a basic grasp of the reading and writing process, then holding them back a year or so might be the fastest and cheapest way to break the logjam of illiteracy at the college freshman level.

Why can't these students read and write? There are three main reasons: (1) the parents don't care enough; (2) many, if not most, teachers of English, are unqualified or under-qualified; and (3) even the qualified ones have too many students and too many classes.

A concerted attack is needed on all these fronts. If the students are held back, the parents will quickly care enough. If they care enough, more school bond issues will pass — and perhaps more of this money will be earmarked for salaries and staff, and less for homecoming games, beauty queens, swimming pools, brass bands, and driving instruction.

The national Council of Teachers of English recommends no more than 100 students and four classes per teacher, to obtain the optimum results. But in my state of Illinois, which is fairly typical, only ten public high schools out of 706 meet this minimum requirement. The pupils can't learn if the teachers can't teach.

Meanwhile, the colleges are flooded with semiliterates, and the whole educational process is bogged down in mediocrity. Maybe it's time to stop the machinery and retool for the next season.

Dual Objective of Education

IN HIS CLASSIC little book of a generation ago, *The Aims of Education*, Whitehead makes the point — too often forgotten or ignored — that education in its best sense really consists of two things, not one. It consists of knowing a great many different subjects fairly well, and knowing one subject very well. A person is not truly educated if — like a doctor or lawyer or engineer in modern America — he knows only one thing very well, and other things hardly at all.

By the same token, the generalist is not truly an educated person, if he has only a smattering — or even more than a smattering — of many subjects, and is able to move easily among them. This is the fault, and fallacy, of a "liberal arts" education that concentrates on nothing in particular.

It is easy to see that the narrow specialist is not educated, for he does not grasp the relationship between his field and other fields. It is harder to see that the glib generalist is not educated either, however fluently he may discourse on a number of "cultural" topics.

The value of learning one subject thoroughly is this: not merely that we come to *know* the subject, but that we come to know what *knowing* really consists in. This is of the utmost importance. Rigorous application to a particular subject — no matter what the subject is — shows the student what knowledge consists of, so that he is aware when he possesses it, and when he does not. For it is the invariable hall-mark of the half-educated person (who is much more dangerous than the plain ignoramus) that he thinks he knows what he does not know.

The whole point of learning one thing well is to learn how extremely difficult it is to attain knowledge; how much labor, patience, and precision it calls for; and how modest and tentative we must be in assuming that we "know" something before we have given it such labor, patience and precision.

The trouble with a specialized education is that it overlooks whole areas of human activity; the trouble with a "broad" education is that it ranges too widely and diffusely, and enables the student to sound (and feel) knowledgeable without having taken the pains to learn exactly what knowledge is, as opposed to prejudice, opinion, speculation, and theory.

Knowledge is like love: it must be directed toward a specific object, it cannot be held in the abstract. Only when we learn to love someone can we detect the counterfeits of love; and only when we know something specific can we compare this knowledge with our ignorance in some other field. In humility lies the beginning of wisdom.

How We Would Treat A Child

I DON'T BELIEVE those white people who are fond of repeating that "the Negro is just like a child." Not only don't I believe that the Negro is just like a child; I don't believe that those white people believe it either.

Because if the Negro is just like a child, why hasn't he been treated as well as we treat a child? If he is not quite up to the rest of us — a little slower or duller — why haven't we treated him as we treat the slowest or dullest child in the family?

If the parents have any sense or feeling, what do they do with a child who is behind the others? Why, naturally, they treat him better than the others, to try to make up the difference. They give more sympathy, special tutoring, extra considerations. And, surprisingly often, this "dull" child turns out to be just as smart as — and much nicer than — the others.

But we in America have done exactly the opposite with the Negro. If we sincerely believed he was slower than the rest of us, and we all belong to the family of man, we would have honored our obligation to give him the most help and understanding, as we would a child. Instead, we have used his alleged "inferiority" first to enslave him, then to break up his family, then to deny him a decent education and livelihood, and make him fit for nothing but servile work.

Many of the unattractive things that white people say about the Negro are undeniably true. But they are true because *we have made them come true.* If you treat someone under your control like a dolt, he will react like a dolt; treat him like an animal, and he will respond like an animal; treat him as an object of contempt, and he will become filled with a self-contempt that must sooner or later erupt in rage, hate and violence.

If we are so insecure that we cannot treat Negroes as equals, let us not pretend it is because they are like backward children — for we treat our backward children with love and patience, encouraging them in their schoolwork, making the biggest fuss over their achievements, and trying to provide them with the greatest security for the future.

If we were willing to do for the Negro what we are willing to do for the retarded, we might find that we are not dealing with a backward child at all, but with a flawed and deprived adult who is capable of all we are capable of — and perhaps much more, having suffered so long, having patiently borne the full measure of man's inhumanity to man.

The Crucial Task of the School

THE BIGGEST PROBLEM our children and grandchildren may
have to face is the growing fact that humanity's technical
equipment is fast outstripping the average mental powers of
society. Sooner than we expect, only a small minority will be
able to understand the processes by which the human population is maintained. And if these processes cannot be understood by the average man, how can the society make any
rational and democratic decisions on basic matters?

In past ages, the social processes were relatively simple and
clear. Power was almost always in the hands of a small oligarchy — whether it was the State, the Church, or the Military.
People knew who their rulers were, what they were doing,
and why they were doing it.

Today, and increasingly in the future, the social processes
have become so complex, so interrelated, so tied in with scientific and technological developments, that the average collective mind of mankind is baffled, confused, and, consequently,
unresponsive. If we do not understand what is happening,
or why, the decisions we are called upon to make will always
be emotional reactions rather than reasoned judgments.

This is a problem that far transcends the current conflict
between capitalism and communism, or the dispute about government versus private enterprise. The entire world, East
and West alike, is going through a transformation of unprecedented magnitude; we might even be said to be moving, at
an enormous speed, from "civilization" to "post-civilization."

In his recent book, *The Meaning of the Twentieth Century*,
Kenneth Boulding, an economist at the University of Michi-
gan, is one of our few contemporaries to grasp the implications
of this cataclysmic change facing our children and theirs. We
are at a watershed of human existence, at which most of our

previous assumptions will be questioned, and many will have to be rejected.

Thus, it becomes even more imperative than ever that our educational system be revamped. What the schools must turn out are people who can think, who can make rational value judgments, who are not bound (intellectually and emotionally) to obsolete ideologies that have little relevance to the unique future before them.

The crucial task of the school is twofold: to ask "What does it mean to be a human person?" and "What kind of society will best fit the needs of this person?" All other questions are marginal and trivial. Unless these two are worked out, society will extinguish itself by the ignorant mishandling of the very tools technology has provided us with.

Learning Faster than Forgetting

IF, THIS JUNE, your son received a Ph.D. degree in aerospace engineering, half of what he knows when he graduates will be obsolete in ten years. For fully half of what he needs to know for the next ten years is completely unknown today.

This "obsolescence of knowledge," especially in scientific fields, is changing the whole idea of what constitutes a "good" college education. And it reaffirms those of us who have been saying for a long time that *learning how to learn* is the most important part of education.

The real reason that vocational and "specialist" training is largely pointless today lies in the rapid outdating of so much technical knowledge and skills. Even our newest profession — that of programming computers — will soon be obsolete, when the computers are built that will program themselves.

What the new society of the future calls for are *versatility* and *flexibility* and *creativity*. These cannot be learned in a technical sense; they are part of a liberal education, which teaches men and women how to think, not just how to put things together and make them work. The new machines will be able to put things together much better than people can.

It is no accident that, for the first time, the prestigious Massachusetts Institute of Technology has appointed a president who is neither a scientist nor a technician. Or that business schools, such as those at Harvard and Columbia, have shifted their emphasis from the technical aspects of business administration to a broader program of liberal arts.

In a recent talk, Dr. Arnold Ducoffe, director of Georgia Tech's School of Aerospace Engineering, remarked that this obsolescence of knowledge is the big reason that today's engineering schools no longer stress the "mechanical," but rather the "philosophical" elements in science — not *how* to do something, but *why* something is true. If we learn the reasons *behind* phenomena, then we can cope with changing conditions.

Our pressing need is for men and women who can adapt to needs and acquire skills that are barely on the horizon today. More and more, the function of the specialist is being taken over by the machines; it is the "generalist," who can make decisions based on an imaginative projection of the future, we so desperately require to keep the wheels turning.

In the past, the average man would change his *job* three times during his lifetime. In the future, we are told, the average man may have to change his *vocation* three times during his lifetime. Unless he learns how to learn, in a philosophical sense, the specialist may become a dropout from the economic community.

Can We Prevent Delinquency?

OCCASIONALLY, I see a boy in our neighborhood whom I would judge to be about 11 years old. So far as I know, he has done nothing wrong yet. He attends school regularly, and has not got into trouble. But I am morally certain that he is going to become an active delinquent in a few years. The signs are all there, if one looks closely at his attitudes.

This is the kind of boy who needs special attention paid to him — the potential pre-delinquent. Even at 11, it may be almost too late, for most experts in the field agree that anti-social patterns are set by the age of 5 or 6.

At 11, however, a lot may still be done to retrain the feelings and reshape the behavior patterns. But how do we go about it? The parents will probably refuse to believe that the boy is heading for trouble; and there are not enough diagnostic or therapeutic centers set up in any community to handle such incipient problems.

Yet, the rising rate of delinquency cannot be halted or reversed, I am convinced, without such preventive measures. In this respect, delinquency is like a cancer: if we can detect pre-cancerous patients early enough, they can usually be saved. Likewise, if we can detect and treat pre-delinquents early enough, much can be done to help them.

Governmental and social agencies spend millions upon millions for coping with delinquents *after* they have got into serious difficulties; and there is no indication that any of these expensive efforts diminish the rate of delinquency. Delinquent crimes, indeed, have gone up four times as fast as adult crimes in the period since the end of World War II.

According to Dr. J. M. Stubblebine, a psychiatrist who has worked with children of this kind for many years in California, it *is* possible to recognize a potential delinquent by a number of traits that most of them share in common. Writing in the October issue of the journal, *Mental Hygiene*, he says:

"Parents, educators, the general physician, family counselors and clergymen must all learn to recognize the pre-delinquent. While it is difficult to 'shift gears' mentally and to regard as potentially dangerous some types of behavior previously thought to be normal, this basic change in attitude would help us come closer to finding both the cause of delinquency and the means of prevention."

It is a difficult task, and calls for more foresight and insight than simply "punishing" or "correcting" delinquents after they are in police custody. But since neither the punishment nor the correction seems to have any lasting effect, perhaps it is time we shifted gears — and funds — into the more fruitful field of detection and prevention.

Why Youths Join the Gangs

THE MOST IMPORTANT aspect of what we call "juvenile delinquency" is usually forgotten or ignored by those who are most distressed by it. The JD does not act as an individual, but as part of a group. There is very little delinquency activity on an individual basis; 90 percent of it is collective. Indeed, the "loner" is looked down upon by delinquent gangs as mentally aberrant.

All persons, of whatever age beyond infancy, have a desperate need for *association* and *identification*. When a teen-age boy joins a gang, and gives it his basic loyalty (even unto death), he is expressing a primitive need that is not otherwise satisfied in the society he has grown up in.

And it is important to understand that the juvenile gang is often the only means a boy has to demonstrate his latent virtues. For the gang requires courage, fidelity, discipline, self-sacrifice, and trust. These are all good and positive qualities, although directed toward an antisocial end.

In the same way, the early communist and Nazi movements in Russia and Germany were able to attract the youth, who had become alienated from the traditional social order. It took their virtues and utilized them in the service of political vices.

The rise of juvenile gangs in our urban society is more an indictment of the society than of the boys who constitute them. It is often the most creative and brightest boys who join and lead these groups — in line with the old Latin tag that "the worst is a corruption of the best."

Boys who grow up bored, discouraged and alienated from their community do not feel like persons in their own right, but like cogs in some impersonal machine that is grinding them down. Since they have a fundamental need to associate, and to identify, with something larger than themselves, the gang becomes the basic unit of loyalty — displacing the family, the community, and even the nation.

We are doing almost nothing about this growing problem. Detention homes and reform schools are futile, if not worse. Social welfare programs are understaffed, underfinanced, and with no clear sense or purpose or direction. The adult community does not know how to communicate with these boys, and would not know what to say to them if it could communicate, for the value systems of the bourgeoisie are meaningless to the boys.

Juvenile crime in the last decade has risen four times as fast as the population growth; and, in the next few decades, there will be more and more younger people under 25. Our greatest threat as a nation may come not from external enemies, but from the millions of disaffected youths who live among us, and off us, but not truly with us.

A Mystery Too Deep for Us

THE TWO YOUNG PEOPLE assured me that they understood each other "perfectly and completely," and no doubt they thought me cynical or even slightly senile when I shrugged and smiled skeptically at their words. But the fact is that, much as they are in love, no person can wholly see another person — and what we cannot wholly see, we cannot wholly understand. We can only have faith, which is quite another matter.

We cannot even see a whole apple, much less a person. Every apple has its obverse and reverse sides; yet who can see them at once, to capture the totality of the apple? In a mirror, of course, we see only a reflection, and not the substance itself. At each given moment, we see merely a part of the apple and build up the rest in our mind's eye from the part we see. But in its fullness, in its third-dimensionality, the apple remains unknown to us. Every object that has depth withholds some secret from us.

And how much more so a person. Hamlet rebuked his false friends for trying to pluck out the heart of his mystery: for his mystery was, quite simply, *himself* — that part unknown to everyone, even to his dearest friend, Horatio, even to Hamlet himself at the end.

Gabriel Marcel, many years ago, wrote a fine book called *The Mystery of the Person*. It is a phrase worth remembering, because in modern times this mystery (which, like all proper mysteries, has a sacred origin) runs the risk of being dissolved into its lifeless components.

There are many today who would consider the person chiefly as Economic Man. There are those, equally prevalent, who would reduce him to Psychological Man. There are the positivists and super-scientists who would admit nothing but Physical and Chemical Man, as if two dollars' worth of phosphates explained love and honor and self-sacrifice.

The whole person cannot be known by human means alone, and he is in danger of being violated when it is tried: his privacy removed, his passions anatomized, his needs prescribed and proscribed, his reactions tabulated on a curve, his ultimate identity reduced to Personnel, Patient, Consumer, Citizen, Housewife, Student, Manager, and, finally, Casualty.

It was sweet and touching that the young couple thought they understood each other "perfectly and completely." Ten years from now, they will not be so sure; and twenty years from now, if they stay together and gain in wisdom, they may have the courage and honesty to admit that they do not, and never did. Nor do they need to: love was devised to carry the current from mystery to mystery — a current so elusive and yet so heavy that no wires of understanding or reason can support it.

Why Some Marriages Fail

I was having lunch with an old friend from the East whose marriage was breaking up, after 15 years of determined efforts on both parts to keep it going.

"What bothers me," he said, "is that I still can't understand why some marriages make it, and others don't. It isn't merely that I feel a failure in this one — it's that I really don't know how much I've learned about having a good second one, and that's what scares me."

Of course, marriage is a subject that everyone knows something about, and no one knows enough about. It's easy to see why the church considers marriage a sacrament — because there is a *mystery* at the heart of it that defies most rational explanation.

In my view, what makes most marriages founder is nothing that appears on the surface, but an unconscious neurotic drive on the part of one (or, more commonly, both) of the partners. And the drive is usually the same: *a desire and a need for contradictory qualities in a mate.* The essence of a neurotic is that he is a personality in conflict — he yearns for opposite things at the same time, and cannot be gratified by either one or the other alone.

As a concrete illustration, consider the common phenomenon of the woman who marries a passive man. She married him because his passivity was appealing to her — but at the same time, over the years, she gradually comes to resent him because he is not more dominating.

If she divorces him, however, and marries a dominating man, she would equally come to resent him in time, because a part of her nature craves the other. She is split in her needs, and until her basic conflict can be resolved, no one man can content her for long.

The same pattern, with many variations (most of them more subtle than this crude example I have given), runs through the millions of miserable marriages we see all around us. In most cases (though not all, by any means), the husband or wife would be just as unhappy with a different kind of mate.

As we grow older, we either modify or discard our fantasies to fit reality, or else we persist in trying to find a "reality" to match the fantasy. The latter task is an impossible one, for the neurotic is not looking for a real person but for an abstract embodiment of childish wishes. And wishes, moreover, that contradict one another.

Our parents and grandparents were wrong in not demanding greater happiness out of marriage than it customarily gave them. But we are more tragically wrong in demanding satisfactions no one person can provide.

The "Right" to Have Children

ONE ANSWER to the population explosion is, of course, more effective birth control methods, and better information about these methods to the people who need it most. Another answer, however, that is neglected in most discussions of the subject is the necessity for changing attitudes toward motherhood on the part of many women.

Many women have children through accident or ignorance; but many more have children because it is considered the thing to do, the acceptable role for a wife. They do not want a child as much as they want the *idea* of a child.

A woman whose heart is not in it should not be encouraged to have children. Yet, while on the one hand we deplore the constant rise in population, on the other hand we somehow seem to suggest that a childless woman is an object of pity or scorn.

Many mothers — too many — did not really want children; this can be seen from the way they handle them. They would like a storybook child: pretty and clean and winsome and obedient, to be put away in a box when the mother is tired of playing with it; not a real child, with a runny nose and torn socks and a sassy tongue and an insatiable desire for attention.

When we talk about the population explosion, most of us are thinking about the underdeveloped countries in the Far East. Not many know that the rate of population growth in the last decade in the U.S. is greater than that of Japan, and about as large as that of India.

True, we can "afford" children more than they can; but our contribution to the problem of space and food supply for the whole world of the future is as substantial as theirs. Moreover, we have access to birth control information and techniques that are lacking in underdeveloped lands.

One of the principal reasons we have not availed ourselves of these techniques as fully as possible has been our social emphasis on "babies for all wives." Many women are pressured by this sentimental fiction into having babies they do not really want and cannot really handle. The emotional consequences to such children, of course, are most damaging. A small child is the most rewarding of creatures if one knows how to love it in the right way, and the most taxing if one does not. The common belief that every woman is "naturally" a good mother is as fallacious as thinking that every piano can make good music.

There are people who should not marry, and there are married couples who should not have children. Contraception is one way to reduce the population swell, but it will not succeed until the only women who have babies are those who want the substance and not just the symbol.

Ten Commandments for Parents

A COLLEGE CONFERENCE on "Parents and Children" has asked me to contribute a few lines to its symposium, since I am unable to attend in person. Knowing full well that almost all advice on child-rearing is futile, I am nevertheless tempted to suggest the following Decalog for Parents:

— Thou shalt honor no other gods but God, steadfastly refusing to make thy child a minor deity in the household.

— Thou shalt make no promises that are broken, whether these be promises of pleasure or promises of punishment; for unless thy child learns to respect thy word, he will not respect any person.

— Thou shalt teach thy child by example, and not by precept; for a parent who teaches a child religion and morality and yet lives by greed, passion and hypocrisy must expect that his conduct will be followed and his counsel ignored.

— Thou shalt worship the Sabbath communally, with thy family, and not seek solitary pleasures which plunge each member of the family into social and spiritual isolation when they should be most together.

— Thou shalt instill no fears into thy child, but rather impress upon him that love casteth out fear; and that he who commits no wrongs because of fear is merely weak, whereas he who pursueth righteousness because of love is truly strong.

— Thou shalt help thy child accept the variety of mankind with joy and wonder in God's creative originality; and not breed in him that terrible false pride of superiority, which stunts and twists the personality of man.

— Thou shalt be not too much a parent, allowing thy child freely to make his own mistakes, not protecting him unduly from the painful consequences of his errors.

— Thou shalt not expect nor demand love from thy child simply because thou art his parent; but thou shalt try to win his respect as a person by justice, humor and understanding.

— Thou shalt not force thy child to develop in thine own image, but assist him in becoming the best kind of person his own nature requires; for we must not judge a child by others, but only by his own potential.

— Thou shalt look daily into thine own heart and examine thy motives; for when thy motives are unpure, love curdles into possessiveness, and thy child is no longer a creature of God, but an instrument of Man's misguided vanity.

Some Feelings Defy Analysis

"Who do you love most?" my five-year-old once asked me, enumerating all the children, including himself. "Don't be silly," I laughed weakly. "I love all of them the same."

He was not to be put off by this shabby parental device. "Who do you love most?" he persisted, and waited for a serious and honest reply. All I could say was, "I love you all the same, but in different ways, because you're different children."

He was not satisfied with this equivocating reply. He looked at me, then shrugged, and gave up the matter. I could see that I had lost a little status in his eyes, as a truth teller and a square shooter.

But how can one answer such a question, when the truth is hardly known, or, if known, barely admitted to oneself? Every parent, I suppose, has one special favorite, one who has captured some secret place of the heart. He tries not to show it, even to feel it, but it is there — and the children know it is there.

Each of us wants to be God's favorite child; Cain, after all, slew Abel because he was jealous that God accepted Abel's gift and spurned his own. It was not so much an act of hate against his brother — there is no mention that they were unfriendly — as a burning resentment against what he considered the partiality of his "father" in heaven. And again in the very first book of the Bible, we are told the story of Joseph, who was the younger son and favorite of his father, Jacob, and who thus became so hated by his older brothers that they sold him as a slave to a caravan going to Egypt.

All children are aware that their parents do not, and perhaps cannot, love them equally. The parents may be, as most are, scrupulously fair in treating them all alike, and even in giving a little extra to those less well endowed — but a child's radar system is frighteningly accurate about feelings we ourselves may not even know we possess.

It is these feelings — hidden even from ourselves — that determine how a child will react, to us, to its siblings, and to the world at large. It is not so much what we do, or what we say, or the actual "techniques" of child-rearing that matter, as much as our emotional substratum.

Parents who tend to blame themselves when a child turns out to have "problems" often ask themselves "What did I do wrong?" or "What did I fail to do?" In most cases, I think, there is no specific act or attitude or omission to pinpoint; and it is futile for the parents to blame themselves for feelings they did or did not have.

"Who do you love most?" is a question that cannot be successfully answered, or successfully evaded. This may be why the child, with its unerring instinct for our weaknesses, eventually confronts us with it.

Evil Outlets for Energy

THROUGHOUT HISTORY, boys have always had a great need to prove that they possess the virtues of courage, endurance and skill. And, until modern times, societies have always provided the opportunities for this.

The 20th Century rise in juvenile delinquency is, of course, the result of many factors. One of the most important, I am convinced, is the lack of opportunity for boys to prove their prowess without getting into trouble.

As we become more and more urbanized and technological, as the frontier disappears, as the challenge of nature becomes subdued, as density of population and congestion of traffic increase — more and more boys are less and less able to find suitable activities for challenging their physical aptitudes. This is one reason, by the way, that organized sports have become so overemphasized in our time.

Adolescent boys in the big cities find it increasingly difficult to grow up in the traditional fashion. If they are venturesome, they get into trouble; if they are aggressive, there are no proper objects around to vent their aggressiveness on, except each other, in tight little gangs. And, most of all, the kind of men they used to model themselves on — the skillful hunter and trapper — have all but vanished today. Their models, therefore, become professional athletes or entertainers or criminals — for these are the only three kinds of people in modern society who seem to live outside the established rules, who can get away with forms of conduct denied to men in more conventional occupations.

In primitive societies, the leaders were wise enough to know the value of the *rites de passage* — the ritual by which a young man proved his emergence into manhood. He was forced to fast, to go into solitude, to paddle through rapids, to engage in tourneys of strength and skill and stamina. All this was done with community approval, and without really hurting anybody else.

Modern society has taken this away and provided no equivalent to drain off the highly-charged kinetic energies of boys. So they invent their own games — playing "chicken" in autos is one of the most dangerous forms — and use adult society as the antagonist. There is no sense of community in what they do; rather, the community has become the enemy.

This has happened in nation after nation, as each country becomes more urbanized and mechanized. It is not so much a moral or a parental problem as it is a "problem of civilization." Much of what we glibly call "delinquency" comes from frustration — for if a youth cannot prove his manhood with tests set and approved by the community, he will prove it to his peers with acts of bravado directed against the community.

Let His Individuality Alone

THE REASON I am against any rigid systems or "techniques" for handling children is that no two children are really alike. They only *seem* to be, to the untrained eye.

A few days after the birth of one of my children, I had a little chat with the supervisor of the nursery at the hospital. "Can you tell the babies apart without reading the tags?" I asked. "They all look alike to me."

"It's an amazing thing," she said, "but after you've worked in the nursery even a short time, you can tell the babies apart within 12 hours after they're born.

"And I don't mean just physically," she continued, "although even their faces are quite different. I mean the personalities are distinctive, too. One baby is quite responsive, another is placid, and a third is fretful. Each has his own individual texture and pattern of personality."

We apply the art of discrimination to our clothes, our cigarets and our motor cars; but it is surprising how few new parents learn to discriminate between their particular baby and the general concept of "infant."

There is no such creature as an "average" baby, except in the minds of statisticians. Each has not only his own texture and pattern, but his own *rhythm* of living. Understanding this rhythm, and learning to work with it, is the first and most important task in rearing children.

(Indeed, perhaps the greatest superiority of a man like Dr. Spock over his predecessors is his insistence on individual differences. Throughout his books, he has emphasized the individuality of the new baby, and warns the parents against trying to make the infant conform to some abstract standard of "babyness.")

One of the surprising findings of psychiatric research has been the large number of older children who feel "rejected," even though their parents showered them with love. Such feelings can be explained only as a negative reaction when parents try to make their baby resemble some ideal baby — to push him with food, to hasten his training, to show disappointment when his development is not as rapid as "the book" baby.

What this apparently means to the child's unconscious is that his parents wish he would be some other kind of child, that they would like to change him or trade him in on a new model which looks like the cover of a baby magazine or the picture on a can of baby food. For the most subtle and damaging way to "reject" an infant is to want to turn him into someone other than himself.

Bad Example Can Be Good

DURING the question period following a talk I gave on children and education, someone in the audience asked me: "Do you try to set a good example for your children?"

"No," I said, "I'm not good enough to set a good example — but I'm bad enough to set a bad example, and honest enough to let the children know it."

This was not just a quip. Most parents are not good enough to set the kind of example they should for their children, and pretending that they are merely makes the children puzzled, then resentful, and finally rebellious.

We are told, for instance, that the way to prevent our children from smoking is to persuade by example — to stop it ourselves. This might be the best way, in the abstract, but many parents are not strong enough to do this. The next best way is to set ourselves up as a bad example.

"I'm hooked on this miserable habit," I tell the children, "because I didn't have any sense when I was in my teens. You can see how it makes me cough, and fouls my breath, and takes away my wind, and dirties up the house. Be smarter than I was, and don't get started!"

Gratifyingly enough, the children respond to this self-deprecating candor much more than they might to a high moral posture on my part, or to a severe prohibition against smoking. They see it as evidence of my early weakness and stupidity, and are resolved not to make the same mistake.

When parents pretend to be better than they are, or try to be better than they can be, the result is almost failure in the eyes of the children. Parents who attempt to conceal their disagreements and quarrels, I am convinced, do as much damage to children as parents who exercise no restraint at all in their bickering.

A child is astonishingly clear-sighted: he can detect our unconscious motivations, he can "hear" through our silences, and he can "know" what has never been verbally expressed. And, to a child, hypocrisy is a much worse vice than any of the other vices parents try to conceal — for hypocrisy shatters trust and belief, without which no family feeling can survive.

If we cannot be good enough (and most of us can't), we can at least try to use our defects and weaknesses for the best possible purpose — to admit them for what they are, and to let the children realize that the prime purpose of parents is to make their offspring better people than the parents were. In the end, they will respect us more, not less, for relinquishing our traditional posture of moral superiority.

The Questions They Can Ask

I'M ESPECIALLY FOND of the little boy I heard about whose father was trying to persuade him to eat his rhubarb at dinner.

"Come now, Billie," the dad coaxed, "there are thousands of children in India who would be glad to have a chance to eat some nice rhubarb like this."

Billie fixed his father with a level gaze. "Name two," he challenged.

That's the kind of answer every sensible child should give to such silly statements. What have the children of India to do with the fact that Billie doesn't like rhubarb? I don't know any *adult* who eats for humanitarian reasons.

Our schools and universities offer many courses in "communications" but the most important communication of all — that between the generations — is neglected in our educational system. Perhaps it cannot be taught.

Most people, beginning with parents, do not know how to talk to children on any meaningful level; and children, quite naturally, reward this ignorance with defiance, indifference, or contempt. Really communicating with a child is a rare and delicate art which only few grown-ups ever master. And it is better that those without this special talent do not try — for they will only sound hypocritical or condescending or too cutesy-wutesy for words. Even someone as versed in the special language of childhood as Lewis Carroll never made the mistake of trying it with boys. He knew that his special affinity was with little girls, and he avoided the company of boys. And when he tried to create a fictional boy, in the character of Bruno, it was a dismal failure, unlike his immortal Alice.

Children think in a different *mode* from adults, and unless that mode is grasped and understood as *a logic of its own*, then we will be forever judging children by the wrong standards, and getting absolutely nowhere with them.

Consider the little boy told by his Sunday school teacher, "Now, remember, we are here to help others." The boy rejoined: "What are the others here for?" Or another boy who was asked, "Can you tell me who made you?" "God made part of me," he answered. "What do you mean by that?" "He made me real little, and I just grew the rest myself."

Children are instinctive philosophers, of their own sort. If their childlike philosophies are laughed at or rebuked or "corrected" in the wrong way, then they close up utterly to adults, and sometimes to themselves as well. Adults who are dull, I am convinced, are those whose childhoods suffered from impoverished communications with adults.

Inspiring a Lust for Learning

At its highest level, the purpose of teaching is not to teach — it is to inspire the desire for learning. Once a student's mind is set on fire, it will find a way to provide its own fuel.

What made me think of this was a luncheon I attended at an Eastern college not long ago, given by the English department of the school. On my left sat a "sound" scholar who knew his field intimately. On my right sat a young whippersnapper who was glib, amusing and superficial. And it was evident that they loathed each other.

Now, of course, the ideal teacher is one who combines both traits: The power and diligence to master a subject thoroughly, and the ability to communicate his knowledge in an interesting and stimulating fashion. Unfortunately, not one teacher in a hundred meets this rigorous standard. If we are forced to take our choice, I should prefer to have college students (undergraduates, at least) taught by the shallow scholar with zest, rather than by the "sound" scholar with dryness, dullness, and pomposity.

Children, for instance, do not "naturally" rebel against mathematics; they rebel against the terrible way it has been taught in the past. Much as a teacher may wince at the thought, he is also an entertainer — for unless he can hold his audience, he cannot really instruct or edify them.

Sound scholarship is necessary in the graduate school, which presumably has weeded out those of limited intellectual attainments. But undergraduates must first be made to feel that a subject is appealing and *relevant* to their concerns; unless this happens, they will not retain what they have learned 24 hours beyond examination day.

Except for the professional schools, teachers should be chosen more for their personal attributes than for their scholarship: For if they cannot make their field seem exciting and challenging to young minds, then they are in the wrong profession, and should devote themselves to research or some other solitary occupation.

The teacher who knows all the answers is not always the one who knows the right questions to ask; the teacher who makes us want to find out the answers for ourselves is the only one who has genuinely contributed to the real end of education — which is, a lust for knowing.

Take the "Guilt" Out of Divorce

IN THE MANY reforms of our criminal code, proposed by a recent President's commission, no mention was made of the matter of divorce. Yet divorce is, in a way, treated like a criminal offense in almost all states.

In suits for divorce, there are the "innocent" and the "guilty" parties. Yet common sense tells us that, except for the most flagrant cases of brutality or drunkenness or desertion, there are no "innocent" or "guilty" parties to a failed marriage — only unsuccessful partners.

England is moving toward realism faster in this area than we are. Last year, a study committee recommended to the Archbishop of Canterbury that there should be only one ground for divorce — the breakdown of a marriage. "Divorce," the committee said, "should not be a victory for one spouse, and a reverse for the other — but a defeat for both."

Appointed more than two years ago, this committee of leading church people, clergy and laity urged that the whole "adversary system" of divorce be abandoned, and that the divorce court of the future "should inquire into the *condition* of a marriage, rather than decide the guilt or innocence of the principals."

Obviously, this makes much more sense (and honesty) than the procedures we now follow. Under the adversary system, most couples perjure themselves in the divorce courts, with the knowledge and connivance of their lawyers. They bring fake charges, give false testimony, and even suborn witnesses to lie in their behalf. And most of it is collusive.

As the British committee observed, if the marriage "breakdown" principle is adopted, adultery, for instance, would no longer be sufficient ground for divorce, as it is today. The whole fabric of the marriage would be examined — with no question of legal guilt or blame — to determine whether it was salvageable or hopeless.

We know that there are no "innocent bystanders" in a bad marriage; that it takes the interaction of two personalities to cause a breakdown in the relationship; and that the law is necessarily blind to most of the psychiatric and social forces that move a marriage toward dissolution. Treating the parties as though they were criminals only breeds disrespect for the law and evasion of its true intent.

Divorce should not be retributive or punitive, but should aim at treating the rupture with fairness and sympathy to all parties. In our present system, it is too often unfair, vindictive, and arbitrary. Unlike all other contracts, the marriage contract belongs more to the field of medicine than to the field of law.

"Getting Tough with Punks"

"WE NEED to get tough with those punks" is the rallying cry of the know-nothings in our society, who are alarmed at the rise of crime and juvenile delinquency. They have a right to be alarmed, but they also have a duty that goes along with that right — the duty to understand the phenomenon, not merely to deplore it.

When a family has a troublesome boy, "getting tough" doesn't make him less troublesome, but more, as all parents have eventually found out. Then why do we imagine that if society gets tougher with its delinquents, we will reduce the severity of the problem?

The fact of the matter is, psychologically speaking, that the only boys who are helped by our getting tough are those who don't need it much in the first place. Every intelligent father knows this: The son who can be curbed by a little punishment is basically a good boy, who doesn't need much punishment. The one who is the real devil only seems to get worse from punishment.

If this is true in the family — and we know that it is — then it must be equally true in the society at large. Punishment works best where it is least needed; it is ineffective where most needed.

In actuality, careful and widespread studies made of delinquent boys have shown, repeatedly and unanimously, that the great majority of them were treated harshly from an early age. More punishment only reinforces their early grievance against society and all authority.

While it may be true, in some cases, that parental leniency and inattention leads to waywardness on the part of some youths, they are a small fraction compared to the number who have been handled brutally, and even viciously, from an early age.

The know-nothings are always in favor of "cures" that are worse than the diseases they purport to treat. Society has had much harsher penalties in the past: The reason they were abandoned was not so much a growing humanitarianism as the realization that they didn't work — in fact, they aggravated the situation, both for juveniles and adults.

Criminality comes out of a social, psychic and cultural matrix; maintaining that matrix, punishing offenders and then throwing them back into it, will be expensive, frustrating and ineffectual. If we destroy the infected environment, bacteria can no longer thrive there; just getting tough with the bacteria, while the environment remains polluted, is more absurdly "idealistic" than the know-nothings accuse us "softies" of being.

Misleading Divorce Data

IT IS TRUE that one out of every four marriages in this country ends in divorce. It is not true, however, that marriage is a failing institution in the 20th Century.

Divorce statistics can be shocking if they are looked at in isolation — but, then, so can any statistics, including those for disease and crime. If we don't know how to use statistics, we are better off without them.

For instance, we all know the figures on the divorce rate — but how many have ever heard that a higher percentage of people in the United States get married today than ever before? In the past, about 90 percent of the population married; these days, the percentage is 95 — which is a lot more people in our U.S. population of 200 million.

Not only do more people get married, but more people get married more than once. Of the 400,000 divorces each year, about two-thirds of the women and three-fifths of the men remarry, and not long afterwards. Marriage as an institution is flourishing, not failing — even though many specific marriages may not be doing well.

Why do we have so many more divorces than we used to?

There are at least five main reasons: (1) people live longer than they used to; (2) they move about more, and don't have the roots they used to; (3) more people have more money and are able to obtain a legal divorce; (4) women have become more educated and more independent, and thus less willing to endure a slavelike marriage; (5) expectations of satisfactions in marriage are higher than they used to be.

In none of these reasons — upon which nearly all sociologists agree — do we find a lowering of moral standards or a cheap and cynical attitude toward marriage. They are changes in *social and cultural conditions*, rather than declines in *personal values*. If anything, the personal values in marriage have been upgraded over the years — for more of the total personality is now involved.

The old-fashioned marriage, which worked reasonably well in the old cultural matrix, fixed the husband primarily in his role as the "provider," and the wife primarily in her role as "homemaker." But such aspects as *sharing*, *self-expression*, and *self-development* were often lacking in the relationship. In today's affluent society, these formerly submerged aspects have come to the surface as basic needs in a good marriage. What we need is not a return to the "old-fashioned" marriage, but a better understanding of the demands of the new kind.

The Art of "Playing It Cool"

ONE of the many things I like about young people today is the whole concept of "playing it cool." To be able to keep their cool is as important to them as keeping "dignity" or "grace" or "honor" or any of the old-fashioned words that previous generations used as yardsticks of excellence.

Keeping your cool means not overreacting to a situation —

not gushing, or panicking, or becoming self-righteous or self-pitying, as so many elders tend to do in time of emergency. It is essentially a medieval and aristocratic attitude — although most of the cool cats would be astonished (and perhaps dismayed) to know it.

But, like any other virtue, coolness has its dark inner lining, which is not so attractive; and many youngsters fail to distinguish between the outer and the inner sides of this quality. To them, coolness has become an *end* in itself, rather than an appropriate attitude. They stay cool even when they should get warm.

Coolness can be motivated by positive factors, or by negative ones. The positive factors are a sense of proportion, of irony, of humor, of philosophic detachment, of stoicism, of awareness that the obvious is not necessarily the real or the good or the true.

There is another kind of coolness — or coolth, if you will — that is motivated by negative factors. These negative factors are mostly kinds of fear — fear of being wrong, fear of displaying emotion, fear of expressing "out" opinions, fear of violating the current dogmas and rituals of the cool society.

This counterfeit coolness is what becomes an end in itself with many youngsters — and, in certain situations, it is as inappropriate as the warmth they are rebelling against. For there are times when we cannot remain detached, we should not be stoical, we must disagree with our peers, we should violate whatever dogmas and rituals we feel to be wrongheaded or wronghearted.

Coolness, to be effective and authentic, must be an attitude, not a *reaction*. It is not a suit of armor to be slipped on, to repel the injuries of the world; rather, it is an internal part of the personality, or it is nothing. A phony cool cat is no better —

and perhaps worse — than the phony members of the bourgeoisie he despises.

Fear is what motivates all phonies, on all levels of society,
from the most conventional to the most outlandish. People
are afraid to be who they are, and become what they think
those around them would like them to be. To be cool simply
because those around you are cool is no more authentic or
life-giving than to be frigid, torrid, or tepid.

Back of the Urge to Steal

WHEN MY WIFE'S CAR was stolen not long ago, a brace of detectives came to the house, lugging a large album of photo-
graphs of known car thieves. Our first surprise was at the
number of them; our second was at their youth. Most of
them looked well under 20.

"Now here's a fellow," one of the detectives said, "who's
just about the best auto thief in the city." There was more
than a trace of admiration in his voice as he added: "This lad
can strip a car clean in less than 30 minutes."

"Are there many that good?" I asked.

"Quite a few," he nodded. "You know, a lot of those boys
are first-rate mechanics, and don't even know it. They can
remove an automatic transmission from a car, on a cold night,
with gloves on, faster than a trained mechanic can do it on a
rack with all the proper tools."

"I imagine they could earn a fine salary as mechanics," I
said.

"They sure could," he said. "In fact, they could make about
five times as much working around cars as they do stealing
them — because the people they fence the parts to don't give
them much over ten percent."

Without meaning to, this detective had confirmed what I
have long said in print about most so-called "criminals." To

believe that they steal for *gain* is a shallow and mechanistic attitude; nor do they steal because they don't believe in "hard work" — what they do is exceedingly hard work, only they happen to love it.

Except for the feeble-minded and the sociopaths (and they are mainly the ones who get caught), professional thieves do not steal for gain, or because they are lazy, or for any other obvious reason. They steal for revenge, whether they know it or not. They steal because they want to get back at society for real or fancied injuries — in most cases, injuries sustained in early family life.

This is why punishment, of the conventional prison sort, is futile. The thief doesn't mind being punished, because his sentence only adds to the stock of resentment he already has against society, and it acts further to ramify and justify his stealing when he gets out. Prison only proves to him that he was right all along in his attitude.

These "good thieves" are bright, courageous, imaginative and energetic. The one quality they lack is the proper motivation to turn their talents in a socially desirable direction. Until we learn to instill the proper motivation, it makes little difference if we lock them up or let them go, for neither leniency nor harshness will change them.

Our Lifeless Fashion Models

I HAPPENED to glance at a magazine lying in my wife's bedside table. It was a foreign fashion magazine called *Élégance*, and in true husbandly form, I looked for the price on the cover. It was $3.

"That's a whacking big price for a magazine," I remarked.

"I suppose so," she said, "but look inside and you'll see why it's worth it."

I shrugged. "What do I know about fashion? One style

looks like another to me." She shook her head, "It isn't the fashions — it's the models. Take a look at them."

I took a look at them, and saw immediately what she meant. The models were women. Moreover, they were human women. They looked as if they moved, talked, thought, and felt. They were real.

"Now look at this one," she said, tossing me a chic American fashion magazine. "Can't you tell the difference?"

No question about it. The models in the American magazine were dead. Their eyes were dead. Their mouths were dead. Their bodies were dead. They looked like clothes hangers, all metallic and angular. And they were profoundly asexual, for all their provocative posturing. Only a necrophile would find them even faintly appealing.

Now, American women are just as womanly as European women. I happen to think we have the best-looking women in the world. And the best-dressed. In Paris, for instance, there are only cheap clothes and expensive ones; the dresses on the rack are abominable, and the *haute couture* is beyond the reach of the middle classes.

Yet, the whole field of fashion in America is dominated by the model who looks like nothing else on land or sea — an eviscerated creature with drooping limbs, bloodless, gutless, and wombless. She would be about as much use to a man as a tuning fork to a turtle.

The European models in the magazine had vitality. They also looked as though they had husbands, children, lovers, and friends, and were not wholly wrapped in the narcissistic cocoon of fashion. The clothes existed for *their* sake; they were not there simply for the sake of the clothes.

The word "model," in its earliest definition in the English language, meant "a representation in three dimensions." And this is precisely the difference: The American model is two-dimensional, lacking the third dimension of depth and warmth and earthiness that distinguishes a living person from a sketch as shallow as a sheet of paper.

That's the Way It Is, Baby

NOTES FOR A NEW COMMENCEMENT SPEECH:

THERE are three ways to be young, and two of them are dumb.

The first dumb way is to be young-simple — trusting, accepting, believing, going along with the crowd.

The second dumb way is to be young-cynical — doubting, rejecting, suspecting, despising whatever the majority does or thinks or says.

The third way to be young is the only smart way — and, like most smart ways, it is a combination of the other two ways.

And this is to be trusting when you must, and doubting when you should.

To accept what has to be accepted, and reject what ought to be rejected.

To go along when it doesn't matter much, and to stand alone when it does.

To be young-simple today is to be a sap. To be young-cynical is to be a sucker for cranks and crackpots and spooks of all sorts.

This is the way it is, baby — a mixed-up world of black and white and gray. With phonies on both sides of the fence — on the Establishment side and on the Rebel side. With patches of goodness, and blotches of badness, and huge globs of indifference between them.

How do you know when to trust and when to doubt, when to accept and when to reject?

You know in two ways — by looking into yourself, and by

looking out at the world. If you concentrate on yourself, you're a fool about the world. If you concentrate on the world, you're a fool about yourself.

It's that simple. And that hard. It calls for balance, for judgment, for coolness, for honesty. Most of all, it calls for deciding things *on their own merit*, not because you read it or were told it or grew up believing it.

The young-simple way leads to stagnation, to dead people walking around repeating high-minded nonsense they don't really understand.

The young-cynical way leads to another kind of stagnation, to living for sensations that offer no possibility for growth.

Life is, if anything, the art of combination. Of discrimination. Of freely picking one's own personal pattern out of a hundred choices. Not letting it be picked *for* you — either by the Establishment, or by the Rebels. Conformity of Hip is no better than Conformity of Square.

This is the way it is, baby. The way it's always going to be.

Double Standard on Children

WE'RE ALL AWARE of the double standard about sex, but few are aware of the even more pervasive double standard about children. I thought of this the other day, while listening to a man talking about the "shiftless" young people in the slums.

This man, I happened to know, has a son who is lazy and not overly bright. Yet he has a responsible and well-paying job with a firm owned by a friend of his father's. The lad was about to flunk out of school, and was given special tutoring over the summer. He finally got his diploma from a third-rate prep school and managed to enter a fourth-rate college, where he barely squeezed through. He has had all the advantages a young person could have — in parents, home environment, counseling, financial support, special schools and camps and tutors. Yet, with all this help, his job is still largely a matter of nepotism. Left to himself, he would sink.

Now this is unfortunate, but no disgrace. He is simply not a very energetic or mentally gifted person. But his deficiencies are skillfully camouflaged by his protective environment.

While this is an extreme example, it is by no means an unusual case of what happens among the more affluent, when their sons find it difficult to cope with the competitive world. Everything possible is done to lift them up to the level of the family's expectations.

But we have a double standard about other people's children — especially if they come from the disadvantaged classes. If they lack parental supervision, have a poor home environment, no counseling, inferior schools, and not much motivation for success — we still expect them to make it on their own, or we condemn them for "shiftlessness."

If the children of the privileged were thrown into the same cultural cesspool, there is no earthly reason to believe they would do any better; in fact, even with their advantages, many still find it hard to make good marks and meet the world head-on. It is a tough race today, even with all the help available.

What is remarkable about the slums is not that so many fall, but that so many rise. That even a minority is able to surmount the nearly-killing environment is a tribute to human tenacity and courage and talent. The ones who make it have to be twice as good as anyone else; and how many of *our* children could we say that of?

Mates Are Really 8 Persons

"WHY DOES marriage seem to be such a difficult relationship?" asked a college boy in a bull session we were having after a lecture. "I look around, at my parents and their friends, and it's a rocky road for almost all of them."

I couldn't refrain from quoting myself — an insufferable habit, but occasionally a timesaving one. "A man," I said, "thinks he is marrying one woman and soon finds, to his bewilderment, that he has married at least four."

"How do you mean that?" he asked.

"Well, there is first of all the woman *he* thought she was; secondly, there is the woman *she* thought she was; thirdly, there is the woman she *really* is; and last, there is the woman she would *like* to be."

Then I added hastily: "And, of course, the same is true for the man in reverse. So that there are at least eight "people" involved in the marital relationship — and that makes a pretty crowded house, even without children."

"It's much too crowded," he agreed. "But what do you do with, and how do you handle, all those people in one marriage?"

"It seems to me," I replied, "that two of them on each side must go. For instance, on the woman's side, both the woman he thought she was, and the woman she thought she was, are figments of their imagination and not real people at all. They are just cluttering the landscape.

"Those two," I went on, "are the ones to get rid of. The ones that have to be kept are the woman she really is, and the woman she would like to be."

"But isn't the latter also a figment of the imagination?" he inquired. "What we would like to be is not what we really are."

"It is and it isn't," I said. "There is always a core of reality in what we would like to be — it represents a potentiality we recognize in ourselves. Unless a marriage can nourish and keep alive this potentiality, it has little to grow on.

"What happens in those rocky marriages you mention," I continued, "is that the spouses reject what their partners really are and what they would like to be, and resent the fact that they don't live up to the idealized fantasy that ignited the whole romance in the first place. They try to make the real person conform to the fantasy, instead of giving up the fantasy and adjusting to the real person. And the first, and hardest, job is knowing and accepting who the real person is among the many ghosts and visions flitting around the house."

Parents' Idiotic Questions

"DADDY, have you seen my sailboat anywhere?" asked my younger son.

"No," I said. "Where were you playing with it last?"

"If I knew where I was playing with it last, it wouldn't be lost, would it?" he retorted.

After boxing his ears for this bit of impertinence, and exiling him for two weeks beyond the reaches of Batman (well, I *thought* about doing it), I reflected upon our little dialog, and decided that my question was indeed a silly one.

One reflection leads to another, and it then struck me that parents probably make more absurd and irrational remarks than their children do. Only we can't hear ourselves saying them.

"Why haven't you done your homework?" is a classic example of a pointless question that a child soon learns to tune out. What answer can he give to that one? "I don't care to do it," or "I was having too much fun playing," or "I'll get around to it when I'm ready," or "it doesn't have to be in until Friday" — the last of which is probably a terrible lie.

Parent noises are boring, predictable, and basically unanswerable. They are not made to elicit an answer from the child (we know very well that the answer to "Why don't you eat your carrots?" is "I hate them."), but to express the parent's anger, irritation, dissatisfaction, impatience, or disgust at the disparity between parental commitment and childish indifference.

There are hundreds of jokes about "the questions children ask," but such questions are models of logic, directness and realism compared with the questions parents ask, every day and every night, with depressing regularity.

"Why didn't you wash your hands?" "How do you expect to pass if you don't study?" "Do you think you'll be strong enough to play football if you don't drink your milk?" "Why are you so mean to your little sister?" "Can't you talk without shouting?" "Didn't I tell you to empty the trash?" "Have you spent all your allowance *already?*" Etc.

When parents sigh that the child "never listens," maybe it's because the child has been listening to so many idiotic questions for so many years that they now come through like radio static. Of course, if David knew where he was last playing with the sailboat, it wouldn't be lost. Pretty soon he'll stop asking his dumb father anything.

3

OF THE SOCIAL ANIMAL

What People Fear the Negro Most?

WHITE PEOPLE in America are feeling very sorry for themselves these days. That is the meaning of the so-called "white backlash" — it is a form of self-pity.

But, actually, who is the real victim of the Negro's alienation from American society? Not the white man, but the Negro himself. For every white person who feels threatened, a thousand Negroes feel even more so. For the Negro is victimized, not merely by the white man, but also by his own worst elements. Their gangs threaten him much more than they threaten the whites. He has to live with it all the time — his womenfolk afraid to walk the streets at night, his children afraid to come home from school.

In our full-blown compassion for ourselves — and in our fear of invasion, attack and injury — we whites tend to forget that the Negro lives with this, and within this, 24 hours a day, seven days a week. He is the one who is trapped in a jungle society — and his desire to move out is not so much an urge to live with the whites as it is to get away from those Negroes who corrupt and debase his neighborhood.

Negroes rob more Negroes than they do white people; kill more Negroes than they do white people; and even in all the "riots," it has so far generally been the blacks, not the whites, who are left bleeding to die.

In the ghetto, the level of life inevitably sinks to the lowest. The ghetto is run by the toughs, by the venal, by the exploiters, by the dregs — for it has no responsible power structure. "Law and order" has little meaning in such a society; it is only raw power that is respected.

We whites have as yet paid a very small, almost negligible, price for Negro servitude. It is the decent, hardworking, responsible Negro who has paid the highest price — being forced to live in an environment where his women walk in fear, where his children grow up stunted and vulnerable to all the vices that accompany poverty and despair.

Whatever the historic causes of this ghetto — and they are complex and contradictory — it is this decent and responsible Negro who must be rescued from the cesspool; his children, at least, must not be allowed to start life with two-and-a-half strikes on them. This is what all the marching and shouting are about — children without a chance.

It is a terrible problem, and there is no easy answer. We are in for a bumpy ride, whites and blacks alike, in the next few years. And we whites who are made uncomfortable by "civil rights" must remember the Negro has lived so long with civil wrongs that he is almost beyond caring to distinguish right from wrong.

Headlines and Faulty Conclusions

ON THE GROUNDS that excessive newspaper publicity prejudiced the murder trial of Dr. Sam Sheppard, the U.S. Supreme Court recently decreed that he be given a new trial in a more subdued atmosphere.

The high court's decision called to mind a study made some years ago by two sociologists at the University of Illinois, who found that jurors who read the newspaper accounts of a case tend to find the defendant guilty more often than those jurors who don't read the papers. Studying a dozen criminal court juries in their county over a period of five years, the researchers reported that those who admitted being "familiar" with the case through publicity always voted "guilty" on the first ballot. "A fair assumption to make about any trial," they concluded, "is that publicity will influence, if not determine, the final verdict."

I think their conclusion was somewhat unfair to newspapers, and too lenient toward readers. Most newspaper accounts of trials are scrupulously fair to all parties — what is often misleading is the headline.

Many persons who say they have read a "story" have read only the headline and the opening paragraph. Now these, of necessity, represent an oversimplification of the complete story. It is impossible to get all the nuances and qualifications of a story into a brief opening paragraph, much less into a headline. "Places Suspect at Scene of Crime" is a typical headline. What else can the poor headline writer do? He is cramped within the confines of space and must pick out the salient feature of the day's development. Such features are generally dramatic in nature.

Later in the story, it may appear that the suspect's appearance at the scene of the crime had little to do with the event; but the man who runs as he reads often does not take the trouble to evaluate these additional facts. (Last week, in fact, I saw the headline "Father Charged in Son's Death," and it wasn't until the third paragraph that I learned he was not charged with murder but with neglect in hiring a sitter without references.)

We are not, on the whole, a nation of careful readers; we

are impatient of nice distinctions and want only the bold out-
lines of the news — upon which we then feel ready to pro-
nounce a firm opinion. What most readers forget is that a
headline is *selective*, not *inclusive*. It is like a sign in a shop
window, telling us that shoes are on sale today — but we have
to enter the store to find out which kind, which colors,
which sizes, and what prices. The headline writer's job is to
turn our heads, not to fill them.

Scoreboard for a Winner: 1

A WINNER says, "Let's find out"; a loser says, "Nobody
knows."

When a winner makes a mistake, he says, "I was wrong";
when a loser makes a mistake, he says, "It wasn't my fault."

A winner isn't nearly as afraid of losing as a loser is secretly afraid of winning.

A winner works harder than a loser, and has more time; a
loser is always "too busy" to do what is necessary.

A winner goes *through* a problem; a loser goes *around* it,
and never gets past it.

A winner makes commitments; a loser makes promises.

A winner shows he's sorry by making up for it; a loser says
"I'm sorry," but does the same thing the next time.

A winner knows what to fight for, and what to compromise on; a loser compromises on what he shouldn't, and
fights for what isn't worthwhile fighting about.

A winner listens; a loser just waits until it's his turn to talk.

A winner would rather be admired than liked, although he
would prefer both; a loser would rather be liked than admired, and is even willing to pay the price of mild contempt
for it.

A winner feels strong enough to be gentle; a loser is never
gentle — he is either weak or pettily tyrannous by turns.

A winner respects those who are superior to him, and tries to learn something from them; a loser resents those who are superior to him, and tries to find chinks in their armor.

A winner says, "There ought to be a better way to do it"; a loser says, "That's the way it's always been done here."

A winner paces himself; a loser has only two speeds: hysterical and lethargic.

A "Liberal" Point of View

MY FRIEND, J. Hawley Smoot, settled himself more comfortably in his leather club chair and muttered, not for the first time, "Too much government. We mustn't let the government get so strong and powerful. It's a menace to our liberties."

"Quite right," I agreed. "It worries me the way the government is shaping the whole economy for our war effort in Vietnam."

"I don't mean that," said Smoot. "Have to do that, you know. Got to beat down those bloody Chinese, no matter what the cost, eh?"

"Well, then," I ventured. "You must like the Supreme Court decisions which clip the government's wings about questioning and holding suspects."

"Hell, no," he said. "We need tougher laws than we have. Can't let those beastly criminals get off so easily. Have to support our police forces to the limit, not handcuff them."

"I see your point," I nodded. "But certainly we have to see to it that the government allows dissent and demonstrations for people who are peacefully petitioning for a redress of their grievances?"

"Bunch of damned Reds and troublemakers," he growled. "The government ought to step in and crack a few more heads, show those dirty beatniks we mean business."

"Then there's all this labor trouble," I went on. "Strikes that really hurt the public and tie up the whole economy for weeks or months. But I suppose that's the price we have to pay for the kind of weak government you like."

"Pah," he snorted. "The country shouldn't allow those things. We ought to force those labor blighters to negotiate. Get an injunction. Haul them into the courts. Show them they can't thumb their noses at the rest of us, even if we have to call out the National Guard."

"And what about the college students," I inquired, "isn't it inspiring that they care enough about what's going on in the country to take political action on the campus and make their voices heard in opposition to such government measures as the draft and so on?"

"Dirty yellowbellies," he roared. "If I had my way, we'd toss the whole bunch in jail and throw away the keys. Put the militia in charge of every campus, and draft all the loud-mouths. This damned administration is coddling those punks instead of leaning hard on them."

"Well, you certainly have thought things out carefully," I nodded, taking my leave. "There's no doubt in my mind that we have too much government. And I'm glad to know there are men like you around who are battling so valiantly against it. With your clear-cut ideas about our liberties, you can't help but win in the end."

Not a Black-and-White Problem

SOMEONE was telling me recently about a British professor at the University of Chicago, who was walking home one night when he was accosted by a group of belligerent Negro youths.

"What's going on here?" he exclaimed. "This is no way to treat a visitor to your country!"

"Where you from?" they wanted to know. "I'm from England," he said in his full Oxonian accent. "Only been in America a few weeks."

"Oh," they said, waving him on. "We didn't know that. We thought you were white."

This true tale is worth remembering the next time we are confronted with what seems to be evidence of "anti-white" sentiment among Negroes. It is not the whiteness per se they object to, but the "American whiteness" — which is a national, and not a racial, resentment.

In much the same way, a lot of what seems at first to be "anti-Negro" sentiment is not anti-Negro as such; rather, it is a combination of fear, anger and guilt at the Negro's poverty, his lack of education, his cultural attitudes and habits which set him apart from the white community. Such people resent the Negro for being "different" from the rest of us, but at the same time resist all efforts to place him in the mainstream of American society.

To the American Negro, an Englishman, a Frenchman, an Italian, a South American is not "white" in the same sense that his fellow citizens are white. "White" is simply a semantic label to identify and define those who, he feels, have let him down and held him down. It is primarily a social and economic antagonism, not a racial one.

Nor can the problem ever be solved on a racial basis, and this is why mere integration is bound to fail. Putting poor Negro children in the same schools as poor white children, and housing poor Negro families next to poor white families — while satisfying the demands of social justice — will only aggravate the tension and conflict, *if nothing more is done*.

The real task, as I see it, is threefold: to provide massive job opportunities for the underprivileged, white and Negro alike;

to upgrade the level of schooling everywhere, and not merely to equalize the mediocrity; and to help reconstitute the Negro family with the father at the head and the mother at home with the children. Tearing down physical slums means absolutely nothing, unless the psychological and spiritual slums are also eradicated.

It is the most enormous internal problem our nation has ever faced. We must pay the price for a century of neglect, and that price will have to be a high one, not merely in money, but in national mood as well.

Bulldozers Digging Our Graves

WHAT IS HAPPENING in Chicago should be a warning to residents of other cities in the nation. Chicago is sacrificing its parks to its roadways, placing traffic above people.

In the last few years, there has been a slow but definite return to the city from the suburbs. Many families are beginning to realize that a city can offer advantages in living that outweigh suburban benefits.

One of the glories of Chicago is its beautiful lakefront, with its parks and beaches easily accessible. Now the highway engineers have begun to defoliate these areas in order to straighten and widen the boulevards to accommodate more cars in the rush hours. If this trend continues, if the engineers are allowed to put utility ahead of beauty and leisure, then the decay of the city as a place to live is assured. Families who have contemplated moving back from the suburbs will be discouraged by the loss of trees and parkways, the shrinking of beaches and the intrusion of more heavy traffic only inches away from their narrow strip of sand.

The modern city — through greed, apathy and shortsightedness — has already become dangerously eroded. Its lack of planning, its failure to zone sensibly, its indifference to slum conditions (except when federal funds are forthcoming), have driven the higher income groups farther and farther into the suburbs. Tens of millions have been spent on expressways to enable these suburban people to enter and leave the city expeditiously; and the more roads, the more traffic; the easier to get into the city, the easier to get out. Those steam shovels on the new expressways are digging the city's own graves.

Cities were made for living in, not just for working in. They should be places of charm and beauty. But if the neighborhoods run down, then the schools deteriorate in quality, and when this happens no amount of high-rise buildings or highways can prevent masses of families moving out to the suburbs.

The highway engineers are only interested in "traffic flow." But more important is "people flow." Who wants millions of cars moving into the city each day, when an equal amount of people move out every evening? And when the city goes, be assured that the suburbs cannot survive for very long, either financially or physically.

When a City's Night Life Perishes

ON MY FIRST TRIP to St. Louis in three years, I took a cab from the airport to the downtown district. It was like arriving in a strange city I had never visited before. Old buildings had been torn down, and new ones put up. Many of the landmarks have disappeared. Expressways and parking lots have changed the whole skyline; even the cab driver was a little puzzled by the detours and dead ends.

This is happening in every large city in America, but of course we can see it more dramatically in a city we haven't visited for a while. It is considered a sign of "growth" and "development," but in my view it is largely a waste of money and energy. The revitalization of downtown districts is not a matter of office buildings and corporate headquarters, of new city halls or banks or post offices. These are just part of the "daytime" city. For every true metropolis has two cities downtown — the daytime city and the nighttime city. Unless the latter flourishes as fully as the former, all the new buildings are simply monuments to pride and vanity, and cannot restore the city in any meaningful way.

In the daytime city, everyone pours out of the office buildings and department stores at five o'clock, and goes homeward — mostly to the suburbs. Downtown then becomes a cavern, dotted only by a few hotels, restaurants and movie houses. It is inhabited largely by out-of-towners, drunks, bums, and restless juveniles.

True urban areas, like London, Paris, and New York, have a nighttime city that is equal to the daytime city. A whole new population takes over after dark — an active and affluent population that uses and enjoys all the diverse resources of the nighttime city: theaters, cabarets, first-class restaurants, and whatever cultural or artistic events the city has provided.

It is the *nature* and *quality* of the downtown facilities that transform it from a hick town to a metropolis, and not the height of the buildings or the cost of the rejuvenation. Unless people are made to *want* to enter the nighttime city by attractions they cannot find elsewhere, all the new buildings and civic centers are doomed to decay.

It takes money to revitalize our drab and dying downtown areas, but money is not enough. In fact, money without ideas is the surest way to speed the disintegration of a downtown, like an oppressively expensive party at which the hosts have supplied everything in embarrassing abundance — except the entertainment of the guests.

Our Apathy to No. 1 Killer

ALL RIGHT, all you good citizens who are so concerned about crime and violence in America. How many of you are willing to support a campaign against by far the greatest menace to life and limb in this nation?

Automobiles take 50,000 lives a year — many of them young children. In July, 1966, motor vehicle deaths reached the unprecedented high of 5,130, a 20 percent increase over the previous monthly high. Disabling injuries for the first seven months of 1966 reached one million, many of whom will never walk again or see again. And the innocent suffer along with the guilty — even more so, for the guilty are scarcely punished under our present system.

The so-called "violence in the streets" that arouses all you good citizens does a tiny percentage of the damage that is done by auto accidents. But there is a very big difference between the two — the violence is committed by *them,* but the auto accidents are by *us.*

Are we willing to discipline ourselves? To submit our cars to more rigorous checkups? To undergo physical and emotional examinations each year? To stiffen the penalties for reckless driving, drunken driving, juvenile driving?

I have seen no evidence that we are. No public committees formed, no meetings held, no petitions passed, no flood of letters to our elected officials, no angry outcries against the senseless "violence" in the streets and on the highways.

For we are afraid of losing our own privileges, and for that cheap and cowardly reason we are willing to permit 1,000 auto deaths a week. We demand tougher laws against criminals and rioters — who comprise less than one per cent of the population — but not against the 99 percent of "respectable citizens" who are responsible for the carnage on the highways.

Not many weeks ago, in the county where I spend my summers, three boys roared through a stop sign at 80 miles an hour, hitting a car and killing five members of the family. The boys were fined a total of $27 and given a 30-day sentence (suspended). I heard nobody complain about this travesty of justice; those who might have complained were all dead.

This happens every week, every day, every hour. It is the largest and most relentless slaughter the world has ever known, claiming more lives than we have lost in all the wars we have fought since the Revolution. Statistically, you are far safer walking down the toughest street in the toughest neighborhood in the toughest city in America than riding along a half-mile from your house. That's where the *real* violence is to be feared. Are you listening, all you good citizens?

Rights and Limits of Dissent

WHEN SOCRATES was invited to escape prison by his friends, who had bribed a jailer, he refused to leave. "I have lived all my life under the laws and the protection of Athens," he said, "and even though I feel I was unjustly sentenced to death, I must stay and accept my punishment."

Most Americans do not understand what is meant by "civil disobedience" — and many dissenters do not understand it, either. In this time of turmoil, it is important that we recognize the rights, and the limits, of civil disobedience.

If a citizen feels that a law is unjust, or that it violates some higher law of conscience or religion, he has a right to resist it, if he does so with two qualifications — first, he must not injure anyone in doing so, and, second, he must not try to evade punishment for it.

A criminal is one who breaks the law, injures others, and

tries to escape punishment. A dissenter — which includes a long and glorious line all the way from Socrates down to Gandhi — is perfectly willing to suffer the penalties for his noncompliance with the law. When Thoreau refused to pay his road tax, and was sent to jail, he objected when friends of his paid his fine and obtained his release. He did not want his conscience bought off so cheaply or so easily.

If a democracy is to have any real meaning, it must respect the right of dissenters to resist the law in a nonviolent manner, so long as the dissenters are willing to face the legal consequences. Else, in time of war or other crisis, a democracy can turn as vicious as a tyranny.

What is called the "positive law" — that is, the body of laws promulgated by a specific government — has no moral force unless it is grounded in the "natural law." For instance, the laws against the kulaks under Stalin, or against the Jews under Hitler, were inhuman perversions of the natural law, and deserved to be resisted, however "legal" they were.

In such countries, "civil disobedience" was impossible — the dissenters would have been summarily executed — and therefore only revolutionary activity was effective. This is why only repressive governments have suffered revolutions; they left no other way out for disagreement.

In a democracy, however, it is still possible that dissenters may change the law through popular opinion, as long as free elections are still available. To deny them the right to influence opinion — through marches, demonstrations, or any kind of nonviolent opposition — is to create an underground, and truly subversive, movement in a country.

We must allow dissenters such freedom, not for their sake, but for ours. Repression, in the end, hurts the majority much more than it injures the minority — not at present, but in the ominous future.

How Not to Solve Problems

A PRIMER IN PROBLEM-SOLVING

CRIME isn't a legal problem.

Education isn't a school problem.

Peace isn't a political problem.

Sex isn't a moral problem.

Poverty isn't an economic problem.

This is why crime cannot be diminished by legal methods.

Why education cannot be much improved by bigger or better schools.

Why peace can't be achieved by political arrangements.

Why sexual conduct can't be controlled by moral codes.

Why poverty can't be overcome by economic means.

For the roots of crime are *sociological*.

The drive and desire for education must come from the *family*.

The attainment of peace must be a *moral and intellectual* imperative, before any political arrangements can be lasting or effective.

Sex is a *psychological* dynamism, whose demands must be met or mastered.

Poverty is a matter of *distributive justice*, not a mere economic mechanism of greater productivity and increased national wealth.

The law cannot reduce crime until the community takes steps to cure the social pathology that is the inevitable breeding ground for crime.

The schools cannot educate properly until the family provides a home setting in which children are motivated to learn.

The nations cannot possibly unite for peace until enough of their individual citizens recognize and act on the assumption that war is an insult to man's reason and a perversion of his ethical sense.

The churches, or other moral institutions, cannot codify or control the patterns of sexual behavior until they revise their notions of "sin" to conform to psychosexual realities as known to depth psychology.

The government cannot eliminate poverty by adding to the Gross National Product or increasing funds for welfare programs, but only by changing the environment, outlook and expectations of the submerged one-fifth of our population who live beneath the level of decent subsistence.

No problem can be dealt with within its own sphere; each is part of another problem, just as the human being is a total organism in which every part relates to every other part. This does not mean that everything must be done at once, but that no discipline can be left to its own experts.

It means, most of all, that solutions overlap and interlock. Perhaps we can only do a little at a time — but that little must come to terms with the whole human organism, not just fragments floating in a void.

Hardy, Tax-Consuming Pioneers

A LITTLE JOKE I read in a magazine not long ago went: "The man whose great-grandfather built a railroad through the wilderness with nobody's OK now has to get a permit to remodel his front porch."

This is a part of the American myth, and it is surprising how many contemporary Americans still believe it. The fact of the matter is that great-grandfather not only needed permission to build the railroad, but he also was subsidized by the federal government for doing so.

We look upon our Western settlers and pioneers as the prototypes of the free enterprise system, as hardy competitive types who struck out boldly for themselves, but this is a gross misreading of American history. Actually, the competition was in the East, in the growing towns and the burgeoning industrial activity of the early 19th Century. Many, if not most, of the men who went westward were not able to compete in that vigorous society. They were offered free land and other inducements by the government. The granting of rights-of-way to railroads, the homestead act, the newly-created land grant colleges — all these were designed to provide an economic cushion as an inducement to get more settlers into the West.

This is not to disparage the admirable traits of some of these settlers, who were courageous, resourceful and hardworking. But it is to suggest that they were *fleeing* competition rather than seeking it, and usually with government promises of assistance and protection against loss.

The pioneers, assuredly, faced hardships — but these were hardships they chose in preference to other hardships. They opted for space and seclusion and withdrawal from the market place, and accepted whatever government help they could get to withstand the adversities and anarchy of life in raw communities.

Indeed, many of them were looking for "security" of a sort they could not find in the Eastern towns they emigrated from. In the hurly-burly of young industrial capitalism, they had only rustic skills that were not adapted to the urban and technical needs of the growing nation. Their westward migration was motivated as much by nostalgia as by the need for independence.

Certainly there were virtues in the pioneer attitude, some of which have diminished or disappeared today. But it is foolish to perpetuate the mythology that those men were rugged individualists seeking new lands to conquer, when in fact they were the foremost beneficiaries of government aid.

Scoreboard for a Winner: 2

A WINNER focuses; a loser sprays.

A winner has a healthy appreciation of his abilities, and a keen awareness of his limitations; a loser is oblivious both of his true abilities and his true limitations.

A winner knows when the price of winning comes too high; a loser is overly eager to win what he cannot handle or keep.

A winner knows that people will be kind if you give them the chance; a loser feels that people will be unkind if you give them the chance.

A winner takes a big problem and separates it into smaller parts so that it can be more easily manipulated; a loser takes a lot of little problems and rolls them together until they are unsolvable.

A winner learns from his mistakes; a loser learns only not to make mistakes by not trying anything different.

A winner tries never to hurt people, and does so only rarely, when it serves a necessary purpose; a loser never wants to hurt people intentionally, but does so all the time, without even knowing it.

A winner is sensitive to the atmosphere around him; a loser is sensitive only to his own feelings.

A winner uses amassing as a means to enjoying; a loser makes amassing an end in itself — therefore, no matter how much the loser amasses, he never looks upon himself as a winner, and he never is.

Sydney Sprouts a Beard

FOUR WEEKS AGO, I began growing a beard. The reasons were simple: curiosity and vanity. I wanted to see how I would look in one, and I hoped that it might give me the authoritative air of a Commander Whitehead or the satyr-like elegance of a Peter Ustinov.

The hardest part of growing a beard is the reaction of the public. You would think it is my own business, but you would be wrong. The public looks upon a beard as an intrusion upon its domestic tranquility. If Americans had their way, they would shave it off the portrait of Uncle Sam.

In the village where I spend my summers, the comments are friendly but puzzled. Am I trying to become a beatnik? I patiently answer that a man close on to 50, with as much gray as black in his beard, hardly qualifies for that category. Do I want to look more "arty"? I just as patiently reply that Moses, Jesus, General Lee, and President Lincoln all wore beards, and none was considered an esthete.

Is it because I'm too lazy and sloppy to shave? Again, I point out that trimming a beard and keeping it neatly shaped is far more trouble than simply shaving the whole face every day. Well, then, am I trying to conceal a weak chin? No, I answer, a double chin.

In this land of presumed individualism, you might imagine that the way a man chooses to wear his hair would be a matter of profound indifference to strangers. Not so. When I used to enter a room clean shaven, I was accepted as just another person. Nowadays, a psychological chain reaction vibrates through the room: here is somebody alien and different, disturbing and possibly dangerous. Watch this man!

It is only a summertime caprice of mine, and I have promised the children that I would shave it off before returning to the city, if they didn't like the way it looked on me. But I am already quavering before public opinion, and have begun to lie about my reasons for growing it.

Sometimes I say it covers a disfiguring scar from a neck operation. At other times I explain that I am growing it for our village's centennial celebration (which was actually held four years ago). And once I told a less-than-adoring female sitting at the counter next to me, that I was paying off an election bet I had made on Fidel Castro as the next mayor of Miami Beach.

Actually, it is beginning to look pretty darn *distingué*, and I have already gained a sneaking affection for my beard. But I doubt that I have the strength of character to persist, in the face of snickers, stares, and shrugs of disgust. "Un-American" is the ugly word I sometimes hear whispered behind my back, and I wonder how Uncle Sam would have handled that one.

"Americanism" Is "Inclusive"

NOT LONG AGO, I read an amusing, but far from trivial, analysis by an anthropologist. He took as his text the statement of an ardent U. S. citizen: *"I thank God that I am a 100 percent American."*

When we break down this sentence, we find that the word "thank" comes from *German* and *Scandinavian* sources, by way of *England;* that God was originally the deity of the *Hebrews;* that the number 100 arises from the invention of zero by the *Arabs;* that "percent" refers to a decimal system created by the *Greeks;* and that the word "American" itself comes from the name of an *Italian* geographer.

It is astonishing, and depressing, how few U. S. citizens recognize what "Americanism" truly consists of. In the first place, it was something absolutely new and revolutionary in the world. It started not as another "ism" added to the old "isms," but as a radical departure from all the others. Its revolutionary quality originated in the phrase "all men are created equal" — equal, of course, in rights and opportunities, not in abilities. Our Declaration of Independence did not say that all "Americans" or all "white men" or all "property owners" were equal — but all *men*, everywhere, regardless of origin or status. Until then, all other political "isms" were *exclusive* — they were regarded as true and operative only for a limited group of persons. But Americanism was conceived as something *inclusive* — anybody who agreed with these rights and freedoms was a member of the human race in good standing and could share in these privileges and blessings.

Therefore, to be a "100 percent American" meant to embrace those qualities and contributions of the Germans and Scandinavians and English and Hebrews and Arabs and Greeks and Italians and anybody else who shared in the ideas and ideals of our nation's founders. The immigrant who came over a year ago could thus be a "better American" than the *Mayflower* descendent — if he better understood and practiced our principles.

"Americanism" is not just one form of nationalism among competing nationalisms. It is the first case in history of men being joined by a *moral idea*, not simply by birth or the accident of geography. And this is why, in its pure and original form, it is superior to all other political "isms."

This is what we should be proud of — our *inclusiveness*, not our *exclusiveness*. Americanism is as broad as the human race, and as deep as the deepest aspirations common to all mankind. To turn it into anything less, anything narrower, anything proud and exclusive and intolerant, is to corrupt and crush this ideal.

Why Not a Week of Truth?

THE ELECTION coming up in Britain soon reminded me of a marvelously rare and honest comment made just before another British election about a dozen years ago, which I have long treasured in my files. It was made by Kenneth Pickthorn, a Conservative member of Parliament, who concluded a political speech with the memorable words: "On this subject, as on so many others, I am amply provided with profound prejudices and superficial information."

Like a dash of sea spray on a muggy summer's day, Pickthorn's refreshing admission made one realize how wonderful the world would be if only for a week all of us could dispense with cant and speak with candor.

The cigaret manufacturer would say to us: "My brand is about the same as all the other brands, with a slightly different flavor, and it won't do a thing for you except reinforce the smoking habit."

The TV commentator would say to us: "I simply don't understand this most recent development in Far Eastern affairs. It's too soon to digest it, and enough facts aren't in yet. Please wait a few weeks until the situation is stabilized and I've had time to study the problem."

The film producer would say to us: " 'Passionate Haystack' is the best picture we could make with the material on hand; it has a few exciting moments, which we hope will compensate for the inferior acting and the absurd story."

The general in Vietnam would say to us: "I suppose I could call this week's maneuvers a 'tactical withdrawal' of our forces, but the plain fact is that we were outsmarted and forced to retreat ignominiously. I'll try to do better next week."

The merchant would say to us: "The fashions are pretty silly this fall, and some of the goods are not what they were when we could rely on honest craftsmanship, but you may find a few things that you like."

The airline would say to us: "There's heavy fog in the west, and the plane may leave in an hour or so, and then again it may not. We have no way of telling, and maybe you ought to call the depot and make a train reservation before it's too late."

The auto manufacturer would say to us: "This year's models are just face-lifted a little from last year's. We made a few minor improvements, but so have our competitors, and there's not a great deal to choose between them except for inessential matters of styling."

The politician would say to us: "I'll give the public as much service as I can, but the organization comes first, debts have to be repaid, and loyalties must be rewarded. All I can promise you is that the opposition won't be any better."

This is too much to expect, of course. But wouldn't it give new zest, and new hope, to the world — if only for one Truth Week?

A Few Things Not to Say

THINGS I HOPE I NEVER SAY AS I GET OLDER:
"IN MY DAY, we kids knew the value of a dollar."

"Why can't they put good old-fashioned *melody* back to music?"

"Anybody who wants a job can find a job, if he has enough gumption!"

"I like girls who look like girls, and boys who look like boys, the way God intended them to."

"The reason they live in slums is that they're shiftless and lazy."

"If I signed Picasso's name to my 9-year-old daughter's paintings, somebody would buy it for $10,000."

"When I go to the theater, I want to see something that relaxes me — there's plenty of trouble in the real world!"

"Hitler and Mussolini did some good things for their people — they just happened to go too far."

"I think people ought to stick with their own kind, and we'd all live a lot happier."

"What we need is a good healthy Depression to make some people realize the value of an honest day's work."

"Those judges are too lenient with delinquents — they ought to throw them in jail and toss away the keys!"

"I say you'll always have wars, because you can't change human nature."

"Kids expect everything to be done for them these days."

"If they'd go out and look for opportunities instead of all this marching and demonstrating, we'd all be better off."

"All we really have to do to straighten out the world is just get everybody to follow the Golden Rule."

"We need more respect for law and order, even if we have to crack a few heads to get it."

"I want you to know I was considered a pretty liberal thinker when I was your age."

"What's the point of having a college education if you haven't learned how to make a living?"

"Of course I believe in free speech and dissent, but in a time of crisis we've all got to band together, even if we think it's wrong."

"The only way to avoid war is to get so strong that nobody will dare to attack us."

A Topsy-Turvy Tax System

WHEN I PUT some expensive improvements on my house, my real property tax goes up. If I let my property run down, my tax would be lower. I can't imagine a more inefficient and illogical way to run a community or a government.

Much of what we currently deplore as "urban blight" is the result of this topsy-turvy state of affairs. It encourages speculators, slum owners, and absentee landlords. It discourages owners who want to improve their homes or their farms.

The real property tax is based on the market quality of the property. If I buy raw land and do nothing with it, waiting for the price to increase (as it inevitably must in our expanding population), I pay comparatively little in taxes. But the more I put into it, the more I must pay. Under such an Alice-in-Wonderland system, it is hardly surprising that the nation's urban complexes are filled with blight, sprawl and greedy speculation; and that any program of urban rehabilitation, construction and development is hamstrung from the beginning.

But what if we took the tax off the improvements and put it on the land? Then nobody would be penalized for improving his property and adding to the value of the community; contrariwise, the incentive to speculate in land would be removed, and both the urban slums and the suburban sprawl would no longer pay rich dividends.

Every year, our living, working and playing space gets more cramped and more expensive. The population explosion is driving more and more people from little towns into the big cities; and from the heart of the cities to the peripheries, where suburban slums are now springing up.

The whole theory and practice of our real property taxes cut across the grain of American history and political economics. We grew strong and prosperous by encouraging people to own and cultivate their property, to make improvements, to add to the wealth of the community. If we took the tax off the improvements — as we take the tax off other activities we want to encourage, such as charitable contributions — then the land-grabber would no longer get rich by sitting on his property until the need for space is so great that the potential buyers are willing to pay almost any price.

And the speculator would no longer profit by squeezing the most housing into the smallest space, as so many of those shoddy suburban development firms have been doing.

Today, the more a landlord lets a building deteriorate, the less he pays in real estate taxes, even though he may be making unconscionable profits by converting three apartments into twelve. And the owner who wants to rehabilitate such a building pays a high premium for restoring the community value. Wouldn't it be exactly the other way around in a well-ordered society?

The High Cost of Compromise

SCHOOLCHILDREN who are taken on visits to Washington generally tour the Library of Congress. There, in a glass cage, they can see a copy of the Declaration of Independence. But this is not a copy of the original Declaration as written by Thomas Jefferson.

The original sheets, which have been seen only by officials and scholars, are kept in a safe, and they contain a clause which was omitted from all later copies. No reference is ever made to it in history classes.

In this clause, Jefferson denounces King George and the British Government for acquiescing in slavery and the slave trade. The clause was knocked out by pressure groups from the South, who agreed to accept other parts of the Declaration only if this part were deleted.

Nobody knows, of course, what history "might have been," but it seems reasonable to assume that the whole social pattern of our country would have been different if the clause against the slave trade had remained in the Declaration, putting the new nation on record as favoring its abolition, along with the other civilized nations of the time.

We would have abolished slavery when it was compara-

tively easy to do so, and the whole tragic and inconclusive
episode of the Civil War would have been averted — an episode for which America is still paying a heavy price today,
nearly 200 years later.

This is the terrible paradox of politics — that, by its very
nature, it is incapable of solving basic political problems. For
the essence of politics is compromise, and Jefferson was forced
to compromise his ideals and his good sense in order to obtain the requisite signatures on the Declaration.

But political compromise usually defers, rather than re-
solves. It closes its eyes to the deeper causes of a problem, in
order to treat its symptoms — and, meanwhile, since the
causes go unchecked, the disease breaks out in more virulent
form in the future.

The delegates from South Carolina and Georgia, who pressured Jefferson to delete the slavery clause, were also politicians fighting for what they thought were their regional advantages. But slavery actually dragged down the South in the
long run, and the Civil War engendered only bitterness and revenge. Slavery deformed the Negro, denigrated the South,
and dragged its evil consequences into the 20th Century.

All political issues, if they are fundamental, are at bottom
moral issues. They cannot be settled at the political level, and
certainly not at the military level. Yet we cannot work out
our moral problems outside the political process, outside the
give-and-take of practical compromise. This is why genuine
progress is so slow: as a man, Jefferson knew slavery was
wrong; as a politician, he had to condone it. And we pay the
price.

Calling the Balls and Strikes

MY EYE was caught briefly by an item on the sports page, reporting that the manager of the Minnesota Twins had threat-

ened assault on an American League umpire for what the manager had fancied was a "bad call."

The item reminded me of a story told by Professor Hadley Cantril, the social psychologist, in explaining the different ways we can approach what is "right" and what is "wrong" in such matters.

Three umpires were discussing the problems of their occupation. One said: "Some are balls, and some are strikes, and I call them as they are." The second said: "Some are balls, and some are strikes, and I call them as I see them."

But the third umpire said: "I see them coming across, and some are balls and some are strikes, but they're nothing until I call them!"

The third umpire was the only realistic one of the three. What is called a "strike" or a "ball" in baseball depends not on the absolute "truth" of each pitch, but on the decision of the umpire. In a real sense, each pitch *is* "nothing" until the umpire calls it. Obviously, of course, if his decisions are too often at variance with the judgment of the players and the spectators, he will not remain an umpire very long — but, except for such rare cases, he "makes" balls and strikes out of pitches.

The attitude of the third umpire has an importance far beyond that of baseball or any other sport. It lies in his candid recognition that objective "truth," or perfect "accuracy," or absolute "rightness" are impossible to achieve in many human situations.

This is the whole idea behind the establishment of an umpire or a referee or a judge. Within the rules of the game — whether the "game" is baseball or a lawsuit — the umpire or referee or judge makes the decision that both sides are bound to respect, even though one side or the other may disagree with an individual decision.

It would be impossible to run a community of any kind

without giving someone the power to exercise this function. Not a town, or state, or nation could run for one day unless we agreed to accept such decisions, even when they go against us.

And this is the crux of mankind's failure in international relations. We have not, and have never had, such an umpire. We believe implicitly in the "rightness" of whatever we do — and so does every other nation — and do not feel bound by whatever decision some "world court" might make. All conferences will fail, all attempts at disarmament will fail, all summit meetings will fail — so long as each nation is calling its own balls and strikes.

Scoreboard for a Winner: 3

A LOSER believes in "fate"; a winner believes that we make our fate by what we do, or fail to do.

A loser blames "politics" or "favoritism" for his failure; a winner would rather blame himself than others — but he doesn't waste much time with any kind of blame.

A loser feels cheated if he gives more than he gets; a winner feels that he is simply building up credit for the future.

A loser becomes bitter when he's behind, and careless when he's ahead; a winner keeps his equilibrium no matter which position he happens to find himself in.

A loser smolders with unexpressed resentment at bad treatment, and revenges himself by doing worse; a winner freely expresses resentment at bad treatment, discharges his feelings, and then forgets it.

A loser is afraid to acknowledge his defects; a winner is aware that his defects are part of the same central system as his assets, and while he tries to minimize their effect, he never denies their influence.

A loser prides himself on his "independence" when he is merely being contrary, and prides himself on his "teamwork" when he is merely being conformist; a winner knows which decisions are worth an independent stand, and which should be gone along with.

A loser is envious of winners and contemptuous of other losers; a winner judges others only by how well they live up to their own capacities, not by some external scale of worldly success, and can have more respect for a capable shoeshine boy than for a crass opportunist.

A loser leans on those stronger than himself, and takes out his frustrations on those weaker than himself; a winner leans on himself, and does not feel imposed upon when he is leaned on.

A loser thinks there are rules for winning and losing; a winner knows that every rule in the book can be broken, except one — be who you are, and become what you were meant to be, which is the only winning game in the world.

A New Kind of Moon Shot

IN THE CURIOUS LOGIC of the emotions, two opposite sides can both be right at the same time. Today, in the ominous confrontation between blacks and whites in America, we have exactly that situation.

The blacks are correct in saying that we have not moved fast enough — not by 100 years — in giving Negroes equal opportunity and equal rights. The whites are correct in saying that we are moving too fast. But how can both sides be right?

Because they use the same words, but mean different things by them. The blacks are legally right, socially right, morally right. The whites are emotionally right.

We are moving too fast not because the Negro is demanding what he should not, but because we whites have not been prepared for it. We have not been prepared for it by our governments, by our schools, by our churches, by all our media of information and persuasion.

After a century of indifference, not to say torpor, we whites are now being asked to do almost overnight what we should have been doing, steadily and gradually, since the end of the Civil War. We are in the position of a man who should have paid $100 a year for 100 years — and now we are being dunned for the whole $10,000 at once.

There is no question that we owe the debt, and the Negro community has a perfect right to present the bill to us, in toto. But it is a staggering sum, after so many decades of delinquency, and we feel somehow that we should be allowed to pay it off only a few dollars at a time.

I think the debt we owe the Negro should be paid, promptly and fully. But it should be paid by the government, on behalf of all white people who lived since the Civil War. It should be paid by taking much, if not most, of the $20 billion we are going to spend to put a man on the moon, and using it to give the Negro a chance to rise or sink with the rest of us.

With this sum, every slum neighborhood in every large American city could be demolished. New schools, new libraries, new recreation facilities could be built. New job training opportunities could be offered. If we just matched the billions we have spent on foreign aid for domestic aid to the submerged one-fifth of our own population, we would be well on our way toward solving the racial conflict.

Integrated housing, morally right, will not do it. Mixed schooling, socially right, will not do it. Access to the polls, legally right, will not do it. What we call the "race problem" is primarily an economic problem — and it is pointless and dangerous to rush ahead on the civil rights front, while we fail to prepare our Negro citizens for the kinds of jobs that will make them stand up straight and live right.

What Is a True "Conservative"?

WHAT is the difference between "convervatism" and "reaction"? I suspect that many persons who call themselves "conservatives" are really reactionaries and don't know it.

I was reminded of this by a letter from a suburban lady who wrote that she wonders "if Abe Lincoln had been able as a youngster to lean on such words as 'disadvantaged' and 'underprivileged,' would he have done as well?" She imagines she is expressing a "conservative" position, but it is really a reactionary one. In the first place, the poverty of Abe Lincoln was nothing like the poverty in the modern urban slum. He was underprivileged economically, but not culturally and socially as well.

In the second place, we don't know what anguish Lincoln might have avoided in later life if his early years had not been so bleak and hard, or how much more he might have accomplished in his personal life, which was not successful.

In the third place, the assumption that being "disadvantaged" and "underprivileged" somehow builds character and enables us to triumph over adversity is not borne out by the very people who utter this cliché. For they give their own children the best advantages, send them to the finest schools, and use their connections to the utmost.

Now a genuine conservative is one who wants to conserve the best that we have; that is, he does not want us to squander our resources. But the most precious resources of any country are the brains and talents of the younger generation. It is absolutely essential that they be utilized to the fullest. True conservatism would demand that every child be given the kind of education and environment that would summon up his full capacities. It would be shocked at the thought that millions of youngsters have practically no chance to demonstrate what they could do under optimum conditions, and that millions of others fritter away their advantages.

The reactionary position — which is often confused with conservatism — is indifferent to this squandering of natural resources. It confuses an economic and social elite — which is one mainly by chance and accident — with an elite of character and intelligence. It wants only to keep what it has, and to get more, rather than to spread the opportunities on the widest possible base.

If underprivilege were such a blessing, there would not be only one Lincoln for a million semiliterates and unemployables; if it were so good for the soul, the suburban lady would sell her house and rear her children in the slums. But of course she won't; disadvantages are "good" only for the great, the dead, and the very remote.

People Are Better Than Politics

FROM time to time, readers want to know why I don't write "more about politics." The only true and honest answer is that I have a profound distaste, not for politics, but for the level at which it operates in our society. If I wrote about it more, I would have to be negative about 90 percent of the time — which is a tiresome stance for a writer, and eventually a bore to the reader.

What could one say that made any sense, for instance, about the race in California between Ronald Reagan, who is in favor of motherhood and against dirty words, and Pat Brown, who can scarcely find his way out of a telephone booth?

What is there to write — partisan politics aside — about the viscosity of Richard Nixon's comments on domestic affairs, or the mendacity of President Johnson's comments on foreign affairs? And who in his right mind would care to choose between these two artful dodgers?

And why waste words over a House of Representatives so lost to ordinary decency that it votes three-to-one to support the unspeakable House un-American Activities Committee, when even the dullest law student knows that both the Committee and the House are thumbing their noses at the whole concept of "due process of law"?

What can one say about a Republican party so intellectually bankrupt that it nominates an amiable ignoramus like Barry Goldwater as its Presidential candidate, or about a Democratic party so steeped in guile that it adopts the very posture in the Vietnam war, after the election, for which it bitterly attacked its opponent before the election?

Only a man who likes to break a butterfly on a wheel would care to dissect Governor Rockefeller of New York. And what in the name of sanity can be said about Lester Maddox of Georgia, or Mrs. Wallace of Alabama, or a score of other political luminaries who — by even the most minimal scale of civilized values — should be manning gas pumps and sweeping floors rather than shaping the destinies of states?

Politics is a farce, when it is not a fraud. It attracts the worst elements — along with a few of the best — because the concept of "public service" in American life has degenerated to a degree that would shock and disgust the founders of our nation. And it is pointless to blame the "apathy" of the voters — when the voters are usually offered a choice between a wrong-principled Tweedledum and an unprincipled Tweedledee.

That's why I don't write "more about politics." I'd rather write about people — in the dim hope that if we can begin to understand ourselves better, we won't expect politics to make the world better.

Patriot versus Bigot

MOST PEOPLE fail to understand the difference between "patriotism" and "nationalism."

Patriotism is wanting what is best for your country. Nationalism is thinking your country is best, no matter what it does.

Patriotism means asking your country to conform to the highest laws of man's nature, to the eternal standards of justice and equality. Nationalism means supporting your country even when it violates these eternal standards.

Patriotism means going underground if you have to — as the anti-Nazis in Germany did — and working for the overthrow of your government when it becomes evil and inhuman and incapable of reform. Nationalism means "going along" with a Hitler or a Stalin or any other tyrant who waves the flag, mouths obscene devotion to the Fatherland, and meanwhile tramples the rights of people.

Patriotism is a form of faith. Nationalism is a form of superstition, of fanaticism, of idolatry.

Patriotism would like every country to become like ours, in its best aspects. Nationalism despises other countries as incapable of becoming like ours.

Just as we fail to understand the difference between patriotism and nationalism so many people fail to understand what "Americanism" really consists of.

"Americanism" was something utterly new in the world when it was conceived by our Founding Fathers. It was not just another form of nationalism — indeed, it was a repudiation of all the then existing nationalisms.

It was conceived as a form of government unrestricted to one geographical place or one kind of people. It was open to all men everywhere — no matter where they were born or came from. In this respect, it was utterly unique. Its patriotism was potentially worldwide.

The word "Americanism" must not be narrowed or flattened or coarsened to apply only to one flag, one people, one government. In its highest, original sense, it asks that all men become patriots *to an idea*, not to a particular country or government. And this idea is self-government by all men, who are regarded as equals in the law.

This is why American patriotism — properly understood — is the best patriotism in the world, because it is for all the world, and not just for us. To confuse it with nationalism, to use it for ugly purposes, is to betray the dream of those who made it come true.

Title Deal Unjust to Clay

WE ALL LIVE, implicitly, by a double standard of "justice." We demand absolute justice for ourselves, but require only relative justice for others. And we don't know we are doing it.

A recent outstanding example was the action of boxing organizations in stripping Cassius Clay of his world heavyweight title because he refused to obey the Selective Service law.

One has absolutely nothing to do with the other. A man does not win the world's title because he is trustworthy, loyal, helpful, brave, clean and reverent, but because he is the best boxer in his class. And he loses the title only when he ceases to be the best boxer. Stripping him of his title because he is presumably "unpatriotic" is as absurd — and as unjust — as sitting down to play poker with a man who wins a thousand dollars, and then refusing to pay what he has won, because he failed to stand up while the National Anthem was being sung.

I have not the slightest affection or admiration for Cassius Clay, in any of his capacities; but at least his decision to go to jail rather than enter the Army is more honorable and more consistent than the decision of the boxing organizations to take away his title. Clay may be wrong in his decision, but he is willing to pay the price, and it will surely be a high one. If he has broken the civil law, he will, and should, be sent to jail; but he has broken no boxing law, and remains the champion no matter if he commits murder, rape, sedition and barratry. What is won by ability cannot be denied because of character.

We are forever confusing the different realms of human activity. We want the idea of "justice" rigidly applied to us when rigidity will help us, and leniently applied when leniency will help us. But when someone else commits an act we disapprove of, then what we really demand is revenge or retaliation rather than justice.

The trouble with this double standard is that once we knock down the distinctions for others, we are knocking them down for ourselves, too. If we can strip a boxer of his title for an act that is wholly irrelevant to his fighting ability, then we can strip a teacher of his job because he wears a beard (which has been tried), or deny a senator his seat because he has embarrassed his colleagues (which has also been tried).

Justice, if it is to have any meaning beyond the rhetorical, must be absolute and uniform for everybody, and not based on preference, or taste, or the passion of the majority. I don't give two straws for Clay, but unless we defend his right to the title, we are signing away our own future rights to be treated fairly.

What Gun Control Can Do

PEOPLE who don't live in big cities find it hard to understand the need for gun control. I was in Montana last month, giving a talk, and during the question period many in the audience were resentful that I have come out for stricter gun laws.

"No laws will stop criminals from getting hold of guns," they keep repeating — and, of course, they are right. Criminals will always get guns, just as addicts will always get narcotics and prostitutes will always get customers.

What they fail to recognize, however — since they live in areas where guns are used largely for killing animals, not people — is that most violence in the city is not committed by criminals. The professional criminals, in fact, shoot only one another; and even the small-time crook is not statistically a great menace with firearms.

I returned from Montana on a Saturday and picked up that night's paper in Chicago. Five separate shootings had been reported — three of them ending in deaths, including one "innocent bystander" to a quarrel. In none of these five separate shootings was a criminal involved.

One youth peppered a police car as he rode past on a bicycle. Two men fought in a tavern; one left, returned with a gun, and killed his antagonist and a stranger at the bar. A 17-year-old girl was shot in the face as she sat on her front porch. An altercation between a tenant and his landlord left the landlord in indisputed possession of his property. He shot the tenant through the head.

This is the pattern of gun killings in the big cities. Most homicides are not professional jobs, in felonious pursuits, but are committed by relatives, friends or neighbors, in the home or nearby. They are sparked by liquor, by lust, by jealousy, or greed, or a burning sense of injustice. And most are committed by people with no previous record of violence.

It is these who will be restrained by stricter gun laws, who will find it much harder to go home, pick up a gun, and shoot an adversary. The liquor will pass, the lust will die, reflection will replace passion if the instrument of death is not so readily available.

No one suggests that tougher gun control will reduce organized crime, or will inhibit the crooks. But the majority of fatal shootings in a metropolis are more emotional than criminal in intent, more impulsive than premeditated. And if the gun isn't there, the impulse to shoot cannot be so hastily gratified.

"The Most Typical American"

PERHAPS the most ironic aspect of the whole racial conflict in America today is the fact that, to most Europeans, our Negro is the "most typical American."

I was having dinner with a group of Europeans not long ago, when the racial subject came up. All of them nodded in agreement when a Swiss gentleman remarked, "You know, we look upon the Negro as embodying most of what we call 'American characteristics.'"

What he meant by this, I found out, was that the very traits we American whites identify with Negroes are called the most distinctively "American traits" by Europeans. These are — vitality, friendliness, openness, disregard for tradition, impulsiveness, generosity, a tendency toward physical violence, optimism, impatience with philosophy or theory, and lack of social polish.

"Every one of these traits, both good and not so good," said the Swiss, "are the ways in which you white Americans characterize your Negro population. And they are precisely the ways in which we Europeans characterize *all* Americans, black and white alike — only the Negroes seem more representative of what we call 'the American character.' "

White Americans tend to look upon Negroes as "childish" — but Europeans look upon *all* Americans as childish. We fear the violence of the Negro in the slums — but Europeans fear the whole Western-saloon inheritance of violence in America's white culture. We regard the Negro as crude or even primitive — but Europeans see a kind of primitive crudeness as an integral part of the *whole* American scene.

Now the point is not whether the Europeans are "right" or "wrong" in their estimate of our national character; perhaps there is no objective right or wrong in such matters, but only stereotypes conditioned by different cultural patterns and varying canons of taste. The point *is* that when we blame the Negro for certain characteristics and modes of behavior, it is possible that we are gazing at an exaggerated representation of ourselves — and nobody likes to see himself in a magnifying mirror, with all his pores enlarged a dozen times.

The modern Negro who calls himself a "black" and turns toward his African heritage rather than identifying with his American background is just deluding himself in seeking for such spurious roots of identity — for, in any sociologist's meaning of the word, he is more "American" in his outlook and reactions than most of his detractors, who bear far deeper marks of their foreign ancestry than he does.

JFK Book: Everyone Goofed

I HADN'T INTENDED to write about Manchester's *Death of a President* squabble, both because I didn't think it amounted to much in the total scheme of things, and because I couldn't find a single positive thing to say about the incident — and an

utterly negative column seems such a waste of my space and
your time.

But so many people have asked me to comment on the matter that, weak reed that I am, good sense has capitulated before public clamor. Actually, I think everybody involved has
been wrong from the beginning.

Mrs. Kennedy was, first of all, wrong — if she sincerely
wanted a first-rate book on the Dallas tragedy — to hire a
third-rate writer. Manchester had hitherto written nothing of
any literary or intellectual consequence, except an ineptly flat-
tering portrait of the late President Kennedy, and there was
no reason to believe that this assignment would transform him
from burlap to brocade.

Secondly, no writer worth his salt, or pepper, has any
right to accept a commission on the terms offered by Mrs.
Kennedy, and still hope to keep his franchise as an independent author calling the shots as he sees them. It is not possible
to respect a writer who submits to such prepublication censorship of his work.

Thirdly, Mrs. Kennedy and her advisers did the most stupid
thing possible in threatening suit if the manuscript were published as written. Nothing could be more conducive in drawing attention to the very passages they wanted cut out; and
this mediocre (and, I suspect, highly distorted) book has thus
been propelled into a prominence it might otherwise never
have achieved — certainly not on its merits alone.

Fourthly, the publishers were wrong in refusing to stand up
to the Kennedy pressure: they should either have published
the book in toto, if they thought they had a clear legal case
to do so, or else have abandoned the whole project — which
would have discredited any subsequent publication of the
manuscript. But, no doubt, they were legally afraid to do the
former, and too financially involved to consider the latter.

The whole incident is a remarkable example of what Professor Boorstein of the University of Chicago has called a "pseudoevent" in American life — an amalgam of vanity, greed, publicity, and hypocrisy puffed up a million times out of proportion to its true worth or significance. It is the stuff that B-films are made of, and not material for a meaningful assessment in the fields of history or biography.

A Republic Isn't Enough

THE RIGHT-WINGERS are fond of making the distinction between a "democracy" and a "republic." They point out that our nation was established as a republic, not as a democracy; and they are ardently in favor of the former, while violently opposed to the latter.

But a republic without a democracy is a hollow shell — and the shell is easily filled by a dictator or an oligarchy. A republic is simply a country without a monarch, which is ruled by representatives of the people. Germany under Hitler was a republic. Spain under Franco is a republic. Both Russia and China call themselves republics in their official titles. There is nothing in a republic that automatically precludes despotism and dictatorship, the rule of violence and bigotry.

A democracy is quite another matter. A democracy is based on the simple and obvious fact that no man or group of men is good enough to be trusted with the uncontrolled power over others. I am not good enough, you are not good enough, and nobody we know is good enough.

Aristotle said that democracy is the *least bad* form of government. Theoretically, we could devise better forms; but, men being what they are, these superior forms would degenerate and become far worse than our bumbling, inefficient, and sometimes corrupt democracy.

When the founders of our nation stated unequivocally that "all men are created equal," they did not mean to state the silly untruth that all men are created similar or identical or without vast differences of ability, energy and brains. What they meant to state was the rock-bottom truth that all men have the same right to determine their own fate; that all men deserve equal treatment, and an equal voice, in the law; that all men must be regarded as ends in themselves, and not as means to other men's ends.

This is what democracy is all about, and this is why it is the only form of government that a free people can afford — with all its weaknesses, inconsistencies, defects, blunders and stupidities. It is not as good as it might be; but we have found nothing better.

Democracy is under great attack in this century from both the right and the left. These extremists seem to be antagonists at opposite poles, but their similarities are greater than their differences. Both distrust and despise ordinary people, while pretending to represent them. Both think they know what is good for us better than we do; and both would enslave us under the guise of liberating us.

We are a democratic republic. The two are indissolubly linked in our history and public philosophy. Those right-wingers who challenge this linkage are just as "un-American" as the left-wingers they oppose.

More to Fear from Facism

THE TRAGEDY, and menace, of communism in the 20th Century is a double-barreled one. First, there is the real threat of Communist domination in many parts of the world. Second, and just as important, there is the "anti-Communist" movement, which is often a cover for reaction and repression.

The rise of communism in our time has made it easier for

reaction to mask itself as "anti-Communist" when it is really anti-people. The diabolism of the Marxists is met by the diabolism of native and disguised fascism purporting to "save" us from Red domination. Communism in itself is not a viable philosophy or ideology. No country has ever freely chosen it; it has no possibility for growth, except through brute force or desperate hunger. Not a single nation with an adequate scale of living has ever voluntarily embraced it.

But the massive irony of Marxism is that it has strengthened and proliferated the forces of fascism more than it has strengthened the forces of democracy. In many parts of the world today, the ordinary people have no choice except between a Castro and a Batista — which is to say, no meaningful choice at all.

In our own country, I consider the militant "anti-Communist" movement to be far more dangerous and pernicious than the exaggerated "Red conspiracy" they warn us about. Even during the worst times we have had, not more than one percent of the American people were attracted to Marxist doctrine — not even the Negroes, who are the only true "proletarians" of American society, were taken in by Communist cant. But because the threat of external communism has been real and pressing in other parts of the world, the professional "anti-Communists" have been able to mobilize large organizations and considerable sums of money to mount campaigns that are essentially fascist in their mood and direction.

It is a bleak paradox that Marx, their sworn enemy, has become their best friend — in the sense that if the Communist movement collapsed throughout the world, these disguised fascist groups would lose most of their emotional momentum and be revealed for what they truly are — not a bulwark against Marxism but a spearhead of hate, intolerance, bigotry, paranoia and violently anti-democratic feelings.

These groups need their "Reds" as much as Stalin needed

his kulaks or Hitler needed his Jews. And if none were around, they would have to invent them — for no Devil theory of history can long survive without its Devil.

Scoreboard for a Winner: 4

A WINNER seeks for the goodness in a bad man, and works with that part of him; a loser looks only for the badness in a good man, and therefore finds it hard to work with anyone.

A winner admits his prejudices and tries to correct for them in making judgments; a loser denies his prejudices, and thus becomes their lifelong captive.

A winner is not afraid to contradict himself when faced with a contradictory situation; a loser is more concerned with being consistent than with being right.

A winner appreciates the irony of fate, and the fact that merit is not always rewarded, without becoming cynical; a loser is cynical without appreciating the irony of fate.

A winner knows how to be serious without being solemn; a loser is often solemn as a substitute for his lack of capacity to be serious.

A winner rebukes and forgives; a loser is too timid to rebuke and too petty to forgive.

A winner recognizes that the only true authority is moral authority; a loser, having little of this, tries to assume more external authority than his character can handle.

A winner tries to judge his own acts by their consequences, and other people's acts by their intentions; a loser gives himself all the best of it by judging his own acts by his intentions, and the acts of others by their consequences.

A winner does what is necessary with good grace, saving his energy for situations where he has a choice; a loser does what is necessary under protest, and has no energy left for moral decisions.

Choking Our Cities to Death

THE CITIES of America are strangling to death in their own traffic. Yet almost all we do is build more highways to take people out of the cities at night and bring them back in the morning.

Has it been wise to build and sell more cars than we can park? In a free economy, I suppose this is a foolish question — as many cars will be supplied as there are people who want them. But, then, shouldn't the people be asked to pay more for glutting the streets with their cars?

During the epic winter snowstorm in Chicago, we saw what a few inches of snow did to the city. Tens of thousands of cars sprawled all over the roads, like huge wounded animals, with no place to go. When the cars were towed off the main arteries, there were not enough garages, parking lots or side street spaces to accommodate them. The snowstorm only made more dramatic the plight of urban traffic. Even in dry weather, the downtown districts are suffocated by private cars, trucks, busses, taxis — so much so, indeed, that many merchants have moved to shopping centers in outlying suburbs. But the same thing is already beginning to happen there: Valuable and productive space is being transformed into parking lots, which are a dead loss to the economy and a blight on the landscape.

If we want the comfort, convenience, and status of private transportation, I suggest we shall soon have to begin to pay a lot more for it. Motorists will have to pay a "use tax" to come into the city — and this tax will go directly toward alleviating the monstrous traffic problem confronting every American city, and many suburbs as well. We may have to start thinking about a "double city" in the downtown districts. This would be a system of either elevated or underground roads for vehicular traffic only. The surface level would then be free for walking, for arcades and plazas connecting shops and theaters and restaurants. Beauty and comfort, as well as utility, would be served by such a plan.

The inner cities are corroding and dying, despite massive efforts at rehabilitation by the municipalities and a few large corporations. They are dying because it is too hard to get in and out; and it is too hard largely because the automobile has delivered almost a death blow to mass transportation. And soon the suburban centers will suffer the same fate, for auto traffic increases far out of proportion to the facilities for handling it. As someone has said, the automobile is the great convenience among nuisances and the greatest nuisance among conveniences. Unless we find a way to diminish its nuisance-value, its convenience will become a Frankenstein's monster, devouring all it overtakes.

Crying "Wolf!" Too Often

IN MOST private arguments, we tend to weaken our own case by pushing it too far, by claiming more than should be rightfully claimed. When we do the same in public argument, it just breaks down any true communication between contending parties.

Last month, the vice president of a large tobacco company told an audience that the government's campaign emphasizing the dangers of smoking "is part of a growing trend to government by big brother." And he went on: "I need not tell you that the foundation stone of our democracy is freedom of choice. If, under the guise of protecting consumers, or any other guise, this freedom is lost, we are all lost."

This is almost a classic example of weakening an argument by pushing it too far. If we agree that the public must have "freedom of choice," then we must also have freedom of access to all information, for if essential information is lacking, our choice is not free, but blind. And the government, indeed, has lagged far behind the medical profession in "emphasizing the dangers of smoking." If we are worried about "big brotherism," the worst way to oppose it is to call for "freedom of choice" when the government is actually offering it to us by letting us know that we smoke at our own risk. It does not stop us from smoking; it simply warns us of the health hazard.

Business and conservative elements in America have continually injured their own cause by shouting "Wolf!" too long and too often, so that the general public no longer believes it when the wolf really begins lurking on the landscape. These constant cries have made it easier, not harder, for government to encroach on private activities.

The way to win the public is by an intelligent discrimination between those government policies which are needed to protect the consumer from his own ignorance, and those which do unjustly interfere with freedom of choice and purchase. By indiscriminately labeling everything the government does as "big brotherism," private enterprise has conditioned the public to accept, rather than reject, statism.

If social security is called "socialism," as it was 30 years ago, and if Medicare is called "socialism," as it was last year, then the public will say, "If this is socialism, then we're for it" — and if thorough-going socialism is ever proposed by the government, it will find a ready audience. An audience created not by government, but by the ill-considered and excessive opposition of dumb conservatism.

What "Police Brutality" Means

WHEN WE READ accusations of "police brutality," we have to understand what the phrase means. Sometimes it means that heads and bodies are hurt; just as often, it means that feelings are hurt. What upsets Negroes, Puerto Ricans, Mexicans, and poor people generally is the fact that they are not treated with the same respect (not to say deference) by the police as are the more affluent members of the community.

There is no question that most police in most cities are acutely sensitive to differences in social and economic standing. A middle-class person is rarely talked to the way an obviously poor person is talked to. The former is treated as a decent citizen until it is proved otherwise; the latter is treated as a suspicious character until it is proved otherwise.

It is the double standard of approach and handling that gives rise to accusations of "police brutality," even when the police have committed no overt act of violence. If their attitude is bellicose and bullying, the "suspect" may even provoke a pushing around in order to justify his dislike and grievance against copdom. To the poor, the police are hated, despised and feared figures — which means that the police get no co-operation from them. Their reaction irritates the police, who then become even more bellicose and bullying, and the circle of mutual distrust is never broken.

What the poor fail to understand, of course, is that the police themselves are fearful in such neighborhoods. They know they are looked upon as enemies — in contrast to middle-class neighborhoods, which look upon them as protectors — and their fear of reprisal makes them talk and act tougher. There is a "psychological feedback" in the police-and-the-poor relationship that perpetuates hostility.

The police, in point of fact, are much less brutal than they were even a decade or two ago; the florid flatfoot who swung his club first and asked questions afterwards is fast disappearing from the force. But, as against this, poor people are more aware of their rights than they were even a decade or two ago, and they are beginning to demand the same civility that is shown to their more affluent neighbors.

"Police brutality" is largely a semantic question, and its solution is more a matter of psychological attitudes than laws. To treat a man like dirt, without reason, may hurt him more than hitting him — and may, indeed, encourage him to provoke physical violence. It may be another decade before our police wake up to this truth.

The Poor Ones Take the Rap

PEOPLE who are alarmed at the rising crime rate believe that "getting tougher" will act as a curb on crime. Nothing in criminal history or past legislation bears out this hope. Severity of sentence has no relation to the incidence of crime.

Americans also mistakenly believe that countries such as England, where the crime rate is much lower than ours, give longer sentences than we do. Actually, the sentences are much shorter in England — but the chance of being convicted and sent to prison is much higher.

It is the *equality of justice*, not the harshness of punishment, that deters criminal activity. Young criminals in America know that the amount of money you have and the lawyer you can afford to hire plays a much more important role in your defense than the enormity of your crime. Therefore, their aim is not to go straight, but to get rich. A successful criminal rarely gets hurt by the law.

The Atlantan, an excellent magazine put out by the inmates at Atlanta federal prison, recently commented on two new prisoners who arrived in two different federal penitentiaries for the same offense: dealing in narcotics. One was a pharmacist, a college graduate, who had smuggled in more than $1 million worth of heroin. With a fine defense attorney, he received a sentence of only five years, with eligibility for parole. The second was an addict peddler, who probably never had over $50 in his pocket at any one time. He was given a lawyer by the court, and received a sentence of 60 years — without eligibility for parole — and cannot be released until he is 97 years old.

These are typical, not unusual, examples. In the same issue, the magazine mentions a convict in New York who had served 34 years for stealing five dollars' worth of candy. If he had stolen a thousand times that much, and had the proper connections, he might have served a year, or not at all. There is almost an inverse ratio in such matters.

"Crime" is not an isolated factor in society. When the crime rate is high, it is generally because the whole system of jurisprudence is perverted. When we "get tougher," it is only the poorest, the clumsiest, the dumbest, who are hurt more. The slick professionals continue to beat the raps, laws or no laws.

There is little democracy in law enforcement in America — and this is what breeds contempt for the law in young criminals. And harsher punishment only makes them resolve to get more successful, not to get honest.

Big Enough to Admit Error

WHILE DOING RESEARCH for a talk, I reread Clarence Randall's book of a half-dozen years ago, *The Folklore of Management*. Randall, as most people know, was one of the most successful and respected of business leaders when he retired as president of Inland Steel.

In a chapter titled "The Myth of the Rugged Individualist" Randall made a statement that could be made only by a big man who was sure of himself in the right way. He is speaking of the broadening of social benefits during the last three decades: "All of this revolutionary social change has come about in my day — workman's compensation, unemployment compensation, social security, old age benefits, company pensions, group insurance, health insurance, supplementary unemployment benefits, insured education plans, and all the rest of our complex fabric of social protection for the individual." Then he makes a most refreshing and remarkable statement: "Almost without exception, I resisted each new change. Almost invariably, I was wrong, as it turned out."

How rarely we hear a man say this, even in private, much less publicly and in a book of wide circulation. Like most businessmen, Randall grew up under the old way, and retired under the new way. But, unlike many of them, he was capable of learning, of changing, and of admitting he had been wrong.

It is a myth, he says, that in the search for security we have lost incentive. On the contrary, "I believe that the modern forms of personal security which now shape our entire society are desirable, in that they give new balance to the economy and bring to the individual a new steadiness of purpose which greatly increases effort." He points to the record to support his view: "The broadening of social benefits has coincided with the greatest surge of industrial expansion that our country has ever known, and with the period of our economy's most imaginative and creative resiliency. If these new measures were all evil, we ought to be in a complete tailspin right now."

There is a gap today, as we know, between government and the business community. What cannot be so easily seen is the gap within the business community — between the top men in large industries, who have a sophisticated attitude toward these social changes, and the heads of smaller companies, who still are fighting on battlefields long evacuated by history. They are not big enough to say "I was wrong."

Horrid Manners at the Wheel

YOU REALLY MUST ride around in a sports car to learn how badly, how competitively, how maliciously most men drive. I have said before, and I repeat, the great wonder of our age is not how high our automobile death rate is, but rather how low it is, all things considered.

The moment the driver of a large, conventional Detroit car pulls alongside my little beast at a stoplight, his hackles go up, his back hairs bristle, and he feels forced to show me how fast he is at the getaway. He will willingly burn a half-gallon of gas and tear two inches of rubber off his tires to beat me at the start.

This is not only juvenile, it is also asinine, because I am not going to race him, and if I did, it would be no contest. I didn't buy a sports car to get away fast at a light, or to exceed any speed laws, but simply because it is surefooted, easily maneuverable, and just plain fun to tool around in. If I wanted to compete, I'd go to Sebring and I'd wear a helmet and take all the precautions necessary. (Incidentally, this is not to suggest that drivers of sports cars are any less adolescent or show-offy than drivers of conventional cars; if anything, most of them are worse, arrogantly weaving in and out of traffic with the cockiness of a little man defensive about his size.)

Much as I agree with critics of the auto industry that it has taken too long to do too little about making safer cars, it must also be admitted that most drivers might use a safer car to commit even more foolhardy acts. Some of them are at least a little inhibited today by the dim knowledge that their overpowered vehicle is not really under their control; given more assurance, God only knows what they might do.

I have heard racing drivers swear solemnly that they would rather take a dangerous curve on a wet track at 100 miles an hour in a race than go half that speed on a straightaway on a dry surface on a typical expressway. "We know what the other racing drivers will do," expressed one, who doesn't even own his own passenger auto, "but even the finest racing driver in the world has no protection against some nut who doesn't even have the sense to be scared."

The sports car driver has a terrifying bug's-eye view of this rampant automania. Other motorists are envious of us, or contemptuous, or just spiteful, and they manifest all the meanness in their souls at every opportunity. On the road, nobody has rights, civil or otherwise.

We are killing ourselves off faster, and in far greater numbers, than we have been able to accomplish in all the wars since 1776. Perhaps this is nature's cunning way of combating the population explosion — at least it's the most efficient tool we've found so far.

Avoiding a Police State

IT is a historical fact that, throughout the history of the world, the liberties of people have much more often been threatened by the forces of "law and order" than by criminals. We easily forget this fact when we worry and complain about crime running rampant, and demand that more power be put into the hands of the various law enforcement agencies.

And it is richly ironic that the very same people who are concerned about the growing influence of government over individual lives are the ones who are clamoring most loudly for increased police powers against lawbreakers. Yet the quickest way to get a police state is to give the police all the power they ask for. I would be much more worried about a police force that had too much power than about a criminal element that was perhaps treated too gently by the courts.

Individual criminals can always be kept in relative control by a police force that is professionally trained, well paid, and free from corrupt political alliances. But a police force cannot be kept in control once its authority has been broadened to a dangerous degree.

Any society has much less to fear from crime — organized or unorganized — than from a usurpation of power by its own law enforcement agencies. Protecting even the worst criminals from unfair treatment is a small price to pay for avoiding the greater danger of police transgressions against the civil liberties of all.

This whole question of "handcuffing" the police by high court rulings is a smokescreen to hide the obvious fact that the police would much prefer to have no restraints on their power to badger, to harass, to intimidate, to wiretap, to wring confessions out of suspects without doing the hard work that good police investigation calls for.

The way to reduce crime substantially is not by giving the police more license, but by giving them more of everything else: more pay, more professional pride, more independence from political pressures, more status, and more serious technical training.

We cannot make criminals any better, if they want to be criminals. But we can make policemen much better, as they do in England and a few other sensible countries. Law enforcement, on the local urban level, is mostly a cheap racket today. When we are willing to pay enough to turn it into a respected occupation, then crime will no longer be so rampant — among the criminals, or among the police.

A Hundred Years of Patience

LOOKING OUT of my office window on St. Patrick's Day, I could see the big parade starting to march through Chicago's Loop — thousands of Irish, with just as many "honorary" Irish marching alongside them.

Being Irish is a pride and a pleasure in America today — so much so that many people like to claim spurious Irish ancestry. The Irish are an immensely likable group, and even their defects are warmly human.

Yet it is worth remembering that it has not always been so. In London, when I was born, the Irish were still considered vaguely subhuman, and generally treated as such. They occupied the most menial jobs, and opportunities for advancement were blocked by prejudice, if not by law. And even in the U.S., until the turn of this century, the Irish were violently discriminated against. "No Irish Need Apply" was a common sign in shop windows in Boston and other Eastern cities for many years. Of all new immigrant groups, the Irish were perhaps the most disdained, feared and shunned by the earlier settlers.

But within a generation or two, in the free atmosphere of a growing and prospering nation, most of this prejudice had dissipated, and today it is only a dim memory that many of the same charges we level against the Negro were once leveled against the Irish.

Yet let us imagine that the Irish had been forced to remain in servitude here; that they had been denied adequate schooling, forbidden to move where they liked, condemned to manual work, and even prohibited from voting. Much as I admire them, I doubt that under such pressing conditions they would have reached a fraction of their present eminence in American life.

What they *would* have done, I am sure — knowing what we do of the mercurial Irish temperament — is rebel against those conditions as strenuously as they rebelled against British domination in Ireland. They would not have waited a hundred years, as the Negro patiently has, before they erupted in passion, violence, and righteous revolution.

We are alarmed today at the manifestations of Negro un-

rest, but instead we should be amazed that there is relatively
so little of it. The Negro has been astonishingly patient,
docile, hopeful and calm in the face of monumental frustration, cruelty and hypocrisy. He has turned the other cheek
often enough to embarrass the apostles of official Christen-
dom, and he is now rebelling because cheek-turning has not
seemed to work too well.

The Negro has practiced what we have only preached,
and now he is beginning to preach what we practice — power.
It frightens us to be confronted with our own attitude staring
balefully back at us.

Paradox of "Free Enterprise"

THE POPULAR PHRASE, "free enterprise," is an interesting example of what the linguists call "telescoping." It is made up
of two separate phrases: "free competition," and "private enterprise."

Private enterprise is what we have in America. In order for
private enterprise to work at its best and fairest, we must also
have free competition along with it. And that's the rub. The
reason that the phrase "free enterprise" has become such a
meaningless political slogan is that many of the people who
believe — as I do — in private enterprise do not at the same
time really believe — as I do — in free competition.

Not long ago, the state of Illinois recovered nearly a half
million dollars from seven rock salt suppliers charged with a
price-fixing conspiracy against the state. All these suppliers,
no doubt, are ardent believers in private enterprise, but they
seem a little short in their fidelity to free competition. Yet
it is impossible to have the one without the other. This
would be "socialism at the top" — companies reaping all the
benefits of private enterprise without running any of the risk
of free competition. Anyone who follows the proceedings of

the Anti-Trust Division of the Department of Justice knows the number and variety of large business and industrial firms which have over the years tried to administer prices, fix profits for the whole field, and achieve a monopoly or dominance that would really stifle free competition. It is hard to escape the conclusion that these companies really do not like competition, or the operation of the free market, and seek to replace it with a closed system that assures them profits and gives the consumer no real choice between so-called "competitors."

Now it may be possible that competition *is* destructive, wasteful, or unnecessarily expensive; and perhaps a few large companies *would* offer better goods at lower cost than many smaller firms fighting each other. But, if such is the case, then we had better stop using the slogan, "free enterprise," and find something more fitting and accurate to describe the operation of our market.

It seems to me that many leaders of our business community want two contradictory things: freedom to make as much profit as possible without interference, and also to protect themselves from the nuisance of free competition. Until they resolve this paradox, they cannot address themselves to the electorate with authority, consistency, or conviction.

Scoreboard for a Winner: 5

A WINNER stops talking when he has made his point; a loser goes on until he has blunted his point.

A winner makes every concession he can, short of sacrificing his basic principles; a loser is so afraid of making concessions that he hangs on to pride while his principles go down the drain.

A winner employs his defects in the service of his assets; a loser subverts his assets in the service of his defects.

A winner acts the same toward those who can be helpful

and those who can be of no help; a loser fawns on the former and snubs the latter.

A winner knows how much he still has to learn, even when he is considered an expert by others; a loser wants to be considered an expert by others before he has even learned enough to know how little he knows.

A winner wants the respect of others, but does nothing with that end in mind; a loser does everything with that end in mind, and therefore defeats his purpose.

A winner's saving grace is the ability to laugh at himself without demeaning himself; a loser privately deprecates himself and therefore cannot publicly afford to laugh at himself.

A winner is sympathetic to weakness in others, because he understands and accepts his own weakness; a loser is contemptuous toward weakness in others, because he despises and rejects his own weaknesses.

A winner hopes for a miracle after everything else has failed; a loser hopes for a miracle before anything has been tried.

A winner goes off the road when he doesn't agree with the direction it's taking; a loser follows "the middle of the road" no matter where the road is going.

A winner, in the end, gives more than he takes; a loser dies clinging to the illusion that "winning" means taking more than you give.

Which "Facts" Do You Want?

PEOPLE who keep saying, "Let's look at the facts" always happen to have a set of facts that fit their preconceptions. But, as any experienced journalist knows, there are as many sets of facts as there are positions that support them.

As an easy, and obvious example, take the case of "affluence" in modern American society. I could array a large, impressive set of facts to show that we are better off than ever before, and that prosperity is increasing across the board for Americans.

Yet, if I wanted to demonstrate the opposite, I could array an equally large and impressive set of facts to demonstrate that our affluence is a dangerous and pathetic illusion. Such as —

Where the age of the head of the family is over 65, two-fifths of all families are making under $3,000 a year. That is, 40 percent of our oldest citizens are living beneath the "poverty" level.

Eight million families make only between $3,000 and $5,000 a year, which is not sufficient for even minimal standards of decent living.

About one out of every five families makes between $5,000 and $7,000 a year — and in this group, 30 percent of the wives work in order to bring the earnings up to this amount. There are 24 million families in the country — families, not persons — with incomes of less than $7,000 a year.

Only 12 million families — or one out of every four — are in the "middle-income" bracket making between $7,000 and $10,000 a year. And two-thirds of these families include at least one child; most of them have two or more.

In the bracket between $10,000 and $15,000 a year, we have only 17 percent of all families; and in order to reach this earning figure, 71 percent of the homes have two or more persons in the family at work.

One-third of all American families have no savings at all, and millions more have savings that total less than $500 per family. An overwhelming majority of U.S. families could not exist for more than a month or so if current income were cut off.

This, as I say, is a "set of facts." Every one of them is true. Just as the "facts" proving our national affluence are true. What we need is less reverence for facts, and more understanding of the human context in which they should be placed. Only then can we begin to have a meaningful dialog on the social problems of our time.

4

OF WAR AND PEACE

Don't Blame the "Beast" Within Us

ONE of the books I enjoyed reading last summer was *The Year of the Gorilla*, written by a naturalist who observed gorilla life more closely and for a longer period than anyone had believed possible. He had read and heard a lot about the "viciousness" and "ferocity" of gorillas, but he found this to be largely a myth. These formidable primates are not aggressive or bellicose; they lead, on the whole, quiet lives, and get along with one another — and with other species — much better than that "higher" primate known as man.

We are all too prone to justify our human aggressions and hostilities as a part of our animal nature; yet nothing could be further from the truth. Human warfare is a *social institution* and cannot be blamed on our "primitive" ancestors or our kinship to the animal world.

A new book published in England this fall, *The Natural History of Aggression*, confirms the observations of the gorilla-watcher, and indeed goes much further into the whole matter of animal aggression. The authors studied the behavior of wolves, shrews, geese, monkeys, lobsters and wasps.

Contrary to popular belief, it was found that animals in captivity are usually more pugnacious than those living freely in their native habitat. Only in captivity do most animals ever engage in fighting against others of their own species.

Fighting among mammals is restricted to those times when food is in short supply or territories are encroached upon. Even then, the battles are only trials of strength, not wars to the death. The battle is formally ritualized, and often stops short of injury. When one wolf conquers another — largely by threat or show of superior strength — the loser throws himself on his back and "gives up," whereupon the winner makes no effort to harm his adversary and allows him to escape.

Men engage in the most frightfully destructive wars not because we are beasts but because we are something quite different from beasts. Our kind of aggression may be said to be a distinctively *human* trait, born of the same brain that has enabled us to invent weapons to be used at a distance. It may be the supreme irony of our species that the very intelligence permitting us to devise such weapons also leads us into the most stupid and subanimal behavior with them.

Nature is not red in tooth and claw, as the early Darwinians believed. The survival of the fittest is as much a matter of co-operation as of rivalry; and the "law of the jungle" is considerably more sensible and humane than the lack of law among nations. What we are learning about animals ought to shock us into the realization that our conduct is somehow a tragic perversion of the biological process. Our social systems have not yet risen to the dignified level of the gorilla.

Men Do Not Like War

IN ANY DISCUSSION of the possible ways to abolish war from the world, one is always likely to hear a strident voice raised in

the ringing declamation: "You'll never do away with war —
because men really like it."

There is not, and never has been, the slightest evidence for
this statement. Anthropologists tell us that primitive man, in
fact, far from being a fighter, was a peaceful farmer, fisher-
man and hunter — until his economic survival was threatened.

Nor is fighting an "animal instinct." The most ferocious
animals do not kill each other, and hunt lesser species only
for food. Darwin's "survival of the fittest" did not mean survival by combativeness but by adaptation to the changing
conditions of the food supply. (Otherwise, the dinosaurs
would have conquered the world, instead of perishing.)

The history of the human race offers more than sufficient
proof that men do *not* like war. If they did, millions would
not have to be drafted, and then carefully trained in sophisticated savagery. Armies spend many months and many millions in making legal murderers out of average men who
would rather switch than fight.

Even in the American Revolution, when the colonists were
trying to overthrow a tyrant and establish self-government,
Washington's most difficult task was getting and keeping
enough troops on hand to meet the Hessian mercenaries hired
by the British. Men had to be bribed and paid increasingly
large bounties — and still not enough volunteers were to be
had. Washington complained to Congress that many recruits
took their bounties and then deserted.

In the War of 1812 and the war with Mexico, three months'
pay in advance plus 160 acres of land were offered to each
recruit — and the results were disappointing. Desertions
were also rife in the Civil War; and, in 1863, when Lincoln
called for another 100,000 militia, only 16,000 responded, and
the Union was forced to draft 35,000 men — of whom at least
25,000 were "substitutes."

Men may sometimes enjoy fighting to obtain release for their animal spirits, but they are not natural killers. In a well-run society, their aggressive drive is safely channeled into sports and other forms of nonlethal activities.

Wars occur because of national pride and economic rivalry, and it is a libel on the human race to suggest that we have a built-in "instinct" for mass homicide. Men may go to war for patriotism, or under compulsion; but no one in his right mind goes to war because he loves the smell of blood.

The Utopian Becomes Realistic

AT THE BEGINNING of 1966, the editor of the "Bulletin of Atomic Scientists" sadly pointed out that "after two decades, the nations of the world have not adjusted their relationship to the revolution in human existence which began with the destruction of Hiroshima in 1945." This revolution, he went on to say, created a reversal of values between what was "realistic" and what was "idealistic." But the governments, and the people, with few exceptions, are still not aware of this reversal of values.

Until the first atomic bomb was exploded, such phrases as "national sovereignty" and "national security" and "military superiority" and "victory in war" had some meaning and made some sense. They were part of the world of reality which nobody could deny. And, until then, such naive phrases as "permanent peace" and "general disarmament" and "common pursuit of common interests by all nations" were little more than utopian dreams, which may have made sense morally and theoretically, but had little practical effect in the world of reality.

Today, the militaristic and nationalistic phrases are utopian and unrealistic, while the peace and disarmament phrases have become the only realistic political program for all nations.

How has this come about? It has happened because modern war is not only *quantitatively* different but also *qualitatively* different from war in the past. Indeed, it has nothing in common with it except the name; and it is by using the same word to describe past and future "wars" that we continue to delude ourselves that we are talking about the same thing.

In actuality, atomic warfare is the direct opposite of past wars. For past wars had boundaries, clearly-defined areas of conflict, distinctions between military and civilian populations, limited aims, and limited capabilities for directing and inflicting damage on the enemy. All this has utterly disappeared in the nuclear age of conflict. The whole world is now the battlefield, the civilians will suffer even more horribly than the military, the capabilities for global destruction are unlimited — and, worst of all, as the rate of nuclear proliferation continues to increase, the larger and more stable governments find themselves powerless to prevent smaller and more desperate countries from building and brandishing nuclear weapons, and thus adding to the probability of war by accident or madness or mere technical stupidity.

We have little "sovereignty" or "security" any more, and our "military superiority" is an infantile illusion. As so often happens in history, yesterday's "utopia" has become our only reliable guide to reality, and yesterday's "realist" is fighting the wrong war.

Let's Let the Moon Alone

SOME MISGUIDED PATRIOT packed a tiny American flag into the Surveyor, which made a soft landing on the moon last month. I suppose this could be the equivalent of planting the flag on newly discovered territory and claiming it for our own. In this symbolic gesture, we did not promote the cause of "Americanism"; rather, we simply extended the earth's anarchy to another planet. If the moon is going to be a "colony" of the earth, we might as well abandon the whole project now.

Science, as we know, is completely international; the men responsible for our technological progress have been Germans, Norwegians, Italians, Swiss, Russians, Englishmen, Frenchmen, as well as Americans. Without their shared knowledge, few of our 20th Century achievements were possible.

If we begin to export nationalism to the moon, we are defeating the very purpose of science and exploration. What will then happen on the moon will be a rapid duplication of what has happened on the earth — claims and counter-claims, invasions and reprisals, conflicts and conquests, all trailing the customary consequences of hate, misery and death. The moon must represent a radical break with human history, or else it will merely provide an enlarged arena for our enmities. If it is to be used and developed, it must be as a huge laboratory for learning more about the universe we live in, not as another source of space and power and exploitation by rival states.

The power structures have always bent and corrupted knowledge for their own special needs; science has always been subservient to politics, and to its logical extension, war. If this terrestrial tragedy is going to be repeated on a lunar scale, then the billions we are spending for exploration on the moon are more than a waste — they are a menace.

It is not inconceivable that some military power might like to use the moon as a gigantic sentry-box from which to rule the earth. This would have seemed like the wildest of science fiction even a dozen years ago; today, it is more than a remote possibility. "Who controls the moon controls the earth" may be the military slogan of the 21st Century.

The need for some abiding form of international law has never been greater, to transform the struggle for outer space into a co-operative effort to harness all the forces of nature to bring a better life to all peoples. This is the only hope left in the Pandora's box which science has flung open into the startled face of modern man.

A World Ruled by Anarchy

FRANCE has recognized Red China. Israel has signed a pact with West Germany. We are co-operating closely with Japan and Italy, our former enemies. Russia is cuddling up to the United Arab Republic.

The day before yesterday, we shot at one another. Yesterday we shook hands. Today we kiss. Tomorrow — will we shoot at one another again? This is the way children play, from day to day, only their shooting is not for real.

Can anyone still take "international politics" seriously? It is deadly serious, of course, in that the possible consequences are catastrophic for the whole globe. But it is not intellectually or spiritually serious, in any high and meaningful sense of the word.

We are "against communism." But whose communism? The Russians'? The Chinese's? The Poles'? The emerging African nations'? The Latin American versions? They seem to be against one another more violently than against us.

The truth is that the world is ruled, as usual, by anarchy; by short-term self-interest; by strategies that cannot deter, deflect, or divert without destroying. The only "policy" of the great nations is to keep on top; of the small nations, to ride with the winner.

We are better than the totalitarian countries in our principles, but little different in our practices. We use the U.N. when it pleases us to (which is not often), and ignore it when we want to (which is often).

We are for "free elections" in foreign countries when we believe our side will win, but against free elections if we believe our side will lose. We willingly support rotten and corrupt reactionary regimes against rotten and corrupt revolutionary regimes.

The citizens of the U.S. do not know what is going on; which makes us even with the citizens of Russia and Red China. We have as little voice in foreign affairs as they do, because matters are too complex, too variable, and too "restricted" for public consumption, discussion and decision.

Tomorrow, Russia might be our friend, and France our enemy. Where will the Turks be at four P.M., and the Yugoslavs at midnight? It is an international game of drop-the-handkerchief — only it is not a handkerchief that is threatened to be dropped. It is everyone's future.

We would not let our children play this way with dangerous instruments. We insist on rules to be followed, for the sake of the whole group, and we punish the child that refuses to follow such rules. But we do not punish ourselves for breaking the rules — and thus it becomes logically and morally impossible for any honest parent to explain world affairs today to any reasonably intelligent child.

What Kind of War Is This?

ON THE FINAL DAY of the Manila Conference, I was watching the proceedings on television when the program cut away from the pompous platitudes of officialdom to an NBC correspondent standing in a public square in Saigon. I cannot quote him exactly, of course, but what he said was a breath of fresh air after the stale and cloying atmosphere of Manila. He was simply reporting the reactions of the South Vietnamese to the conference.

Most of the people there, he said, were supremely indifferent to it. All they wanted to do was survive. About 80 percent of the population live in villages, and they couldn't see how burning their villages was going to bring them a better life. They regarded the conference as purely political, a prop to support Premier Ky and his military cadre. Neither communism nor democracy, as ideologies, mean much to them, and they feel that neither China nor the U.S. cares about their welfare, but are just using the country as a bloody chessboard for power politics. If the war continues much longer, they are convinced their country will be ruined, no matter which side "wins." And they have no more faith in their own political leaders than they have in ours or China's.

This correspondent's cool and candid report reminded me of an Associated Press dispatch from Saigon I clipped out of the paper this summer. It ran: "North Vietnam's order for partial mobilization and a stepped-up war in South Vietnam brought shrugs in Saigon today. 'Today is Sunday, the people go to the movies,' said a young Vietnamese, who had succeeded in obtaining a discharge from the army. Premier Nguyen Cao Ky was sailing off a scenic island in the South China Sea. Many of his generals were either gambling, visiting friends, or basking in the sun near swimming pools."

What kind of war is this, in which we are "saving" a people who show no desire to be saved, "protecting" a country by burning its villages and destroying its crops, promoting "democracy" by supporting militarists and opportunists, and

"defending law and order" by violating three treaties and the
U.S. Constitution?

If we feel we must fight, if we feel that communism must
be opposed everywhere at all times at all costs, let us say so
and do so; but let us not mouth the cheap and transparent cant
that we are doing so because we care about the Vietnamese
or an abstraction called "social justice." Nobody, not even
our uneasy allies, believes us.

The Fight for Raw Power

LET'S ASSUME that the hawks are right — which I don't for
a moment believe — and that our presence in Vietnam is imperative in order to "contain communism" in that part of the
world. Let's assume further that we "win" the war in Vietnam, whatever that means, and the Communists withdraw to
lick their wounds. Then what have we really got?

What we have got are a dozen other Vietnams, ready to
spring up in a dozen other parts of the world. As soon as one
fire is put out, another one will begin to roar elsewhere. We
cannot doubt this. The next World War could start anywhere — in the Middle East, in Africa, in South America.
For communism is no longer something that is "exported" by
Russia; it is more like a spontaneous combustion that can happen in any bitter, frustrated and underprivileged nation.

Today there seem to be only two main forces in the world
— reaction and revolution. There is no effective "third force"
to temporize between the two. There is a Batista, and he is
followed by a Castro. And the sad history of our country in
the 20th Century is that of supporting a Batista until he is
inevitably followed by a Castro.

The whole continent of South America — which we ignore
at our peril — is rent with the conflicting forces of reaction

and revolution. Adherents of the democratic process are piti-
fully few and weak in almost all South American countries.
The decent people have little real choice.

And the same is true in many other parts of the world. The
poor people choose communism in preference to reaction, and
the affluent people (along with the military) choose reaction
as the only way to stop the march of communism.

Between these two vicious extremes, truth and justice are
crushed in the middle. And the U.S., which is supposed to
represent the viable center, has in its obsession with the communist menace, too often given aid and comfort to the forces
of reaction.

How can we beat back communism in Vietnam with a
military dictatorship as shaky and cynical as that of General
Ky's? How can we win the common people to our side anywhere by supporting their oppressors and exploiters? With
the best of intentions — at least, let us assume so — we have
only succeeded in alienating most of the world's people.

"Winning the war" in Vietnam is meaningless, even if possible. When we abandon law and resort to force — as we
have there — we give sanction to the abandonment of law
and the resort to force of all nations. If we are no better than
our enemies, what do we fight for but raw power?

The Best of All Bargains

WE KNOW what a "good bargain" is, from our point of view
— it is a transaction in which we feel we have come out ahead.
But what is a "best bargain"? Is it not a transaction in which
both parties feel they have come out ahead?

Certainly this is the case in marriage. Those marriages we
regard as the happiest are those in which each of the partners
believes that he or she got the best of it, that the other mate

is really better than we are, and perhaps better than we deserve.

Conversely, the worst marriages are those in which one of the mates feels "cheated." It is a bad bargain, and bad bargains usually end in the divorce court. And even when the balance is redressed, so that the scales tip more equably, we still would like to feel that we have the best of the bargain.

Nations are like families in this respect. Within the family of nations, each wants to get a "good bargain" in its relationship with the others. Yet a good bargain is one in which we get more and the other gets less; in such cases, the other will try to get more and give us less. Such conflict ends not in the divorce court, but in war.

What we have to aim for, in these parlous times, is awakening the realization of every country that peace represents the "best bargain" of all — because it is the only condition in which each nation can get back more than it is giving.

In our present state of national rivalry, this country or that can get a "good bargain" in one part of the world or another, in one economic area or another. But such bargains are more illusory or real — because it usually costs more to keep the advantage than it did to gain it.

In the best bargain — which is a firm structure of world law, assuring world peace — each country would receive much more than it gives. If we and the Russians, for instance, stopped spending so many billions on armaments (which nobody really wants to use), the returns of putting that money to productive use would bring a hundredfold benefit to all of us.

If we warred jointly on poverty, disease, illiteracy, prejudice, pollution, mental illness, crime and a dozen other common enemies of mankind, each nation and each person would get back infinitely more than he contributed. This is so obvious as to be banal — but it is precisely the obvious that is the most difficult in human affairs. War, in the 20th Century, is no longer even the "good bargain" it seemed to victors in the past. There is no time left for anything but the best bargain.

Old Enemies and New Friends

WE ARE TOLD that the United States "won" the Second World War, while Japan "lost." If this were not a matter of historical record, there would be no way of telling the victor from the vanquished — except that the vanquished seem to be doing rather better than the victor.

Japan's economic growth rate is unmatched in any other industrial country. In the 10 years from 1955 to 1965, the Japanese economy's growth rate was an astonishing 13 percent *yearly*, and it shows no sign of letting up.

Japan has no nuclear forces, no fleets, no bases, and pays only one percent of her Gross National Product for defense. She contributes nothing to U.N. forces, and makes no contributions to the East-West confrontation in central Europe. While business is booming internally, foreign trade also thrives — Japan's trade with the Soviet Union last year topped the $400 million mark for the first time, and her exports to Communist China were in excess of $150 million. And while we fight in Southeast Asia, Japan's exports to that area rose by a whopping 17 percent last year.

Twenty years after we utterly defeated Japan in World War II, we are still spending the bulk of our national income on non-productive tools for war — income that could be spent for poverty, for schools and hospitals and roads and parks and pollution and a dozen other social needs.

We are committed to "maintaining security" all over the

world, mostly by ourselves. We are now "allies" with our old "enemies," Japan, Germany and Italy; and "enemies" with our old "ally," Russia. We are building bigger and worse bombs every year. We are embarked on a costly and dubious adventure in Vietnam that even our closest friends want no part of. We are enveloped in the very spirit of "militarism" which aroused our anger and opposition to the Kaiser and Hitler, and against which we fought in two World Wars.

We "won" those two wars. If we "win" the third, such a thing being possible and the earth being still livable, does anyone doubt that we will then feed and aid and restore our enemies, and then turn them into allies when new "enemies" thrust their heads up elsewhere?

Must we go on like this unto eternity or oblivion? And how can we blame it all on the Russians or the Chinese, when it has been going on since the infancy of mankind, and maturity is not yet in sight anywhere?

Maybe We Need a "Peace Chief"

ONE OF THE CHIEF conceits of so-called "civilization" is that war and conflict were more prevalent in what we call "primitive" societies. But most anthropological research does not bear out this view.

Studies of primitive tribes, whether in Africa or among the American Indians, indicate that only as the tribes advanced further into more "civilized" states did they relax their efforts at peace-keeping and intensify their warlike activities.

Indeed, most of the North American tribes had "peace chiefs" as well as "war chiefs." The peace chiefs engaged in elaborate ceremonials with other tribes to enable potential conflicts to be resolved amicably without loss of face on either side.

And these "primitives" were so psychologically shrewd that sometimes they arranged for the tribes to engage in mock battles, with the exchange of hostages, to drain away the hostility and release pent-up emotions without going through a real war.

The higher the level of civilization, the fewer provisions are made by society for resolving conflicts. Every modern nation has a department of war; none has a department of peace. As society becomes wealthier, stronger, and more technical, more of its resources are allocated to military preparations.

A good case could be made that the Johnson administration's decision to stay in Vietnam — despite the rapidly deteriorating situation — is not based on military, political or moral considerations, but simply is an unwillingness to lose face there. Politicians, even more than most people, hate to admit they were wrong; phrases like "national honor" are often used as a camouflage for persisting in such tragic mistakes.

Methods of maintaining peace were part of the essential fabric of primitive societies, because it was realized even then that deterrence did not deter: tribes that prepared for war went to war, unless there was some means of turning off the war machinery and turning on the peace machinery. This is a lesson we seem to have lost in our advancing technological society.

For several years, we have been involved in "disarmament negotiations" in Geneva, but nobody pretends that these are much more than feeble efforts to strike a moral posture, while at the same time most of our energy and funds go into building the most powerful armament factory the world has ever known. It is a ludicrously unequal contest between the "war chief" and the "peace chief" in our tribe — especially since no one knows who the peace chief is or what he is really doing.

Perhaps it is time we dropped the illusion of being "civilized," and restored some of those "primitive" methods of keeping our young men alive.

Runaway Births and War

IT IS INTERESTING, and rather depressing, to note how most people tend to think in airtight compartments. What education should do is teach people to relate one subject to another — but this is a rare and apparently difficult art, even for presumably educated persons.

The prime example of airtight thinking in our time is our general concern over the "population explosion," and our inability to link it up with that other major problem of conflicting nationalisms. Every study has shown, for instance, that the lower the standard of living, the higher the birth rate. Countries decrease their rate of growth as they become more opulent, more literate, more hopeful for the future of their children.

What has happened in the past generation is that the new drugs and medical advances have enabled us to cut the mortality rate in the underprivileged countries, while the birth rate remains much the same. It is the poorest nations, with the densest populations, that continue to have the most children.

How can this alarming tendency be controlled? Only by raising the standard of living in such countries to that critical level of education and affluence at which the birth rate naturally begins to decline.

This, obviously, cannot and will not be done in the current atmosphere of conflicting nationalisms. The world is now spending about 120 billion dollars for the arms race; this leaves only a minimal amount to raise the living standards of the have-nots. If much, or most, of these funds could be diverted to aiding the underdeveloped countries, we might see dramatically satisfying results within a generation or less. The physical and medical sciences have already reduced disease and infant mortality sharply in such countries, but this only adds to the problem unless the prime birth rate is also reduced.

The only alternative seems to be the extermination of millions of people through nuclear warfare. Thus, the problems of population, poverty and war are indissolubly linked: poverty generates an increase in population, and the increase in population generates pressures that result in war or revolution.

We can no longer afford a world divided into the have and the have-nots; and it is highly doubtful if we can any longer afford a world divided into competing nationalisms which are forced to spend the bulk of their wealth for weaponry. If the human race cannot work out some fair and sensible plan for disarmament and world federation, we shall either all suffocate together or all go up in smoke together.

Will the Past Bury the Future?

IN 1966 we entered the last third of the 20th Century. More drastic and fundamental changes have taken place in the world during the last 30 years than in the 300 years preceding. More significantly, the *rate of change* has accelerated to a dizzying degree; science can hardly keep up with itself, and nothing else can keep up with science.

The whole nature and direction of the human problem has changed in one generation. Throughout the entire past, man's prime purpose was to get food and shelter from a hostile or indifferent environment, to obtain a decent measure of goods and security. Almost all our social, political, and economic institutions were founded on the premise of a world of scarcity. But it is no longer for many of us, and need no longer be for any of us, a world of scarcity; it is now possible to share the abundance technology has made available.

Yet our modes of thinking and feeling and acting are still attuned to past centuries, not to present needs and capacities. Today's problem is, simply and massively, *learning how to live together*. It is not a scientific or technical or political problem, but a *moral* one, in the broadest and deepest sense of that much-abused word.

Man's relationship to the earth he inhabits has undergone a radical transformation in our time. Wars in the past were fought mainly for *sources of energy* — for slaves or coal or oil or gold that could be turned into labor and thus into wealth. There was not enough to go around, and war was the classic means of getting more.

We are now on the threshold of the release of thermonuclear energy, the most Promethean breakthrough since man discovered how to use fire. It will soon no longer be necessary to compete for scarcity; modern technology will be able to provide abundant energy everywhere on the globe. This is the great promise of nuclear fission.

But the great promise is matched by an even greater threat. As rational, moral creatures, we are still at least a century behind our scientific times. This "cultural lag" cannot be deplored too often or too strongly. Most of our ideas are obsolescent, most of our social and political arrangements are unfitted for today, much less for tomorrow. This is lamentably true on both sides of the iron curtain.

Is it man's tragic fate to be demolished by the most sophisticated weapon on behalf of his most archaic passions? The real race is not between nations, as we mistakenly think it is, but between man's new power to provide a decent life for all, and his ancient reactions of fear, hate and suspicion. Will we allow the past to bury the future?

Why Not Protest Foreign Policy?

A SOCIAL PSYCHOLOGIST could write a fascinating paper on our "national schizophrenia" about government. Many of us act like two different persons when regarding our government's domestic policy and regarding its foreign policy.

On the domestic front, we question the wisdom, the prudence, even the motives of the federal government in many of its ventures; we complain that the individual is "losing his freedoms." No one doubts that we have the right to make such complaints if we sincerely believe them. On the foreign front, however, most of us are outraged when a minority of students and others who dislike the government's policy in Vietnam protest and demonstrate against it.

Yet it is entirely possible that the U.S. government is wrong in Vietnam; a week, or a month, or a year from now, this might be admitted and our policy might be reversed. The public doesn't have enough facts one way or the other to make a rational decision about our policy in Vietnam, or anywhere abroad, for that matter.

I have no clear idea whether we are right or wrong; all I have are my suspicions. But it does seem clear to me that the students have as much right to march and protest against our involvement in Vietnam as the rest of us have to march and protest against any domestic policies we find repugnant. They have the right even if they are wrong — this is, basically, what distinguishes democracy from dictatorship.

The *means* they use to express themselves are quite another matter. If they are violent and repressive means, they cannot be permitted. If they are peaceful means, they must be permitted, or we prove ourselves to be little better than the Russians.

What frightens me much more than the marches and demonstrations is the ugly attitude of the general public toward them. Patriotism is a splendid thing, but, as Nurse Edith Cavell said when facing a firing squad: "Patriotism is not enough." To blindly accept the government's position in Vietnam is as senseless as blindly following its domestic program. This is not patriotism; this is abdication of free citizenship.

Except for the neurotic fringes — which all such movements attract — I do not believe that these young men are cowards or in any way "anti-American." I think most of them are acting on high moral principles, and if they happen to be wrong, their attitude is a luxury a democratic society can afford. We do not need, and should not want, the kind of "consensus" that a Soviet Russia or a Nazi Germany demands of its citizens.

There is nothing holy about a government's foreign policy; neither the Congress nor the people have voted for any "war" in Vietnam. If we stifle the voices of protest under such conditions, what hope is there for freedom if and when full involvement in a war becomes the order of the day?

Only the "Improbable" Is Left

"WHEN you have eliminated the impossible," Sherlock Holmes told Dr. Watson, "whatever remains, however improbable, must be the truth." This piece of reasoning applies to much more than just the solving of crimes.

From my study of history, for example, it seems clear that

everything we have tried in the past to keep the peace has been impossible of success. Pacts, treaties, balances of power, even conquests — perhaps conquests most of all — have given us only an uneasy truce for a few years.

The idea of some kind of world government is fraught with peril — it is utopian, idealistic, the time is unripe, the people are not ready, and it could pave the way for a world dictatorship. It does not have one chance in a thousand — but nothing else seems to have any chance at all.

The idea of a genuine democracy, likewise, seems highly improbable, for many of the same reasons — there are not enough people who are mature enough to make the important decisions influencing the course of history. Yet, again, no other system is workable, and all others we have tried are worse. As Aristotle said, it is the least bad form of government, in a practical sense.

What is so puzzling and distressing about the human race is that *we are more willing to keep trying the impossible than to take a chance on the improbable.* We want easy answers to hard questions, even though history, again and again, tells us that easy answers are no answers at all, and only raise harder questions when they fail.

We do not want to pay the price for world unity, which is giving up some of our sovereignty; we do not want to pay the price for democratizing society, which would mean spending more on education for intellectual growth and emotional health than for our physical plant and our military hardware. So, in the end, the price we will pay must be incalculably higher.

We want to choose between the good and the bad, but we do not have this range of choices — usually we have to decide between the relatively bad and the absolutely bad. And since the absolutely bad — like settling national disputes by war — never works, we have to take our chances with the relatively bad.

The development of nuclear weaponry has eliminated all past ways of "solving" our problems as impossible. The resolution of conflict by other means is difficult, delicate, hazardous, demanding a maturity most statesmen and citizens do not possess. But, however improbable, it is the best we have left to us. May we only know it in time.

When the Pros Get Together

ALL PROFESSIONS and activities — if they involve skill and dedication — seem to unite men everywhere. Politics is the only profession that divides men. How can we solve this problem, especially on the international front?

Last fall, Colonel L. Gordon Cooper, who had flown in space longer than any other man, told his professional society that he foresaw greater space co-operation between the U.S. and the Soviet Union. Cooper and Commander Conrad, he went on, had found the Soviet space pilots "mighty nice fellows" who "appeared to be very happy that we could get together and talk." He said "we have already begun to make some break-throughs" in the weather program and elsewhere.

Astronauts, scientists, researchers, mountain climbers, chess players, architects, chefs, relay runners — any occupation that calls for more than routine ability — binds its practitioners together, regardless of their national origin.

On a man-to-man basis, people with shared interests find that these interests surmount language and geography and ideology; they respect one another for prowess and knowledge and have no trouble in co-operating to promote their shared interest throughout the world.

This makes it only the more tragic that in the world's greatest shared interest — the need for peace — we are able to attain so little trust and respect and co-operation. The profession of politics seems by its very nature divisive rather than unifying.

Yet man, as Aristotle remarks at the beginning of his book, is a political animal. We cannot abolish politics or simply do away with all politicians; someone is needed to do the work they perform.

What is significant, however, is that no people are as bellicose as their leaders. No people desire war until they are inflamed by their leaders. No people could not settle their disputes amicably, unless the pride, the struggle for power and prestige on the part of leaders, made such settlement difficult or impossible.

Everything in the modern world is more united and more interdependent than ever before — except the world states themselves. Our trend toward co-operation is self-evident in every field, from weather programs to food supplies. The globe has become too small, too crowded, too complex, for the self-willed anarchy of the past.

Some way must be found to replace the divisive element in world politics with a unifying element — something stronger and deeper than a paper organization like the U.N. If American and Soviet astronauts can get together and talk like "nice fellows," why must countries be so much worse than people?

The Weakness of Our Strength

THE STRONGER we get, the weaker we are. This is rapidly becoming the paradox of military strength in the modern world. And this is why the whole nuclear arms race is such a grim travesty of "defense" and "security."

As more and more smaller nations acquire the ability to

make and deliver nuclear bombs, the strength of the United States and Russia becomes less and less important. For we and the Russians have the most to lose, and neither of us can afford an "incident" that might escalate into nuclear warfare.

The H-bomb is wiping out differences in size and strength; indeed, it is reversing these traditional differences. In another decade, perhaps a half-dozen powers will have the bomb; and then another half-dozen. What does it matter if we can kill our "enemies" 20 times over, if they can do it even once?

The diplomatic and military frustration among the large powers today comes from what the behavioral scientists call "cognitive dissonance." All that fancy phrase means is that we know one thing, and we believe another. We believe in a "strong America," but we know that strength of arms has become a dangerous, or fatal, illusion. We are like a giant walking along a busy thoroughfare, carrying a load of dynamite in both arms. A Nasser can tweak our nose, a newborn African nation can kick our shins — but we cannot drop the dynamite to retaliate, or everybody will go up in smoke.

When we were weaker, when the world still had only conventional weapons, then we were stronger. We could move ships and men and planes in some decisive way, and both sides knew there was a limit to the damage that could be done. Past war was never "civilized," but it was finite. It ended when a specific goal was achieved.

War of the future, however, is irreversible. Once set into full-scale motion, it cannot be halted when a city has fallen or an outpost been captured. War now has a built-in self-defeating mechanism — no longer "us or them," but "all or nobody."

Every responsible leader — political, military, scientific — on both sides of the Iron Curtain knows this to be a fact. But our whole inherited system of beliefs and ideologies will not square with this fact; and so we keep going from strength to strength, getting weaker as we go, making more certain that if the ultimate confrontation comes, nothing at all will be left. This is what we call "a strategy."

Death Sentence Without a Trial

IN FLORIDA recently, a pair of unsavory characters were acquitted after a long and nasty murder trial, because the jury found a "reasonable doubt" of their guilt. This was quite just and proper.

At the same time, however, thousands of American boys are being drafted and shipped overseas to their possible death while there still exists a "reasonable doubt" that the war we are waging in Vietnam is either valid or necessary. This doubt has been expressed by responsible members of the U.S. Congress, by a Supreme Court Justice, by an esteemed military leader, and by scores of professional, technical, and scientific figures who have seriously addressed themselves to the problem.

Putting aside for the moment all the pro and con arguments about our involvement in Vietnam, what strikes me as grotesque is our insistence that no individual be sent to death while a "reasonable doubt" remains — yet our willingness to send thousands of our sons to the bloodiest of battlefields in a cause that many good men think is unreasonable and unjust. Nations, apparently, consider themselves above the rules and laws which they invoke for their citizens. The United States has broken three treaties and is in violation of the U.S. Constitution in its undeclared "war" in Vietnam — and how can we ask citizens to observe laws when nations feel free to break them at will?

We may be right or wrong in doing what we are doing

there, but that is not the point of my objection. Even if we are right, we do not convict an individual as long as a reasonable doubt remains; yet the doubts many of us have about Vietnam are reasonable, and still they do not impede the flow of human sacrifices to the battle front.

A nation, of course, cannot always wait until everyone agrees, especially if it is seriously threatened. But there is no evidence that we are threatened or under attack; indeed, many of the neutral nations, and some of our so-called allies, privately regard *us* as the threateners and attackers in Southeast Asia.

There is much conflicting evidence in this matter, much still to be debated and weighed and analyzed. While we do this in a trial, we do not at the same time send the defendant marching along to the electric chair. But nations are like the Queen in *Alice in Wonderland*, with her shrill, hysterical cry of "Sentence first — verdict afterwards." And if the verdict turns out to be "not guilty," how redeem the lives of these young men?

Speeding Toward Destruction

THE "Nth Country Problem" is a term widely used by scientists and technicians in discussing the possibility of atomic war breaking out. It means that *the probability of any nation using atomic devices irresponsibly or accidentally increases as more countries become able to make these devices.*

If two autos, for instance, are alone on a highway, the chance of an accident between them is slight. It becomes greater with three or four or five cars; finally with enough cars on the highway, an accident becomes statistically inevitable. This is the "Nth Country Problem" in atomic warfare.

How is it possible to dissuade or prevent more and more nations from making the bomb? It is only a matter of time and money before most of them will be able to do so; the scientific knowledge is common property. There are no "atomic secrets," because science is international and cares nothing for flags or ideologies or borders. Given the technical resources, there is no country which cannot stockpile its own supply of atomic bombs.

In this precarious "peace" under which the world lives from day to day, it is obviously vital (in the true sense of the word) that the smaller nations be restrained from the use of force — because the accidental spread of small wars can easily lead to a large-scale nuclear confrontation which would involve all of us.

But how can the larger nations counsel the smaller ones to refrain from force, and use U.N. peace machinery, when the larger ones don't heed their own advice? How can a parent or teacher tell a child not to strike out in anger when the parent or teacher himself is striking out at the same time?

When the U.S. advises Israel and Jordan to stop bickering, or when Russia attempts to mediate the conflict between India and Pakistan, those countries tend to be skeptical and scornful of peacemaking efforts. If a show of force is "right" for the big powers, then the smaller powers cannot be dissuaded from strong-arm methods.

The annual cost of world armaments has soared to $180 billion — which is 50 percent higher than a U.N. estimate of three years ago. The U.S. and Russia account for more than four-fifths of the world's military spending. All the other nations put together spend only 20 percent as much as we and the Russians do for arms. How can we keep the "Nth Country" off the road while the first and second countries are speeding down the highway to death?

"*Who's Trying to Stop War?*"

"IF I get drafted when I'm 18," asked my son the other day, "where do you suppose they'll send me to fight?"

I looked at him. He is just 11 — barely old enough to join the Scouts. And asking about his military service.

"I don't know," I said. "Maybe there won't be any war by then."

He shook his head in a mixture of scorn and sorrow. "Sure there will, Dad. Who's doing anything to stop it?"

When I was 11, war was something remote and fictional and dramatic. Today it is not only immediate and real, but it seems a permanent state to youngsters. Life consists of going to school, then getting drafted and getting shot at.

"Who's doing anything to stop it?" Nobody, I thought, almost nobody. Fathers give their sons the best they can, but once the boys turn 18, we are powerless to protect them from killing and being killed.

It used to be called "defending your country," which is a glorious concept. But it is foolish to pretend today that war "defends" anything. War can only destroy the victors as well as the vanquished, the women and children as well as the combatants. In some way, the children understand this better than their parents do. They have grown up in the shadow of the bomb, and they know that the fingers that press the buttons — kill here, die there — are beyond their parents' control.

We pretend to be knowledgeable and authoritative and ethical figures; but when the showdown comes, our children are painfully aware that we have little to say about it. We will do what we are told to do, will sacrifice our lovely boys to whatever slogan we are ordered to chant.

We instruct them in morality — but the monumental immorality of war laughs at our petty sermonizing. We give them the finest education — but, before they are barely civilized, they are trained in barbarism. We hold out promise of the "future" — but turn it into a nightmare for them.

Of course, we are fighting for "freedom." So is every country, since prehistoric times. The freedom to fight another war, some other time, some other place, with some other fathers' sons, for some other slogan which will be forgotten or repudiated the day after Armistice.

Where do you suppose they'll send him to fight? Seven years is not so long, if we make it. Seven years to fatten him up, smarten him up, make him strong and capable and virtuous and loving. And ready for death at 18. Why not? Who's doing anything to stop it?

Masters at Fooling Ourselves

"Why aren't more people actively concerned about the possibility, and prevention, of atomic war?" a college student asked me recently, during the question period following a seminar I had taken part in.

There are many different answers to that question, but I think the one that covers the greatest number of cases is the "cognitive dissonance" theory — a new concept that psychologists have found most fruitful in studying behavior variations. Cognitive dissonance is the difference between what we *know* to be true and what we *want* to be true. Cigaret smoking is an excellent example: smokers know it is harmful to their health, but they do not want to believe it — so they set up various psychological mechanisms to conceal or distort or deny the facts.

Automobile accidents are another prime area for cognitive dissonance. We know how dangerous driving has become, and we also know which precautions should be taken — in checking the car, in wearing seat belts, in obeying speed limits, in exercising courtesy and restraint on the road. But we do not observe these precautions, which could save thousands of lives a year.

In the case of smoking, we prefer to believe that lung cancer is something that happens to other people, but cannot happen to us; in the case of auto safety, we prefer to believe that fatal accidents happen to other people, but cannot happen to us. And we indulge ourselves in all kinds of irrational arguments to hide the dissonance between fact and fancy.

This same mechanism is operating, I am convinced, in the matter of atomic warfare. We know what unrestricted thermonuclear war would mean in terms of the human race, and we also know that the nations of the earth are doing little — if anything — to prevent its occurrence. Yet, at the same time, we can't afford to believe that it will really happen to us, to our family, to our community, to our country.

To conceal this dissonance, we lull ourselves with various untruths and half-truths: "Political leaders won't let it happen." "What can one person do to stop it?" "Weapons are so terrible that no one will dare to start an atomic war." "If we build up enough defense, no one will attack us." "After all, nations didn't use bacteria and gas in the last war, even though they were available." And so on and so on.

We get actively concerned about elections, budgets, taxes, zoning laws, civil rights, the right to profit, the right to work. But the right to live, which precedes all else, is tucked away in the bottom of the mind, the way a child desperately represses what it most fears.

The Conflict in Our Attitudes

SEVERAL READERS have asked me to explain and clarify the phrase, "cognitive dissonance," that I used in a recent column.

It was first introduced by Leon Festinger in 1957, and has since received much respectful attention from behavioral scientists of all schools.

The term indicates a conflict between incompatible beliefs or attitudes held at the same time by the same person. Sometimes these beliefs are unconscious, and sometimes they are conscious; what is important is the way we handle the "dissonance."

In a simple example, given by Professor Edwin Boring, the Harvard psychologist, consider the man who likes to smoke and continues to do so, even though recent studies convince him that smoking may lead to lung cancer. Confronted with this dissonance of attitude, he can do one of four things: (a) change his behavior by stopping smoking; (b) change his cognition by ridiculing the cancer scare; (c) suppress or ignore the dissonance, by refusing to read anything further on the subject; or (d) doing something in between, like rationalizing or distorting the cognition ("I know smoking is bad for me, but driving a car is just as dangerous," or "if I stop smoking I'll get fat or nervous, which is just as bad").

"Any serious decision," he notes, "made to resolve a doubt when no additional evidence becomes available, creates dissonance." When 50-50 evidence changes to 60-40 evidence, one may decide to act on that percentage, even knowing that there still exists a good argument in back of the 40 percent.

Man must inevitably operate in the face of dissonance in belief and attitude. Few important decisions are clear-cut and certain in all their consequences. Our job is to cope as best we can on the basis on what we know, even though such knowledge is partial and incomplete.

Faced with the smoking problem, for instance, we may either stop smoking or not stop; the evidence in favor of stopping is at least 60 percent. If we refuse to stop, however, it is immature and self-defeating to change our cognition, suppress the dissonance, or rationalize and distort the evidence. We must accept the fact that a dissonance exists, and remain ready to change our behavior when the odds become large enough to convince us that it should be changed.

Dissonance is hard to live with, for most of us like to be consistent at all cost. But the cost of distorting or suppressing knowledge is too high to pay. We cannot wait for certainty to resolve conflicts; by the time the experiment is concluded, the experimenter may already be dead.

Sound Reasons for Paradoxes

"You're so fond of finding paradox in other people's viewpoints," said a college student to me in a bull session following a lecture. "But what about paradoxes in your own viewpoint — can you think of any ways in which your own position is mocked by its contradictory?"

Indeed, I can. A very obvious and important one comes to mind: the question of nationalism versus internationalism. I am utterly convinced that some kind of world government is necessary if humanity is not to blow itself up; and the closer we move to this ideal, the safer we are.

Yet — and this is the paradox at the heart of the matter — it is precisely the nationalism I deplore that has, in recent years, kept the world alive for freedom.

Without the resurgence of nationalist movements behind the Iron Curtain, there would be little hope in our conflict with a monolithic communism. And the new nationalism in India and Africa has just as effectively prevented any one ideology from capturing a large bloc of peoples and suffocating them in its tyrannous embrace. The world should be growing closer; instead, it is fragmenting into nationalistic groups. And it is only this fragmentation that stands as a barrier against world domination by any one creed or dogma.

This is precisely why history is so tenuous and tortuous a subject, both to understand and to apply to current affairs. The idealogues of the left and the right see history as a straight-line, clear-cut process, in sharp black and white, in which everything has its opposite, and opposites never meet.

In point of fact, however, history is a crisscrossing of trends and tendencies, a blending of opposites, a polarity of tensions between one view and another. To be an internationalist, as I am, should not mean to be blind to the virtues and necessity for nationalism at a given time; and to be a nationalist should not mean to be blind to the virtues and necessity for internationalism at a given time.

Yet, this is a difficult attitude for an individual to take: to admit that what he dislikes may be imperative. Most of us are encapsulated in our beliefs, and the more we argue for them, the less able we become to see any merit in the opposite beliefs. It is this petrification of the intellect that makes political arguments so tedious and fruitless. What we need, above all else, is the ability to see the paradox inherent in any given position, and to know that if we relentlessly drive that position to its ultimate conclusion, we are driving it to bankruptcy. This may well have been Marx's *arrière-pensée* in his ironic statement: "I am not a Marxist."

Two Distinct Kinds of Freedom

IF we cannot agree upon or define or pin down such seemingly obvious terms as "marriage," and "unemployment" and "delinquency," what chance is there that we can agree on what we mean by so broad and loose a word as "freedom"?

One reason we cannot understand, or come to grips with, the problems of peoples in underdeveloped countries is our lack of a common basis (and common experience) for talking with one another. What I mean has been succinctly expressed by

Felix Greene, in his book, *Awakened China; the country Americans don't know.* Writing about Red China, he explains:

"When a Chinese worker or peasant says he is freer today than he has ever been in his life, he means it . . . Perhaps he does not mean it in our way, for he has never known the particular forms of political and social freedom which have been the product of our own historical past and which are the fruit of our relative physical security.

"A Chinese uses the word 'freedom' in a very personal, down-to-earth sense. He is not talking about abstractions, but about experience. He means that he is at last free to eat, and not to starve; he is free of the landlord and the moneylender. He is free to learn to read and write, he is free to develop skills that would otherwise have remained hidden; he is free to send his children to school, and when they are ill, there is a doctor to help make them well; he is free to look at the future with hope, not despair. For him, these are all new freedoms."

This is how communism "conquers" underdeveloped and poverty-stricken nations — by abrogating all political and individual freedom (which means little to a starving man) and replacing it with food, housing, medical care, schools, and technical training. It strikes a bargain that the peasants and workers are only too glad to pay — for the "freedom" they have given up is one they have never been allowed to exercise.

Western capitalism has not understood this simple equation. Our political and individual freedoms are precious to us because they are the "surplus value" of a society that has never known famine and pestilence and tyranny as a normal way of life. But a hungry man, as Cato said long ago, has no ears; he votes with his stomach.

It is the *human person* who needs and desires our sort of freedom; but we do not become persons until our animal wants are gratified, until we no longer live from day to day and hand to mouth. Communism appeals to the biological man; we to the political man. At this stage of the world's development, it seems an unequal contest.

Putting Untold Energy to Work

THE WORLD is ruled by energy, in one form or another. This is the meaning of much of what we call "history" — the wars, conquests, explorations, revolutions. Men were looking for newer and greater sources of energy that could be transmuted into wealth.

In the early days, slaves were energy, along with water and wind, coal and wood. There was never enough energy in the world, never enough production of goods, never enough wealth to do away with the gross inequalities among men and nations.

Today we stand on the threshold of a new liberation of energy — an impending revolution that makes Marxian doctrine as obsolete as the dinosaur. Most of the reasons — the physical reasons — for conquest, war and revolution are simply out of date, or will be soon. It is our tragedy that we do not know it yet.

The first element in this liberation is the rise of automation. Rather than fearing the specter of automation, we should welcome it, plan for it, adjust our social, political and economic theories to it. It can be damaging only if we arrive at it unprepared and unwilling to pay the price for it.

One of the most respected men in the field, Herbert A. Simon of the Carnegie Institute, has recently published a book, *The Shape of Automation*, in which he makes the categorical statement: "Acquiring the technical capacity to automate production as fully as we wish . . . means that our capacity per capita to produce will continue to increase far beyond the point where any lurking justification will remain for poverty or deprivation. We will have the means to rule out scarcity as mankind's first problem and to attend to other problems that are more serious."

Secondly, it is probable that this last third of the 20th Century will see the Industrial Revolution enter its final phase — the liberation of thermonuclear energy, for use everywhere on the globe. This breakthrough would move us into an entirely new phase of human history, making obsolete the old concepts of work, of production, of economics.

But the great disaster of our century may be that we are hurtled into a catastrophic world conflict on the basis of ideologies that are outmoded, rivalries that are meaningless, and power struggles that have no rational goals — before we have time to demonstrate that the future need not be like the past. We desperately need a new set of attitudes, a much broader perspective, to match the revolutionary aspects of our new technology.

The Right to Ask Questions

PEOPLE are never going to agree, so we have to learn *how* to disagree. This is the basic task facing society; all other tasks are subordinate to it. The extremists of the right and the left want to make all people agree — by coercion, if not by consent, by imposing an official attitude upon us, with absolute standards and severe penalties for dissenters.

But most of us, who belong to neither extreme, have not yet solved the problem of learning *how* to disagree. In a crisis, we become as dictatorial as our enemies; beyond a certain point, we will not tolerate disagreement.

Consider our attitude toward the protesters against our Vietnam policy. We do not distinguish between those who disagree, and those who violate the law; between those who assemble peacefully to protest, and those who foment riots.

Yet, the reason we have all this agitation about Vietnam is our failure to disagree in the *past*. There has been no real public dialog on foreign policy: our commitments have not been explained, our mistakes have not been ventilated, our objectives have not been clarified.

As a result, we are in the dark about foreign policy; we must accept on faith the statements of our government leaders that what we are doing is both just and necessary in this war that is not a war against an enemy who is not an enemy.

The tragic events in which we are involved today began in 1954. A decade has gone by in which the American public, on the whole, took no interest in Southeast Asian affairs, and in which the successive administrations were not particularly informative on the progress of events.

But a democratic society cannot operate in this fashion and still keep its franchise. A democratic society — if that phrase is to have any meaning beyond mere rhetoric — must learn how to engage in creative disagreement. If it does not, then when things go from bad to worse, there is no room for disagreement — the worst time to saw off a limb is after you have crawled out on it.

We cannot afford the luxury of being apathetic about foreign affairs. We are too rich, too strong, too important in the world. If we have the right — and I think we have the duty — to question our government's wisdom in domestic affairs, we have an equal obligation to question our government's conduct in foreign affairs. Otherwise, by the time we object, it is too late; by the time we ask questions, the only answers have been forced on us by circumstance.

Leaders from the Stone Age

If we are alive then, we won't recognize the world 20 years from now. A dozen different revolutions are taking place — in industry, universities, medical clinics, laboratories, government projects. These revolutions are changing every field of human activity: transportation, communication, merchandising and marketing, health, weather control, education, the whole structure of work and home life and leisure.

Only one thing is not changing. The most important thing of all — the way in which we conduct our relations with other countries. And this one thing may easily negate all the other things we are doing.

What the professionals call "conflict resolution" is limited largely to a few textbooks and lecture halls. No money is being spent on it, little research is being done, and hardly any progress is being made. Our machinery for aiding people to live together amicably on this alarmingly shrinking planet is still as creaking and rudimentary as it was 2,500 years ago when the Athenians and the Spartans ruined themselves in a war that meant nothing and settled nothing. All the lessons learned by philosophers, social scientists, economists, psychologists and historians in these 2,500 years have not moved us one inch closer to a rational resolution of national conflicts.

This is the most fantastic, and frightening, paradox of the late 20th Century — we seem able to control and improve everything except the one factor that may spell the doom of the human race. In this area, we are still living in the Stone Age — but with the capability of blowing up the whole earth in one day.

We are employing our best brains and talent — and immense sums of money — to enable people to live better and longer, to enjoy leisure, to take full advantage of our brilliant technological breakthroughs. But whether any of us will survive the next decade still depends upon the ancient (and proven ineffective) devices of power politics.

The world's leaders are the same kind of men they have always been: but we can no longer afford that kind of men, any more than a modern corporation can afford to have a caveman as its top executive. The world desperately needs professional managers to integrate and implement the new knowledge of the 20th Century, not the same old power-driven, honor-ridden, cliché-mouthing politicians.

The disparity between our New World technology and our Stone Age statesmanship would not be tolerated for a moment in any company, or college, or hospital, or any other institution of our time. Only in the field of government — most crucial of all — are we still trying to operate with the crude instruments of a vanished age.

A Half-Century of "Progress"

IT was exactly 60 years ago this summer that the great "civilized" nations of the world ratified the Hague Convention of 1907, which was widely hailed as a tremendous step forward in "humanizing" warfare. Under the terms of the Hague Convention, all the great nations agreed that the "laws" of war did not allow unarmed civilians to be killed, and that belligerents did not have unlimited rights to injure the enemy by any means at their disposal.

Since that time, of course, the civilized nations of the world have become more, not less, barbarous. The First and Second World Wars were bad enough, in terms of civilian atrocities; what has been going on since then is enough to make Attila the Hun seem like Florence Nightingale.

War is now nothing less than wholesale murder. Nuclear weapons make no distinction between fighting men and their women and children. The latest weapons permit us to press a button and annihilate millions of people halfway across the world. Wars are no longer "declared"; battle lines mean nothing; and "international laws" are laughed at, both by those who espouse them and those who flout them, when it suits their diverse purposes to do either.

I repeat these truisms at length, because their truth has not yet been absorbed by the millions of people who are now sleepwalking to their own possible — nay, probable — destruction. Most people still think and talk about war as though the old conventions and restraints were still operable. But they have long since been morally repealed.

As Lieutenant General E. L. M. Burns of the Canadian Army has remarked in his new book, *Megamurder,* the nightmare of the Western World and of the Soviet Union is that at any day instantaneous death may come to millions upon millions of our population, with the simultaneous destruction of our cities, structures, machines, and the stored knowledge upon which civilization depends. "The military profession," this general points out, "derived whatever respect it enjoyed (in the past) because it was supposed to protect the lives and property of the noncombatant populations. Now, in the conception of nuclear war, the armed forces of each side take the civilians of the other side as their targets, and are unable to safeguard the lives of their own people." In 1907, he observes, it was declared to be against the laws of war for armed forces to take hostages whose lives would guarantee submission. Now, whole populations are hostages. Does anyone suggest we have made "progress" in the intervening six decades?

Where Politics Can't Serve

ONE of the great, and dangerous, myths of political life is the belief that "politics stops at the water's edge." Ever since we entered World War II, America has preached what is loosely known as "bipartisan policy" on foreign affairs.

Whether this should be so or not is a topic for another column. What I'd like to point out today is that we don't practice what we preach in this crucial matter — and that's one reason we're in such trouble.

The conflict in Vietnam is *not* a nonpartisan war, even though both Democrats and Republicans may support it. It is a venture whose "success" or "failure" may easily determine whether President Johnson is reelected in 1968. If we "win," he will reap the benefit in votes; if we are still bogged down, or make major concessions to the Vietcong, he may be swept out of office.

Naturally, then, there is great political and psychological pressure upon him to establish a glorious "victory" before the 1968 election. It is for this reason, more than any other single consideration, I believe, that our military efforts are being stepped up to a frightening degree in Vietnam now.

But if the conduct of foreign affairs were genuinely a bipartisan policy, then the President would appoint a special commission of both Democrats and Republicans who would be jointly responsible for the course of the conflict, under his chairmanship. The decisions made, and the course taken, would then depend upon many factors — political, economic, moral — and not be based upon narrow considerations of the President's popularity or chances of reelection. The war would be wholly taken out of the political arena.

In such a case, President Johnson would receive neither exclusive credit nor exclusive blame for the course of the war. It would cease to be largely a political football, and we could then have responsible and open debate upon the fundamental issues involved. This is, indeed, the only way to diminish the "credibility gap" — which is just a polite way of saying that the American voter is being hoodwinked and lied to.

A half-century ago, Clemenceau made his famous remark that "War is too important to be left to the generals." In the atomic age, it is even more imperative that war not be left to partisan politicians who may be more interested in the next election than in the next generation. For it is the next generation who will die in order to give the next election to the man who calls the winning signals.

On Living with Communism

WRITING in the Catholic publication, *Commonweal*, Conor Cruise O'Brien says in a brief paragraph what needs to be read and reflected upon by every responsible citizen on this side of the Iron Curtain: "The problem of our age is not how to stop, fight or eradicate communism. It is how to cope with its challenges and its appeals in such a way that the competing systems on the planet may produce more benefits to mankind than threats and suffering."

And this is what most dedicated anti-communists are not able to see — that it is not enough today to be *against;* and that if communism were utterly wiped off the earth, we would still be faced with huge problems of injustice, bigotry, starvation, ignorance, disease, and poverty. All these existed long before communism, and will continue long after it has been eradicated — *unless* we are able to help the whole world move into the 20th Century. In this affluent technological age, people are no longer willing to accept their status or deprivation as an act of God or fateful necessity. They want a chance at more of the good things of life, and nothing is going to stop them.

It is not enough to demonstrate that our system works relatively well for *us*. If it won't work well for them, they won't want it. We have to show how our particular fusion of capitalism and democracy can pull them out of the mire — and if it can't, they will turn to some other socioeconomic mix.

Communism is appealing only to people who see no other way out. It is a creed of despair more than of hope; a goal for those who feel they have nothing to lose. And the best way to "fight" it is by helping them get something to lose, by giving them a real stake in society.

What is stupid about the passionate right-wingers is regarding communism as a *cause*, instead of a *symptom*. It is a symptom of a deep malaise in the social organism, and if Marx had never been born, and the whole apparatus of communism had not been formulated, there would still be the same agitation and unrest under a different name.

You don't cure measles by rubbing off the spots, and you don't eliminate the profound disturbances in a social order by getting rid of the revolutionaries. If the *causes* remain, the symptoms will reappear, in even more virulent form. This is an obvious truth that despots and doctrinaires of both left and right cannot seem to grasp.

Germs May Inherit the Earth

OF ALL LIVING THINGS on earth, which is the one most resistant to nuclear war? No, not the elephant. Or the whale. Or even the cockroach or the beetle. It's the disease germ.

What does this tell us about the evolutionary process "culminating" in man? When we finally see fit to blow up the earth — in a temper tantrum over who gets the most toys — the best chance for survival lies with the disease germs.

This is not my jaundiced opinion, nor the whining of some sentimental pacifist. It comes out of a computer programmed by the Rand Corporation, that cold-eyed, logistical, unemotional research company that is financed mainly by the U.S.

Air Force. In its last of 22 reports on the biological and environmental consequences of nuclear war, Rand also projected that four families out of five would lose at least one member; that an attack in which 54 percent of the general population would die would also kill 74 percent of all children and 87 percent of all persons over 65. Along with us would go virtually all animal life, fish, birds, invertebrates, and you name it. Only the little bacilli which transmit diseases to living creatures stand a good chance of shrugging off such exposure to nuclear radiation.

When the dove of peace lies dead on the ground, a wilted olive branch dangling from his beak, the germs shall inherit the earth. At least, according to the latest mathematical formula calculating expectation of loss of life in proportion to exposure to radiation. And those who live by the Rand shall surely die by the Rand.

Then we shall have — for the first time on earth — true survival of the fittest. For the fittest, in the ultimate nuclear showdown, is neither man nor beast, American, Russian, Chinese, or Eskimo — but a tiny creature we cannot see with the naked eye, a thing scarcely to be called a living organism, a silent invader who has been waiting patiently for millions of years to assert its dominance over this little patch of dirt whirling in space.

And if, eventually, the evolutionary process should be started up again, millions of years hence, when the protozoic slime is again fit for living — what a new Bible could then be written! It would make the Book of Genesis sound as prosaic as a railroad timetable. For who then, in the new epoch, would believe the myth that Man himself — expressly forbidden to kill — had killed himself and every other living creature but the disease germ?

How do you like them apples, Adam and Eve? For what

we are on the threshold of doing makes your caper seem like a Sunday school picnic.

Fatalism: Sin of Our Times

SOME PEOPLE like to imagine they are being "philosophical," when they are only being fatalistic. To me, in these days, such fatalism is simply funk or a failure of nerve. It is not true understanding.

"Look at history," they are fond of saying, "and recall that about 20 major civilizations have risen and fallen in the 6,000 years of recorded time. Our civilization is just like all others — fated to flourish and decline, and to be followed by some other."

This view, I submit, is a painfully shallow misreading of human history. It is true that in the past civilizations have been cyclical, have fallen and been replaced by others — but we are now at the end of the line. There is now a qualitative difference in the world.

No living man has studied the lessons of the past more carefully than Arnold Toynbee. In his historical essays, he warns us that it is dangerous to draw parallels between past civilizations and our own, or to suggest that "civilization can go shambling along, from failure to failure, in the degrading but not utterly suicidal way in which it has kept going for the first few thousand years of its existence." The reason it cannot, Toynbee points out, lies in the recent technological inventions of the modern West, which have given us infinitely more power over nature, but not over ourselves. Civilizations of the past have died from one, or both, of two diseases, he says — Class and War. Class has destroyed them from the inside, or war from the outside — but new societies could always spring up again.

Today, however, "Class has now become capable of irrevocably disintegrating Society, and War of annihilating the entire human race. Evils which hitherto have been merely disgraceful and grievous have now become intolerable and lethal, and, therefore, we in this Westernized world in our generation are confronted with a choice of alternatives which the ruling elements in other societies in the past have always been able to shirk."

Unless united mankind can abolish both War and Class, Toynbee concludes, this time they would win a victory over mankind which "would be conclusive and definite." Nothing will be left for the "new civilization" to arise in, and the complacent "cycle" theory of the fatalists would be terminated by oblivion.

We have been able to destroy individual specimens, but we have not been able to destroy the species itself. Now race suicide is easily within our grasp; and fatalism about that is the sin of sins.

War a Far Cry from a Game

ONE of the most sickening aspects of the news coverage in the Vietnam war is the daily scoreboard: 14 VIETCONG AMBUSHED; ONLY 2 YANKS KILLED. That sort of thing. It makes the war seem like a football game — so many downs, so many yards gained, so many opposing players knocked out. Only the players are knocked out forever.

Apart from the vulgarity and banality of listing such figures, there is the psychological impact upon the public. After a time, we no longer regard the contending soldiers as human beings: they are numbers, just like the numbers galloping down a football field. But the Vietcong are not just numbers, any more than our soldiers are numbers. They are boys, no better and no worse than ours. They are fighting because they are told to fight, and most of them are just as confused about the reason as our boys are.

War dehumanizes people as it progresses, and it dehumanizes the noncombatants. We are in the stands, cheering as the other side fumbles the ball and our side makes a recovery. But our cheers mingle with cheers from the other side of the field, and after a while it is hard to tell the fans apart.

Every day, we read the scoreboard; and every day we become more insensitive to the fact that these are our sons — and their sons — being killed. They are not "Yanks" or "Vietcong"; they are boys who were meant for better things, who were not born to die in a senseless conflict over policies that could change in the next Conference.

Twenty-five years ago, we were fighting the "Japs." They were terrible people then, and now they are our friends. But that war resolved nothing, any more than the First World War did. There is more trouble all over the globe today than at any time in our century.

Nor will the end of the Vietnam war resolve anything. The Bad Guys will continue to run wars, and the Good Guys will continue to fight them. The old men will plan, and the young men will die. The power structures will push the buttons, and the people will blow up.

So many of us are worried about "the power of government," but few seem to be worried about the greatest power of all — the power to call and conduct a war. And this is the one power the people of the world can no longer afford to grant their governments, for nobody can be trusted with the new weapons of warfare.

War is not only too serious to be left to the generals, it is too dangerous to be left to the politicians. In the next World Bowl, the score will be 0-0, and the stands will be empty.

Wars Just Make Us Worse

IN 1917, the year I was born, we went to war against Germany for the first time. One of the chief reasons we gave for entering the war on the side of the Allies was the terrible "militarism" of the Kaiser. And the worst symptom of this militarism, we said, was the fact that Germany had compulsory conscription. Young boys were drafted against their will into the Kaiser's army, even before a war was declared.

Now, 50 years later, we are engaged in an undeclared war in Vietnam. We have a system of compulsory conscription, and have had it ever since Selective Service was set up in World War II, a quarter-century ago. And nearly everybody here takes it for granted. We may differ and argue about the *form* of the draft, but almost all Americans agree that compulsory conscription is a necessity in today's world. We beat the Kaiser, but the Kaiser's militarism has eventually won. We have become what we went to war against our enemy for being.

And this is the great indictment of war as an institution. It reduces everyone to the lowest common denominator of humanity. It makes the victors almost indistinguishable from the vanquished.

One war, and one generation, after we had fought the Kaiser, we fought Hitler's Germany. We were appalled when the Nazis bombed Coventry and Rotterdam, undefended cities, killing tens of thousands of civilians — men, women, and children. The Nazis said they were doing it as an act of humanity — for it would bring the war to an end sooner. We rejected this horrible hypocrisy, and condemned the Nazis as bestial barbarians.

Then, not much later, we bombed the undefended cities of Hiroshima and Nagasaki, killing tens of thousands of civilians

— men, women, and children. We said we were doing it as an act of humanity — for it would bring the war against Japan to an end sooner. And we did not, and do not, call ourselves bestial barbarians.

Now, one war and one generation later, we are burning peasants in Vietnam, destroying villages and devastating the countryside — because our enemy is forcing us to behave in this frightful fashion. We say we have no choice; we must fight fire with fire.

Where do we stand now, compared to that day in 1917 when we first went to war to "make the world safe for democracy"? If the Kaiser had won, would it have been any worse? Indeed, it was because the Kaiser lost that Naziism was able to take root in Germany. Does war do anything but perpetuate itself, in more hideous form, a generation later?

5

OF THE MIND AND PASSIONS

Right Question Isn't Easy

ONE REASON I am not easily impressed with the results of surveys or polls, in which people at random are asked to give their opinions, is not that I mistrust the answers but that I suspect the questions. For it is much harder to devise a fair question than to give a fair answer.

Many scientific experiments have shown how careful one must be in asking questions. For example, two different groups of scientists held two different theories about the sense of smell. A few years ago, the researchers on the problem asked people to estimate the relative strengths of certain odors. It was found that a quite simple change in the way the question was worded would make the answers conform to either one or the other of the theories. The difference in the wording was so slight that it took the researchers a while to discover what was wrong — the question was psychologically slanted (unintentionally, of course) to evoke a particular kind of answer.

Such unconscious slanting is even more common in non-scientific polls and surveys. It is easy to phrase the same question in three or four different ways, and get as many different "majority" opinions.

If one asked a random sampling of Americans, "Do you believe in the principles expressed in the Declaration of Independence?" the replies would be overwhelmingly, "yes." However, if one asked, "Do you believe that all men are created equal?" the answers might be 50-50, even though "created equal" is the basic principle in the Declaration. And this is because most people do not know what the phrase really means.

"Do you believe we should continue to prosecute the war in Vietnam?" would, I believe, receive the assent of the majority of Americans. Yet this could easily be rephrased so that a majority would answer "No." And it could be so ambiguously put that about half would reply affirmatively and half negatively.

This kind of experimenting has been done, for instance, on the subject of capital punishment — where it was found that one set of questions would get most people to be against it, and another set would get most people to be for it. It is the emotional reaction that is evoked, rather than the objective question, that determines the kind of answer we give.

All trial lawyers know the absolute importance of phrasing a question in precisely the "right" way — which means, for them, eliciting the answers that will benefit their side. Until we refine our method of forming questions, our "surveys" tell us less than we think.

When Understanding Fails Us

I HAVE JUST finished reading the new play, *Tiny Alice*, by Edward Albee, which I intend to see in New York later this month. I did not understand the play after reading it, but hope to do so after seeing it.

What interests me, however, are the different reactions of people to works of the imagination they do not understand. Many persons become immediately indignant; they think it is the job of the creator to make everything crystal-clear on immediate inspection. Others deride the work as meaningless or purposely cryptic or pretentiously empty. Not one person in a hundred will blame himself for his encrusted habits of mind that prevent him from grasping a new idea or a novel insight.

Yet, faced with a mechanical or scientific object beyond their comprehension, most people either accept its value, or at least suspend judgment. This is because the scientific or technical object seems to "work," and thus justifies its existence. In our pragmatic age, we feel that whatever works must somehow be right.

But this is demonstrably not true. Einstein overthrew most of the scientific concepts of the preceding 300 years; but, in a gross and obvious way, these concepts "worked" better than his theory. Mathematics, for instance, is the exact science *par excellence*. Yet even in mathematics, some of the "simplest" questions still confound the best mathematical minds. In the last century, an enormous effort has been made to clear up the chaos in "group theory" — and mathematicians still can't answer some of the basic questions about finite groups, which raise dozens of unsolved problems.

None of this bothers the layman, of couse, who is wholly unaware of scientific complexities and differences. When he confronts a work of art, however, he wants it to have unity, simplicity, coherence and significance — and, moreover, he is disturbed if the critics disagree about its worth.

Tiny Alice may be a great and profound play, or a silly and muddled one. I may not understand it because the author is confused or because I am too limited or too closed. Indeed, the author himself may not "understand" it, and yet it may have meanings that will reverberate for a long time. T. S. Eliot could not really explicate his *Wasteland*, which was the most influential poem of the early 20th Century.

We are all intellectually modest in the presence of scientific theories, but intellectually arrogant when confronted with artistic inventions. But the purpose of art is not to get down to our level; rather, it is to lure us up to a level beyond our ordinary selves.

The Critic and the Mirror

READING a sassy and shallow review of a new novel I happened to like, I recalled a recent comment in *The Author*, a journal put out by the British Society of Authors. In a perceptive piece on book reviewing, John Rowe Townsend expressed the core of the problem in a simple paragraph, when he wrote: "The great menace in reviewing is not the lazy or biased man, but the one who is more anxious to write a lively piece than to deal fairly with the book under review. Literary editors can tell at a glance whether a review is lively; they cannot easily tell whether it is fair; and as the newspaper industry is highly competitive, this particular kind of meretricious reviewing is hard to eradicate."

As every professional writer knows, it is much easier to jeer or sneer than to make a balanced estimate of a book's worth; a calm or favorable review often sounds dull, while a panning review is often quoted and reprinted and enjoyed by people who have never read the book.

The desire to be "lively" is a laudable one in writing, for the author's first duty is to hold his audience. But at what price, at what expense? Surely not at the expense of fairness, of reliability, of responsibility toward the book reviewed and toward the public.

A review should be a kind of magnifying glass, in which the critic permits the readers to see the flaws and the virtues in the object under scrutiny. In too many cases, however, it's a looking glass, in which the reviewer revels in his own expressions and attitudes, using the book only as a *point d'appui* for his own verbal acrobatics.

The problem is a human one, and not merely a literary one. It is a melancholy fact that critics are best remembered for their jests and japes, not for their sober appraisals. When Benchley was reviewing plays for *The New Yorker* magazine (and quite capably), he was invariably quoted in his attacks, never in his praise. This so hurt him — for he had an essentially kind nature — that he left the field for good.

Acerbity and mockery are not only easier to write, they are easier to recall, they make amusing conversation, they serve as a substitute for judgment, and, most of all, they satisfy the snob that is latent in all of us. But this kind of "liveliness" should be the sauce — sparsely used — and not the main course. A review might be garnished with wit, and perhaps even a soupçon of wickedness, but when these become the substance, a reviewer has relinquished his magnifying glass for a mirror that diminishes everyone, including in the end himself.

Some Things We Can't Fathom

IT IS NEARLY impossible to understand someone else doing what we cannot imagine ourselves, in any circumstances, doing. This is why the world was so baffled in December, 1965, when Jean-Paul Sartre refused the Nobel Prize for Literature and the $50,000 that goes with it.

I had read only a brief and unsatisfactory version of his reasons for refusing, until the *New York Review of Books* translated his full statement appearing in the French journal *Le Monde*. Shortly before that, I had appeared on a television panel in which the participants were asked why, in our opinions, Sartre had turned down the prize. We said, variously, that (a) he didn't need the money, (b) it was a shrewd publicity stunt, (c) it was a peculiarity of Sartre, and (d) it had to do with his political sympathy for the Eastern bloc.

None of these "reasons," it turned out from his statement, was anywhere near the truth. My own guess had been no more near the mark than those of the others — for I, also, could not conceive of myself rejecting this high honor and the considerable sum attached to it. His reasons, summarized baldly, were twofold: unwillingness to be transformed into an "institution" and unwillingness to align himself with the cultural forces of either the Western or the Eastern bloc of nations.

Agree or disagree with these views, there is an honesty, consistency and authenticity about them so far removed from the mixed and shabby motives of the ordinary person that we are compelled, in psychological self-defense, to impugn his motives and seek for some subtle ulterior ones instead.

The point I am making is not that Sartre is right or wrong in refusing the prize, or even that his reasons are valid or invalid; it is simply that hardly one man in a million is prepared to live fully up to his professed creed when so powerful an inducement as this award comes along — especially since, as he regretfully pointed out, he could have used the money to advance the organizations and movements he considers important.

When confronted by this sort of behavior — exemplifying a morality and an inner coherence we pay lip service to but do not follow — it becomes terribly necessary for us to devalue such behavior down to our own level. This is why we on the panel were so ready to chalk up Sartre's refusal to riches, or publicity, or psychopathology, or his socialist sympathies. These things we can understand and accept. But we cannot really understand people who act much worse, or much better, than we would in similar circumstances. For what we call our everyday decency is little more than a spiritual mediocrity that can neither sink to depths of depravity nor rise to heights of nobility.

Dream Girl à la Computer

An outfit called Com/Pair Systems in Princeton has offered, for the paltry sum of $6, to match me up with a woman through an RCA-301 digital computer. It has also promised me two extra "compatible counterparts" at no added cost. This bargain seems too great to pass up. I have avidly sent for the questionnaire to be filled out and fed through the machine, although I could save Com/Pair a lot of time and trouble by telling them exactly what this woman will be like.

My "one and only," when the computer tracks her down, will be a woman of immense beauty, but no vanity, who spends practically no time in putting herself together. She will be exquisitely feminine and dainty, but at the same time able to change a tire while I sit in the car and wait, and put up storm windows while I loll in an easy chair reading. She will be a superb housekeeper, able to run a 20-room house without help; a *cordon bleu* cook, whipping up a dinner for ten couples in less time than it takes to tell it; and a magnificent *raconteuse*, equally adept at diverting an 8-year-old child and an 80-year-old dowager.

Although a woman of immense inherited wealth, she will be utterly free of the foibles, foolishness and snobbishness that so frequently flaw the possessors of long-term solvency. She will be a mature woman — but innocent; a virginal woman — but experienced; a sensual woman — but athletic; a sophisticated woman — but enthusiastic; a maternal woman — but erotic; a complex woman — but uncomplicated; a rational woman — but intuitive.

She will be submissive but not cloying, amusing but not fatuous, serious but not solemn, efficient but not officious, discriminating but not captious, intriguing but not devious, and dependent but not demanding. She will know where to buy a $300 gown for $16, or how to buy a $16 one and make it look like $300; she will be an accomplished linguist, researcher, typist, historian, philologist, and clinical psychologist; at the same time, equally proficient in the skills of plumbing, carpentry, nutrition, decoration, landscaping, and repairing broken bicycles.

I do humbly recognize that all this may be a trifle too much for one woman — which is why Com/Pair offers those two extra "compatible counterparts" to take up the slack. On second thought, I've asked the company to forget about the questionnaire. Just send me the RCA-301 digital computer, and we'll march down the aisle, arm in armature!

Greatest Machine of Them All

OUR VENERATION of the machine in this computer age has led us to a subtle but definite downgrading of the human brain. We forget that in order to make a machine that seems smarter than man, man must be smarter than the machine.

The human brain contains about ten billion neurons; each of these cells is connected with hundreds, and sometimes thousands, of others. No machine ever devised by man could approach the complexity and versatility of the human brain.

According to Arthur Samuel, consultant to I. B. M.'s research department, the chance of constructing an artificial brain that could duplicate ours is about the same "as the chance that every American will be stricken with a coronary on the same night."

In the new book, *The Computer Age,* prepared by Gilbert Burck and the editors of *Fortune* magazine, the cost of duplicating the brain's cells and connections is estimated thus: even at the ludicrously low cost of only five cents per cell and one cent per connection, the cost would come to more than $1 quintillion, or $1 billion billion — more money than all the governments in the world together possess.

Samuel, by the way, is the man who taught a computer to play checkers so well that it now consistently beats him. But checkers is a relatively simple game, with a finite number of alternative moves. Chess is a different matter; no machine yet programmed can play very much better than a good novice. The number of all possible moves in a chess game is something like 10 to the 40th power; to examine all these, even the fastest computer would take longer than the age of the universe, which is estimated at about two billion years.

Doubtless, the vast funds we are spending for computer research are worthwhile, for the more we can get machines to do for us, the more will our own faculties and energies be released for specifically human projects. But at least an equal amount should be spent on developing the brains we have, the unused potential that resides in each of us, and especially in our children. My own guess is that all of us utilize no more than between 10 and 20 percent of the intellectual capacities we have — and that adequate research could show us how to exploit the enormous mental powers that are lying unused at the mind's bottom.

It is not enough that a few brilliant men can create computers to "think" for us; for the greatest thinking machine is inside each of us.

Just What Is Obscenity?

BEAUTY, we are told, is in the eye of the beholder, and I believe it. But where, then, is obscenity? Is it in the mind of the beholder?

This vexing question has agitated the American community all the way up to the Supreme Court, and down again. The latest Supreme Court decision in the field holds that material conveying any "social importance" may not be considered as obscene.

Unlike beauty, however, it seems to me that obscenity resides in the mind of the conveyor. And who can look into another's mind and know his motives? Why did Henry Miller write *Tropic of Cancer*? Not even Mr. Miller could tell us the real reasons, for he does not know them.

The Supreme Court's decision is, of course, absurd. It is a makeshift device to prevent the local authorities from banning whatever works take their displeasure. As such, it was a necessary decision, in view of the asinine censorship regulations in most cities and states. But it does nothing to clarify the meaning of obscenity. I believe it cannot be clarified in any legal way, for it is not a legal problem, but a philosophical one. Cleanliness, like godliness, cannot be defined in the statute books.

We are an oddly inconsistent people. On the one hand, we resent laws, we cherish what we call our "personal liberty" and our individualism. On the other hand, we want the law to proscribe what we find personally offensive and appalling. We loudly call upon the police and the courts to prosecute pornography; but when the courts demand equal social treatment under the law for all races, we protest that "you can't legislate human feelings." What we are asking is for the courts to refrain from interfering with those feelings we enjoy, and to help eliminate those feelings that distress us.

But we cannot have it both ways. If we are going to allow city police and local courts and post office officials to decide what is "obscene" and what is not, then we cannot turn around and demand "personal liberty" in other spheres of conduct. We have to decide which is the lesser risk to the community.

My own strong feeling is that our crusade against obscenity is a "displacement" which enables us to get rid of our own guilt by attacking the "dirtmongers." There is much more important "dirt" in our society, which we do little about, from the actual dirt of air pollution to the soiled state of politics and social inequities. Obscenity will disappear when the need and demand for it disappear. It is only a symptom of a deeper malaise in the social organism.

Is It "Contrary" or "Contradictory"?

Do you know the difference between "contrary" statements and "contradictory" statements? Or do you imagine it's just playing with words, merely a semantic distinction with no practical application?

It can be shown, I think, that much of our confusion and conflict over political and social matters arises from our inability to distinguish between statements that are "contrary" and those that are "contradictory." I don't mean that better logic alone would change our opinions; but it would make us look elsewhere in support of them.

"The wall is black" and "the wall is red" are contrary statements; that is, they cannot be true together. But they can be false together — the wall might be green, neither black nor red. The falsity of one statement ("the wall is black") does not imply the truth of the other. "The wall is black" and "the wall is not black" are contradictory statements; that is, they cannot be false together and they cannot be true together. The truth of one implies the falsity of the other, and vice versa. They are mutually exclusive terms; there is nothing in between them.

What we do, however, in much of our political and social talk, is to take contrary statements and turn them into contradictories, so that we get what the semanticists call a "two-value orientation."

The two statements, "Communism is the best system" and "Capitalism is the best system," are contraries, not contradictories. It is not possible for both statements to be true together, but both may be false together. Another system, combining their elements, might be better than either communism or capitalism.

But if we take these contraries as contradictories, then we are automatically against everything the communists are for, and for everything they are against — even when they happen to be against the right things for the wrong reasons. If we adopt such a posture, then no real communication or cooperation is at all possible. It is one of the worst faults of Marxist ideology, indeed, that it does adopt such a posture.

Each side denies that there can be more than one other side — and this denial is the essence of the "two-valued orientation," which is shared by Nazis, communists, and the radical right. They are all somehow incapable of seeing that the wall may be neither black nor red, and that the falsity of their opponent's position does not imply the truth of theirs.

Oversimplification is one of the most dangerous attitudes facing us. This is especially so in our complex and interrelated modern society. It is tempting to look for simple answers, but when we turn a contrary into a contradictory, we make it impossible for our answer to correspond to reality, or to find any solution in reasonable terms.

Who, Not What, Gets Our Ear

WHEN WE HEAR a statement, or a summary of facts, or an argument (in the debating, not quarreling, sense of the word), what do we really listen to — who says it, how it sounds, or what is said?

Most studies made have shown that we listen least to *what* is said; we pay more attention to *how* it sounds; and most attention of all to *who* says it. The symbol influences our reaction much more than the fact.

In one study I read about recently, college students were given a list of 14 statements, all of them made by Samuel Johnson, but attributed to other persons. Seven statements were attributed to "favorable" persons, such as Abraham Lincoln and Winston Churchill; and seven to "unfavorable" persons, such as Hitler and Castro. The students were asked to indicate whether they agreed or disagreed with each statement.

Two weeks later, they were given the same set of statements — but this time, the attributions were turned around, in order to see whether the students would pay more attention to who made the statement than to what was said. On the second exposure, a total of 324 changes were made, almost one-fourth of the number possible. And 70 percent of the changes were in the anticipated direction: they agreed with favorable personages and disagreed with unfavorable ones.

Along the same lines, a study by Hovland and Mandell exposed college students to a talk favoring leniency in the treatment of juvenile delinquents. A guest speaker was introduced to three different groups: first as a judge in a juvenile court, second anonymously, and third as an ex-delinquent who was now out on bail after arrest on dope peddling charges. He gave the same talk each time; but the one by the "judge" was deemed fair by 73 percent of the audience, while the talk by the ex-delinquent was deemed fair by only 29 percent. Moreover, the group hearing the talk by the so-called judge favored more lenient treatment than those hearing it from the ex-delinquent.

Another interesting study was a talk on devaluation of the currency. First, the speaker was introduced as the head of a large importing firm; next as an economics professor at a leading university. Although the content and conclusion of the speeches were identical for the two, the audiences tended to "mistrust" the importer and "trust" the professor — because the former's motives were believed to be influenced by self-interest. He was considered to be "less fair and honest" than the other.

Obviously, the expertness and general trustworthiness of a person is an important part of any communication he makes. But the person should not overshadow the statement, and even great men have been grievously wrong. Abraham Lincoln never said it, but it's true.

Choosing Our Life's Work

A GROUP of college students in an English class recently asked me: "Why did you become a writer?" I shrugged and said, "Because there was nothing else that I was good at."

But it was a serious question, and I fluffed it off only because there was no time to discuss it in depth. Actually, no one ever really knows why he "goes" into any profession or occupation, unless it happens to be sheer chance or accident. And I don't believe there is much accident in such matters.

Why do certain men become policemen? If we knew the whole complex of reasons, we might have a better understanding of law enforcement, and how to improve it — especially in the human relations aspect, which is deplorable in most cities.

Why do men become doctors? There are many surface reasons, of course — prestige, scientific curiosity, family background, and so on. But the unconscious reasons may be as strong, or even stronger, in motivating a young man through the obstacle course of medical training.

One suggestion I recently ran across comes from a widely respected doctor, Dr. Herman Feifel of Los Angeles' VA Hospital, and the author of a pioneering study, *The Meaning of Death*.

Dr. Feifel contends that one important reason men become doctors is to control their own excessive fear of death. By becoming a doctor, he says, a man "secures himself against the jeopardy of death, and obtains dominion over his own anxiety, by having the power to cure."

This may seem like arrant nonsense to most doctors, but patients who have observed many physicians "playing God" and assuming the mantle of omnipotence may not so quickly pooh-pooh the notion. There is a "magic quality" in medicine, for the doctor as well as for the patient; and the primitive witch doctor is not as far removed from the modern specialist as we sometimes like to think.

What about writers? Their deeper motivations, too, may have little relation to the art of words or expressing thoughts. Perhaps they were not listened to as children; perhaps they, too, use words as a kind of magic to ward off the anxieties of realistic living. And, quite likely, they adopt the "might of the pen" to serve as lance and armor against some real or fancied weakness in their own nature.

Knowing why we "become" certain things is not merely an exercise in introspection or a self-indulgence — for such knowledge can be used as a professional tool to deepen our relations with others, and to help us guard against those negative, or hostile, motives that inevitably color and deform our higher, and more conscious, goals in life.

The Deviate's Double Life

THE MOST interesting aspect of that squalid Jenkins case during the 1964 election was never discussed, or even raised. It had nothing to do, of course, with politics, but with the organized idiocy of the social order.

The chief objection to Jenkins was that he posed a possible "security risk" by being a homosexual in a sensitive government position. Why did he pose a security risk? Because homosexuals are notoriously susceptible to blackmail.

Why are homosexuals notoriously susceptible to blackmail? Because the blackmailer threatens them with public exposure of their deviation, which would cost them their careers, at the very least.

Why should this threat affect them? Very simply, because our social order does not accept their deviation, and forces many of them to lead wretched double lives. In a sense, the homosexuals are "driven into crime" by the attitude of society.

Obviously, the way to remove the "security risk" that attaches to homosexuals in government service is to accept their deviation openly, as a condition as old as history, and thus to remove the pressure that makes them easy prey to blackmailers. But this is not the rational way in which a social institution works. Instead, we must pretend to ourselves either that the problem hardly exists, or else that by ostracizing and punishing these people we are somehow solving the problem or reducing the consequences.

Quite the opposite is true. Our codified hypocrisy simply intensifies the problem in all areas. It makes the homosexuals more apprehensive and more furtive, forcing them into shameful and "illegal" activities; while at the same time, it strengthens the hold that sinister and subversive elements can exert upon them. Moreover, society's attitude channels them into an "underground" movement of their own, and cuts them off from the mainstream of community life. Like all persecuted minority groups, they strike back by forming cabals, by "taking over" certain spheres of activity (in the arts, for instance), and by purposely provocative behavior.

If our society were mature enough to ignore or accept their deviation, much of their unattractive social behavior would disappear, since most of it is based on an overreaction to public opprobrium. It is we who make them not only "security risks," but who give them an extra layer of neurosis on top of their own internal conflicts. The Jenkins case was more illustrative of our irrationality than of his.

Living in Caves of the Past

ONE of the basic definitions of a "neurotic" is that he is a person who is living in the past. He is tied, with unconscious chains, to his childhood. His present responses are overconditioned by the past, not by the reality around him.

By this definition, today's society is 90 percent neurotic. Most people are not living in the world of 1966 at all, but in a much earlier world. And the "solutions" they propose for current problems are grotesquely inappropriate to modern conditions.

For instance, both the left-wing and the right-wing political syndromes are fantastically outmoded. The left-winger sees "capitalism" as it was 50 or 100 years ago, not as it is today; beginning with Marx, all the left-wing leaders grossly underestimated capitalism's ability to change and to transcend its earlier limitations. Likewise, the right-winger is living in a nostalgic dream, by trying to equate our complex, interrelated economy with the frontier society of a century ago. Birchism is not a political point of view, for it has no relevancy to the modern world; it is a form of emotional regression.

But it is not merely the extremes of left and right who suffer from this neurotic clinging to the past. The vast bulk of us who are somewhere in the political middle also display our own severe symptoms of cultural neurosis. For the hard, cold fact is that nearly every aspect of human life needs to be reexamined and reevaluated in the light of today's needs, demands, expectations, and possibilities. This is true in education, in housing, in work, in family relations, in leisure, in sex, in religion, and perhaps most of all in international relations.

The chaos, confusion and conflict we see everywhere around us is not so much a result of rapid change as a result of our *psychological failure to grow up to this change.* In our medicine, our science, our technology, we rapidly adapt ourselves to new techniques and solutions; but in our thinking, our feeling, our accommodation to social, political, cultural and economic problems, we remain enslaved to tribal memories.

It is hard and painful to grow up individually. It is even harder and more painful for a whole society to grow up, to throw off its early prejudices and preconceptions, to take a realistic look at what is happening in the world. Unless we can control and subdue the influence of the past, we shall have less and less control over the future.

Letting Others Do Dirty Work

A WOMAN in Kansas wants to know how it is possible that a friend of hers — "a sweet and generous woman" — can have as another close friend a woman "who is a malicious gossip of the worst sort." She is puzzled by what her friend "finds" in the gossip.

What she finds, I expect, is a deeply repressed part of her own personality. Some of us do our own dirty work; others must get someone else to do it for them. For we become friends with people not only for their virtues but also for their vices.

Her example reminds me of married couples I have known, in which the husband was mild, quiet and courteous, while his wife was loud, aggressive and contentious. People observing them in action would invariably ask, "Why does he put up with it, why does he let her get away with such behavior?"

The only answer that makes sense is that he covertly enjoys such behavior. She is acting out for him some real need to attack others — a need he is unable to express directly. A large share of her initial attraction for him, no doubt, lay in his (perhaps unconscious) realization that she would be glad to do some of his dirty work for him.

The "sweet and generous" woman who has a malicious gossip for a confidante probably resents being so sweet and generous all the time, but lacks the temperament to be otherwise. So, with the cunning with which our infantile needs take revenge upon us, she seizes gratefully upon a "friend" who allows her to enjoy malice without suffering any of its consequences.

What we consider "odd" friendships or marriages can hardly be explained on any other basis. Each of us has actualized only a part of his full personality; the unactualized parts (which are unacceptable to us) often find their expression through the friend or mate (or gang) we choose. This is the true meaning of the maxim that "opposites attract" — they attract because they are not really opposites, but complementaries. They expand our possible range of reaction to the world.

It works both ways, of course. The malicious gossip is in the grip of a compulsion she cannot understand or control; and so she buys an indulgence against her sins by making friends with someone who, in turn, expresses a buried part of the gossip's nature. For just as no one can be "all that sweet," no one can be all that malicious, without release.

Why should the German people have chosen Hitler? I look upon it as more than a political or economic choice — that Europe's most orderly, most industrious, most rational, most educated, most instinctually repressed nation should have voted in the arch demon of irrationality.

How "Projective Tests" Fail

A FRIEND of mine, who happens to be the president of a large business firm, was asked by his personnel department to permit giving "projective tests" to applicants for executive jobs. He turned down the request, saying, "If I had taken such a test 20 years ago when I came to the company, not only wouldn't I be its president now, but I wouldn't even have been given a job."

He is absolutely right. The use of psychological tests for business and industry may have some limited value, but not in predicting who will make a good and successful manager. I am not talking here about the older type of "aptitude" tests for determining specific skills, such as those given to airline pilots, bus drivers, and so forth, to determine their dexterity

and coordination. In such cases, we know what we are looking for in the job applicant. But nobody really knows what
it is that makes a good manager good.

One of the leading British authorities in industrial psychology, Dr. J. A. C. Brown, makes this point emphatically in his
recent book, *Techniques of Persuasion.* He writes: "If it were
possible to know every single detail of a person's private life,
we would still not have the faintest idea of whether or not
he would make a good manager in a particular firm. The
concealed fallacious assumptions," he goes on, "behind the
use of 'personality tests' in industry are (a) that we know
what makes an individual a good manager, and (b) that the
normal person is more efficient than the abnormal. The facts,
however, are quite otherwise; for all the indications are that
most of the greatest leaders in industry have been highly neurotic. It is their neuroticism which gives them their drive in
situations where a truly 'normal' individual without mental
conflicts would simply sit down and do nothing."

Because some neuroses make people incompetent at work,
he explains, we tend to assume that those without a neurosis
would be competent, "whereas the truth is that . . . Since
neurosis is socially defined, we ignore the great bulk of brilliant people who are successful precisely because they are
neurotic."

The modern projective tests are highly scientific, and can
tell us a great deal about the individuals tested; but when used
for a grossly unscientific purpose, it is precisely the one thing
we want to know that they are incapable of telling us.

Childishness Among the Learned

IT IS HELPFUL to be intelligent, but it is not enough. It is useful to be educated, but it is not enough. There is no indication

that people who are intelligent and educated are any more rational or co-operative in their behavior than those who are not.

I was thinking of this while discussing with some highly informed persons the matter of government grants for scientific research in the universities. Something like a billion dollars a year is currently being handed out for such research, and the sum will rise even higher in years to come.

Yet, the chief obstacle to fruitful results in scientific research comes from the fact that the men who get these grants — very intelligent, very educated men — are dead set against co-operating with researchers in allied areas. They want their own separate empires.

If one thing is sure in modern science and technology, it is the increasing interrelationship among the disciplines. Physics and chemistry and biology and mathematics — these are all drawing closer to one another, separated only by hyphens rather than by periods. At the same time, however, the recipients of these massive grants are not drawing closer to one another; each jealously guards his own little domain and resents any possible encroachment upon it. The most modern research techniques are being conducted in the most old-fashioned way: by a single professor and a handful of assistants in his field. These men are generally so highly specialized that they are unaware, or uninterested in developments in the allied sciences.

C. S. Lewis once said that today's university could rightly be called a "multiversity." That is, rather than trying to unify and correlate human knowledge, it scatters and departmentalizes it into fragments, none of which makes much sense divorced from the total picture.

One of the men I discussed this matter with made the pertinent observation that all scientists who receive their doctorates become "doctor of philosophy," not doctor of science. This means that they are supposed to be able to relate their fields to other fields, and to philosophize about the common needs and objectives in all the disciplines.

Exactly the opposite has happened in contemporary academic life. Specialization has nearly turned into anarchy; there is no cohesive, unifying force, and little sense of cooperation. Rather, there is frantic competition for more grants, more money, more equipment, more staff. If our most intelligent, our best educated, conduct themselves in so childish a fashion, what right have we to expect more of the so-called common man?

All Demonstrators Aren't Kooks

Do you know the difference between a "convertible proposition" and a "nonconvertible proposition"? If you don't, the chances are high that you can't reason accurately or realistically about many issues and conflicts in the modern world.

Suppose I suggest the proposition (which is true) "Neurotic people are usually unorthodox." Do you then turn it around into the proposition (which is false) "Unorthodox people are usually neurotic"? If so, you are committing a fallacy in logic, and a sin against truth.

Yet, we do this all the time, in dozens of obvious and subtle ways. One of the most obvious ways today is our estimation of events like student demonstrations on campuses. We take the true proposition "Most kooks and beatniks will participate in these demonstrations," and we convert it into the false proposition "Most students participating in these demonstrations are kooks and beatniks." If we believe this second statement, then we become totally incapable of understanding the meaning and the thrust of student action.

Another common (and false) conversion is from "Communists support this position" to "Those who support this position are communists." However, the second statement does not at all necessarily follow from the first. It may, or it may not.

Some propositions can be converted, and some cannot; it is important that we recognize the distinction between the two, if we are to discuss and debate important matters rationally. But what most of us do in argument is the equivalent of saying that because "All cats are animals," therefore "All animals are cats."

Going back to the first proposition I cited, it is true that most neurotic people are usually unorthodox, because neurosis tends to make such people alienated from their fellows. Even when they are right, it is for the wrong reasons. But it is not true that most unorthodox people are necessarily neurotic. Some are ahead of their time; some have more courage or wisdom than the rest of us; some hold their individuality in higher regard than most of us; some have too much creativity or imagination to be content with conventional attitudes.

We must not let the fact that kooks and beatniks and neurotics seize gleefully on campus demonstrations blind us to the even more important fact that thousands of serious and dedicated students also take part in them, for reasons that are worth listening to. If we persist in converting propositions that cannot be converted, we shall continue to be vexed by the patterns of the present, and baffled by the forms of the future.

Lending an Ear to Our Foes

SUPPOSE that an editorial in the communist newspaper *Pravda* said, "The scenic resources of the United States have been so ruthlessly exploited by real estate developers, by polluters, by the raw material extractors and other private interests, that relatively few stretches of unspoiled, high-quality, esthetic natural environments are left along the nation's waterways or anywhere else." We would look upon this as typical Soviet propaganda, wildly exaggerated, and bitterly biased against the "private interests." Our initial reaction would be to rebut this unqualified attack upon us.

In point of fact, the sentence I quoted comes from a recent editorial in the *New York Times*, a highly respected middle-of-the-road newspaper and one of the bastions of the Establishment in the U.S. As such, the statement was calmly received and given thoughtful attention by readers.

A long time ago, Don Marquis wrote: "An idea isn't responsible for who believes in it." We have yet to learn this lesson. A statement by a Klan leader or a communist, by a civil rights worker or a pacifist, will be judged more by the source than by the content. The intrinsic truth or falsity of the statement is usually obscured by its origin.

This is the height of folly on our part. We can often learn more from our enemies than from our friends; those who disagree with us can, in many cases, help us broaden our own viewpoint and escape from a "closed system" of thinking that tends to entrap most of us.

We know this is true in personal relations. The astringent comment by someone who doesn't like us may reveal an unattractive part of our personality that we are unaware of, and that our friends would never disclose, even if they saw it.

Likewise, in social and political matters, if we talk and listen only to like-minded people, we will hear nothing but what we want to hear, we will merely be confirming our prejudices and comforting our preconceptions. This is why any private club is so insular and so stultifying, whether it is a club of reactionaries or revolutionaries.

When we refuse to listen to our adversaries, or automatically discount their comments as "propaganda," we have relinquished a valuable tool for self-discovery and self-improvement. The best argument for full freedom of speech is a practical one: that clamping down on unpopular sentiments is as self-destructive, in the long run, as listening only to doctors who tell you that you are well, and repressing those who suggest you are ill.

Nobler Motives Come Slowly

IN THE DEVELOPMENT of the individual, from babyhood onward, there is *an order of appearance* in motives, a kind of "evolutionary process" of the personality. The first, and lowest, motive in the baby is physiological, like hunger. A baby, first of all, must be fed. Next comes the safety motive, which creates fear. When a baby is no longer hungry or fearful, it moves to such motives as love, esteem, and self-realization.

This is the thesis of Dr. A. H. Maslow, in his book, *Motivation and Personality*, which appeared about a decade ago. I think he is largely right. And what is important in this theory is that *a higher motive usually does not appear until the ones below it are satisfied*. If a love drive is inhibited by fear, the fearful person will not let himself go. If the hunger drive is great enough, it will overcome fear of punishment. Only when the lower, primary instinctive motives are satisfied, can the higher motives come into play.

To understand this hierarchy of needs in the human personality is to understand why we cannot expect too much of people living in slums, where life is a continual daily struggle to appease hunger and to ward off fears.

When hunger and fear are reduced, love motives can ap-

pear. When love motives are permitted to flourish, then the
motives of esteem and self-realization can develop. But it is
nearly impossible to have the higher motives until the lower
ones have been gratified.

It is foolish and Utopian to expect underprivileged people
living in the degradation of the slums to pull themselves up
by their psychic bootstraps. A few extraordinary persons
may be able to do this, but the vast bulk are crushed under the
weight of their condition. Wanting the esteem of society, and
possessing self-esteem, are later and higher motives in the development of personality. To ask the underprivileged to care
about art and science, civic responsibility and financial integ-
rity is like asking a hungry and frightened baby to "pull itself
together."

Man has evolved not only as a species, but each man (and
woman) evolves as a person, stage by stage. When a whole
stratum of society is confined to satisfying its primitive drives
— for food, for jobs, for safety — in an affluent culture, only
the most insensitive and supercilious would blame such people for "not making more of themselves." Out of such soil,
what flowers can grow, except by a miracle of grace?

We Need Security to Do Our Best

ONE of the reasons that organizations don't work as well as
they might — and I am thinking here, particularly, of large
business organizations — is that most of us have a defective
theory of human motivations. We think, for instance, of "security" and "initiative" as being opposites, in the sense that
the more security a person is given, the less initiative he will
display. This seems to me a gross misreading of human behavior.

In modern industrial society, the best rewards and the most solid developments are achieved by those organizations that are willing to make innovations, that are unafraid to take risks and to question the conventional wisdom of the past. When leaders and executives fail to take such risks, it is more usually because they are *insecure*, rather than being *too secure*. They are fearful of their position, scared of being wrong or thought wrong, dubious about their talents, or uncertain about their status in the organization. It is this kind of anxiety that makes for conformism, timidity, and a lack of initiative.

Giving a man security — so long as his performance justifies it, of course — is giving him a firm place to stand. Without a firm place to stand, he will be afraid to move, lest he topple over. The chap whose philosophy is "Don't rock the boat" is the one who feels that the first wave will knock *him* out of the vessel, not the one who is securely tied to a cleat.

As Wilbert E. Moore remarked in his provocative book, *The Conduct of the Corporation*, which won the most distinguished prize in sociology a few years ago: "The freedom to disagree, to suggest improvements, to question time-honored but irrational formulas, requires for most men in most times a relatively stable place to stand . . ."

We can perceive the same tendency in that embryonic organization called a school: the child who is anxious about his academic status, who is too worried about keeping up or passing, will do much worse in his studies than the one who feels that as long as he is doing his best, he will not be thrown to the wolves. A sense of assurance motivates us positively; a sense of fears motivates us negatively, if at all.

Oppressed, insecure and frightened people show little initiative; they are not free enough from inner conflict to stand up boldly and say new, and possibly unpopular, things. Only the strong can practice freedom, and only the (relatively) secure can feel strong.

Death Penalty and Deterrence

PEOPLE think they are talking facts and logic when they are talking emotions. It is extremely hard for any of us to see that our "reasons" for holding a certain opinion are based on feelings we may scarcely be aware of, and not on the "facts" we trot out in defense of such opinions.

Consider the vexing question of "deterrent punishment" for criminals. Most penological studies have shown that "deterrence" does not deter, but the advocates of capital punishment refuse to believe this evidence.

In Great Britain, the Homicide Act of 1957 changed the law relating to murder. The Homicide Act abolished the death penalty for all homicides except for a group called "capital murders" — those committed in furtherance of theft, in escaping arrest, murdering a policeman or prison officer. These exceptions, of course were aimed at habitual criminals. It was argued that the Act would have a deterrent effect upon them, making them less ready to carry weapons, lest they accidentally kill someone while doing a job and be convicted for capital murder.

In an evaluation published by the British Home Office in 1961, it was found that exactly the opposite had occurred. The increase in murder taking place since 1957 has been precisely *in that group;* the habitual criminal has actually become more homicidal, even though he may hang for it.

Contrariwise, it was feared, when the Act was first passed, that if the death penalty were relaxed for particular kinds of offenders, murders by them would multiply greatly. But such has not been the case. As Dr. Howard Jones, the British sociologist, remarks in his new book, *Crime in a Changing Society*, it is among those for whom the deterrent, in all its horror, has been retained that murder has increased.

In those American states in which the death penalty has been abolished, there has been no rise in the homicide rate; while those states still administering the death penalty have a murder rate just as high as, or higher than, the states that have abolished it.

None of this, of course, will have any effect upon those who want murderers to die. They will find one "reason" or another for clinging to their viewpoint. Because crimes of violence are on the increase, they are frightened (as we all should be); but rather than seeking to correct the underlying causes of violence, they want society to retaliate with its own kind of institutional violence.

This is an emotional reaction, not a rational one; it is illusory, not realistic; it strikes at symptoms, rather than probing the psychosocial origins of murder; and it merely legitimatizes the taking of human life. Like war, capital punishment is a mark of man's inability to master his most primitive strivings.

"Obscenity" Is Matter of Intent

THE MOST RECENT Supreme Court decision on obscenity — in which the judges divided five against four — only further points up the utter impossibility of deciding what is "obscene" in any legal sense. Not only does one generation disagree with another about what is "obscene," but within the same generation, different classes and groups of people will disagree about it. There may be some absolute standard, but no one has found it yet.

It might be useful here to compare the idea of "obscenity" with the legal concept of "fraud." In order to prove fraud in

a court of law, it is first necessary to show "intent to de-
fraud." If it can be shown that a man did not intend to commit fraud, he may be guilty of something else, but he is not
guilty of fraud.

In the same way, "obscenity" resides in the intent of the
author. And how can one demonstrate such intent, or lack
of it? The court has used as a yardstick "whether the material has some redeeming social value." But this is a foolish
criterion: I might write a novel consisting of 90 percent pornography, and put in 10 percent of "redeeming social value,"
simply to placate the authorities and satisfy the letter of the
law.

"Intent" is a highly subjective matter, and does not easily
lend itself to legal probings. I have seen, for instance, foreign
movies which the average person would unhesitatingly call
"obscene," yet in my view they sprang from an honest attempt to depict reality as the scenarist saw it.

On the other hand, I have seen Hollywood movies which
the average person would call "light sex comedies," yet in
my view these have been more obscene than the foreign films,
for their whole intent seems to be to titillate the subject of
sex in a coy and vulgar manner.

Who is right or wrong about this? There is no way to tell;
it is a matter of taste, judgment, background, conditioning,
and cultural atmosphere. It may be that obscenity, like
beauty, lies in the mind of the beholder; or there may be
an *evolutionary morality*, as Teilhard de Chardin put it, whose
value depends on "collective feeling, common insight and the
culture of the time."

Furthermore, I don't happen to believe that obscenity, of
any sort, is as harmful as some people seem to think. The profound immoralities of our time are cruelty, indifference, injustice, and the use of others as *means* rather than as *ends*

in themselves. If everything deemed indecent or obscene were wiped out overnight, it would not make for a conspicuously better world, or for a more "moral" citizenry.

The Censor's Lust for Power

IN 1966 the U.S. Supreme Court struck down the federal obscenity conviction of a Nashville man and wife who took nude pictures of each other and received prints through the mail.

It indicates how asinine our obscenity laws are if a husband and wife cannot take any pictures of themselves they care to take and have the prints sent only to themselves. Surely the law against sending "pornography" through the U.S. mails was not passed to stop this kind of thing, foolish or vain though it might be.

And this is the whole trouble with obscenity laws. They never stop at any reasonable point, but pursue their way to the peak of the ridiculous. Was it not unfair and absurd that this Nashville couple had to go all the way to the U.S. Supreme Court to reverse their conviction for an "offense" that means absolutely nothing?

In his new book, *Fresh Every Morning*, Bishop Gerald Kennedy writes: "I have come to the conclusion finally that censorship is wrong and that it raises more questions than it solves." And, recently, even the Catholic Church has done away with its famous "index" of banned books, on the sensible grounds that it is more useful to instruct the public in what it *should* read than to fulminate against those books it shouldn't read.

All censorship is negative — and negative injunctions have never prevented anyone from doing anything bad he wanted to do. "Thou shalt not kill" is the most ignored commandment in the Decalogue: nations punish their citizens for killing, but then turn right around and kill their enemies with a clear conscience.

Only by training young people how to care for others (and such training must consist largely in setting an example) can we stop killing; and, likewise, as Bishop Kennedy says, "only by raising the tastes of all men so that the filthy and obscene will have no appeal" can we do away with pornography. If most people continue to read junk, what difference does it make if the junk is pornographic or not, for even nonpornographic junk deadens the mind and the spirit.

Moreover, censorship, besides being ineffectual because it does not go to the roots of human motivation, by its very nature is totalitarian and continually wants more and more under its control. It is a form of political persecution, and does not recognize any legitimate limit to its goals — just as the Nazis, who began with repressing the communists, could not rest until every element in society was shackled.

It seems to me that our nation has more to fear from the militantly censorious than from the married couples who take nude photos of each other, presumably in preference to staring at nude photos of strangers.

Good PR Formula: "Listen"

As YOU MAY imagine, someone who writes a daily column is bombarded with hundreds of pieces of mail a month from "public relations" people. They all want something favorable printed about their clients.

What fascinates me about this flourishing business of public relations is that not one firm out of 20 seems to understand the main purpose of a program of public relations. Most of them look upon it as a one-way street: a means by which the company communicates with, and persuades, the public to some attitude or action. They think it is their job to *talk;* when the most important part of their job is to *listen.*

What is wrong with most large companies? The chief defect is the isolation of the executives at the top, who rarely know what is happening at the bottom until it is nearly too late to do much about it. Just like the husband, the top executive is generally the last man to learn about infidelity.

Good public relations does not consist so much in *telling* the public as in *listening* to it. It provides a feedback that is otherwise lacking in the organizational structure. And it keeps reducing corporate fantasy to the proportions of reality — not at all an easy task.

For one of the great myths of American social life is that the business leader is a hardheaded realist with his ear to the ground. In some respects he may be, but in relation to his company he is a starry-eyed idealist who is unwilling to see the worst until it is full upon him. The corporate executive cannot believe that his subordinates are unhappy, or that the company isn't living up to its claims, or that its product isn't the greatest ever turned out, or that the customers aren't thrilled to pieces to see a picture of the plant and the founder. No love is as blind as that of a man infatuated with his own firm.

The value of public relations ought to be, and most often isn't, bringing the company down to earth, forcing it to listen to ugly sounds from its employees and customers, and turning communication into a genuine two-way street. Only in this way would the public relations counselor earn his magnificent fee.

Ninety-five percent of the mail they send me goes directly into the wastebasket, where it belonged in the first place.

They are just self-congratulatory messages, designed to massage the ego of the company's directors, rather than to provide information for the public. And the best information that could be provided would be the good word that the company is dying to hear what the outside world thinks of it.

Challenge of Psychic Cancer

THE DAY that the "Guilty" verdict was brought in by the Speck jury, I overheard a group of people at the luncheon table next to mine discussing the trial and conviction. "Why does the state go to all the trouble, time and expense?" asked one of them. "He's guilty — everybody knew it — so why not give him the electric chair, or put him away for life and forget it?" Everyone else at the table nodded in strong agreement.

I didn't nod in agreement, even mentally. One must recognize that theirs is the attitude of most people, but I happen to think it is a wrong, dangerous, and ignorant attitude. Quite apart from the civil rights involved in the matter — and the blackest villain is entitled to the same trial rights as a cherub, or the law means nothing — there is another equally important consideration: We learn absolutely nothing by sending such a man to the chair, or even by putting him away to rot in prison for a lifetime. If he is mad, we should study the causes and course of his madness; if he is bad, we should study the origins and evolution of his badness. If he is a mixture of both — as we might suspect — we should study the relationship between moral character and emotional sickness.

Society hates, fears and resents such men, and wants to obliterate them. But such obliteration does not deter or prevent similar occurrences, nor does it help us to detect, in the early stages, the behavior patterns of other men who might do likewise.

It seems painfully obvious to me that if we understood more about such matters, not only might the eight nurses be alive today, but also the young sniper who committed mass murder from his tower in Texas could have been spotted as a potential menace long before that dreadful day. Such actions are almost always prefigured in early behavior — if we are alert to the deeper meaning of such behavior.

Acts of what we call "senseless violence" are increasing enormously in this age. But though such acts may seem senseless to us, they make a kind of insane sense to the persons who perpetrate them; and if we obtained a better grasp of their convoluted mental processes, it might help us prevent incidents of this tragic kind — just as an improved knowledge of symptoms enables us to prevent physical illness from worsening to the incurable stage.

What is a "waste" is not the long and cumbersome trial, but the fact that after the trial little is done to probe the psychic cancers of such men. Simply to execute them or shut them away is the surest guarantee that future tragedies will be neither prevented nor anticipated. If we handled physical disease the same way, who would be alive?

Just Like the General's Mule

WHEN a famous German general, long ago, heard one of his staff officers venture the sententious remark that "Experience is the best teacher," the general snorted: "Nonsense — my mule has been through ten campaigns with me, but he knows no more now than he did before the first one!"

Experience can be a very bad teacher, indeed, or no teacher

at all. It is like the silly phrase, "Practice makes perfect." In most cases, practice merely confirms us in our errors, and the longer we do something the wrong way — that is, without enlightenment and instruction — the more fixed we become in our folly.

To take a trivial example in my own case: I began playing tennis as a boy, and had many years of experience. I also practiced incessantly. But because I did not understand the basic principles of the game, the more experience I had, and the more practice I took, the more deeply I fell into the grip of bad form and losing habits. It finally became necessary for me to take lessons if my game was to improve at all — and most of the lessons were spent in *unlearning* everything that "experience" and "practice" had taught me!

This, of course, made it twice as hard for me to become a truly proficient player. With a beginner, the coach merely instills good habits and proper form; but with me it was necessary first to break the deeply ingrained bad habits of years and reduce me to the rank of ignorance before I could learn to rebuild my game the right way.

Young people today are fond of believing that "experience" in and by itself is a good thing, and that we automatically learn the right after we have experienced the wrong or the dubious. But older people know — through painful examination of their own lives — that this is not usually the case.

Many people go from one bad experience to another, from one kind of mistake to a different kind, learning perhaps to avoid the kind they made in the past, but having no rational guideline to prevent them from making other, and more disastrous, mistakes in the future. The millions of multiple marriages in American society are tragic proof of this failure to profit from mere "experience."

Of course, we cannot learn without "living." But "living"

means not only inviting new sensations and experiences; it means also studying, analyzing, generalizing, anticipating, and judging from mankind's accumulated wisdom of the past. Otherwise, our experiences do us no more good than they did the general's mule.

Prayer and Cabbage Prices

THE MOST tiresome quotation in the world has turned up on my desk again. Every few weeks it is reprinted in some publication or other, and it wasn't even true in the first place. It runs like this: "The Lord's Prayer has 56 words. Lincoln's Gettysburg Address has 266; the Ten Commandments, 297; the Declaration of Independence, 300. But a recent government order on cabbage prices has 26,911 words."

Nobody has ever been able to produce that "government order on cabbage prices," because it doesn't exist. A Washington correspondent once spent half a week looking for it — or for any other government order on any other vegetable price that ran to 26,911 words. Nothing.

Even if this coy little piece of propaganda were true, however, what would it prove? An embarrassing truth — that the Lord's Prayer, Lincoln's Gettysburg Address, the Ten Commandments, and the Declaration of Independence are the most flouted, ignored, misquoted, misinterpreted, and practically repudiated pieces of prose in human history.

If even ten percent of us actually believed ten percent of what those statements say, and acted on our beliefs, the whole course of history could be changed. But we don't, and it isn't.

In point of fact, not one American in 100 would honestly sign the Declaration of Independence today. It is a highly "seditious" and "subversive" document, as anyone will find out who takes the trouble to read it carefully. It is "revolutionary" in the best and highest sense of that word, and we are in no mood to tolerate revolutionary documents.

As for the Ten Commandments, everyone is proud that he doesn't break the minor ones, and thus conceals from himself the fact that he breaks the important ones every day — especially the first, which prohibits us from worshipping false gods.

It is easy — for most people — not to kill or steal or beat their parents with a club; but it is much harder to avoid the idolatry of worshipping sex or money or position or race or nation or intellectual achievements, or any of the dozen other things that we make gods of. Everybody mumbles the Lord's Prayer, and hardly anyone takes it seriously, in acting out his life. Lincoln's Gettysburg Address has become a piece of oratory, more noted for its brevity and pathos than for its magnificent plea for reconciliation and its tragic awareness of the futility of war.

Cabbage prices, people listen to, if they care about cabbage and prices. Great thoughts are quoted and memorized, but not listened to — whether they are expressed in 26 words, 260, or 26,000.

Too Much Power for Critics?

PRESUMABLY worried because its drama critic has too much life-and-death power over the new plays opening on Broadway, the *New York Times* recently appointed a second critic to share the power — and the blame.

This is an old problem in the theater, and in all the other arts. I remember, more than 15 years ago in Aspen, Olin Downes, then music critic of the *Times*, lectured to us on the function of the critic. He admitted that the newspaper critic in a large city has entirely too much power. The two morning paper critics in New York — both in music and in drama — could blast reputations at will, and make it almost impossible for new talent to obtain a second hearing.

One solution he suggested was for papers to change their critics every couple of years. Another was that different staff members cover plays and musical events, on a rotating basis, supplemented by commentaries from practicing members of the arts or crafts.

Lord Acton held that all power tends to corrupt, which is an extreme view. Socrates, I think, was closer to the truth when he observed that "the only men who deserve to be given power are those who do not want it."

The real difficulty in these situations is that the men — be they politicians, militarists, critics, or what you will — who get the power are generally those who go after it. And since these are most often the men with the strongest views and most aggressive natures, they are the ones who can least be trusted with power.

Criticism is necessary to civilization, and the public taste is steadily raised by those critics who are a little ahead of their time. The complete abolition of public criticism would be more of a blow than a help to the arts — but the critic must not only be *professionally* competent (which many are not), he must also be *emotionally* stable.

Indeed, it is not corruption in any sense of the word, but the emotional temptation to play God — or Lucifer — that turns so many critics into power-drunk pundits parading their prejudices as ultimate truths. The problem of finding men who have the intellectual capacity to recognize quality, plus the emotional balance to temper their judgments with compassion, goes far beyond the role of critic.

It applies even more strongly to statesmen, teachers, judges, and everyone who passes verdicts on the acts of others. The reason many people gravitate to authority is their unconscious urge to abuse it.

Buying Off Our Consciences

A FEW DAYS after the Clay-Terrell fight, I was having a cup of coffee with a friend, when he pointed to the front page of the paper. A lady cellist in New York had just been arrested for performing with a bare bosom during an avant-garde concert.

"I wish you'd explain to me," he said, "why this event is considered 'obscene conduct,' and the Clay-Terrell fight isn't. Why are we so repressive about sex, and so permissive about violence?

"I watched the Clay-Terrell fight," he went on, "and by my definition, it was an obscene performance. After the seventh round, Terrell was just a punching bag. And Clay was as ugly and vicious as a man could be. Yet the public pays millions to watch such spectacles, and feels cheated when one of the fighters doesn't end in a bloody pulp on the floor."

It wasn't hard for me to agree with him that we have a perverted sense of values in Western society, insofar as sex and violence are concerned. It seems absurd that a bare bosom is considered in any way "lewd," while the brutal batterings of two anthropoids are applauded and approved as a great sporting event.

Neither a prize fight nor a cello concert cum nipples would attract me as a customer, but I fail utterly to see why one is given police protection while the other is subjected to police persecution. The lady cellist wasn't hurting anybody, or doing anything intrinsically wrong, and her bosom is certainly no more an offensive sight than Terrell's bloodstreaked chest.

I am almost convinced that this curious inversion of values — where violence is condoned if not actually sanctified, while sex is still shrouded in shame — explains in large part the shifting sexual morality of young people today. A society that is so willing to send them out to be killed, that is so indifferent to human life, and yet at the same time that places so many safeguards against sexual activity, seems unworthy and hypocritical in the eyes of many youngsters.

Unnecessary *pain* of any kind is what is "obscene" in human conduct, while pleasure may be good, bad, or indifferent, depending upon the other values involved in it. Surely the display of the body is not lewd by and of itself, with or without a cello; nor is there anything lewd about the mutual enjoyment of sex by two consenting adults. It may not be prudent, but that is quite another matter.

Is it possible that our strictures against sex are the way we buy off our collective conscience for our obscene addiction to violence?

LSD Offers a Wrong-Way Trip

ONE of the loftier reasons given by LSD users for taking the drug is that it "expands consciousness." During a trip, they say, the whole world takes on a new and heightened significance, beauty, and unity.

There is no doubt in my mind that what the human race urgently needs is "expanded consciousness." Indeed, I would say that unless we achieve a breakthrough in this area, the future of our species looks exceedingly dubious. Our present consciousness is too limited for our survival.

But the kind of expansion I foresee is not dependent upon drugs, which only serve to separate and isolate the individual. The breakthrough we desperately need is one which expands *by joining* — not only by joining person to person, but also by joining the different parts of our own personality.

In his new and fascinating book, *The Savage and Beautiful Country*, which deals with man's unconscious needs, Dr. Alan McGlashan points out that "full human consciousness is still to be won. It is waiting to be born from a marriage that only can take place at the deepest level of the psyche — the marriage between thinking and feeling."

When operating in isolation, Dr. McGlashan suggests, each of these functions is essentially destructive. And, except in moments of high crisis, thinking and feeling tend to be antagonistic to each other. While this remains so, human consciousness is a "crippled thing." "Isolated thinking and isolated feeling are, in fact," he goes on, "classic forms of madness: They constitute the two dangerous, closed-in worlds of the schizophrenic and the manic-depressive. But to marry thinking to feeling is not merely to restore sanity to the operations of the human mind; it is also to open new and urgently needed dimensions in human consciousness."

As an example, he cites the thermonuclear bomb as a typical end product of the kind of thinking that is disconnected from feeling. And, likewise, the kind of feeling that is disconnected from thinking has as its end product — war. Autonomous thinking provides the weapon, and autonomous feeling supplies the emotional setting in which to use it.

Drugs such as LSD liberate the feelings, but damage the mental processes. They represent a triumph of the irrational, a subjugation rather than a marriage of thinking and feeling. Like all revolts, they go too far and commit the opposite sin. In the name of "unity," they sever the thinking animal from his feeling body.

Few of Us Know How to Listen

I WAS HAVING a discussion with a woman I had just met at a party, on the general subject of education. About ten minutes after I had made a certain point, she returned to it, and re-stated what she thought I had said.

I shook my head in disagreement. "Isn't that what you said?" she asked. "No," I replied, "that's what you heard, but not what I said." And I carefully repeated my original statement, which was quite different from her version.

Even highly trained persons don't know how to listen. Some years ago, two psychologists at Cambridge University made a recording of the discussion which followed a meeting of the Cambridge Psychological Society. The recording was made without the knowledge of the members present. Two weeks later, they wrote to all who had attended, asking them to write down everything they could recall about the discussion. The reports were then checked against the recorded version, and it was found that the average number of specific points recalled by any individual was less than ten percent of the total re-corded.

But the really remarkable thing, according to Professor Ian Hunter, in his book, *Memory*, was that "of these recalled points, on the average no less than 42 percent of them were substantially incorrect." Hunter goes on to report: "A large variety of errors and confusions appeared. Happenings were recalled which had never taken place at all or which had taken place on some other occasion and were wrongly recalled . . . What was recalled was not only fragmentary but also distorted and much was recalled which, in fact, had never happened."

It is the unconscious process called "interpretation" which falsifies and distorts so much of what we hear and read and see. We begin with certain preconceptions, and then we try to make experience fit into these preconceptions. It is terribly hard to dislodge them from our minds. For example, when I am working a double-crostics puzzle and fill in a couple of letters of a word, I have already begun "interpreting" that word. And if, as sometimes happens, those letters are wrong, it is difficult for me to "erase" my mental picture and start afresh. The greatest enemy of finishing a puzzle is this kind of "mental block."

Many courses are offered on "how to speak," but none that I know of on "how to listen" — an infinitely rarer and more precious trait.

What Shape's Your Mind In?

It is true that minds are of different sizes, just as bodies are of different sizes. But it is also true that minds are of different *shapes*, just as bodies are of different shapes. And the shape can be as important as the size.

A considerable number of people feel inferior or inadequate in the mental department, when they compare themselves with mighty minds. This is mistakenly placing too much value on mere size, and not enough attention to shape. A mighty mind can also be mighty dull, mighty ponderous, and mighty closed in its frame of reference. I have known many intellectual persons, with massive brainpower, who had ungainly "shapes" to their minds, and were not nearly as interesting, amusing or stimulating as persons with smaller but more shapely minds.

There is no reason to feel inferior because God has seen fit to give us a mind less vast and powerful than some others. We can do nothing about that; but we can do something about the shape of the mind, just as we can make the shape of the body more graceful and attractive.

The people I most enjoy are not necessarily those with the largest mentalities, but those who know how to use what they have with charm, humor and individuality. A four-cylinder mind, properly tuned and expertly driven, can generally run rings around an eight-cylinder mind that is cumbersome and self-satisfied.

A nicely-shaped mind, like a nicely-shaped calf, need not be large. It is the trimness and the curve that are appealing, not the bulk. And anybody who sincerely tries can improve the shapeliness of his or her mind, by getting rid of the superfluous fat of banality and conformity.

Indeed, what I personally would call an "intellectual" mind has little to do with brain size, and even less to do with formal education. It is much more a matter of shape — of a kind of grasp, a kind of attitude, a kind of approach to the world and one's self. It involves a humorous detachment from the obvious, and a profound awareness of the personal equation in all "objective" opinions.

Many large minds are muscle-bound, just as many large bodies are. Our aim should not be to "expand" the mind, for this simply cannot be done, but to improve its contours, to enhance its charms and graces and whimsies, to trim off the ugly fat deposits of encrusted nonthinking. Given the proper exercise, our minds, like our bodies, are capable of twice as much activity — and appeal — as we ordinarily display.

Facing Truth in the Mirror

ARE YOU TELLING THE TRUTH TO YOURSELF —
WHEN YOU SAY that if you had happened to take a different crossroad at some earlier time in your life, things would have been much better?

When you complain that favoritism, office politics, or log-rolling have held you back and have given the less meritorious preferment over you?

When you claim that if only your husband or wife would

change some habits, you would be able to get along really well?

When you insist that you "know myself," and therefore have no need to delve more deeply into the personal source of problems that plague you?

When you shrug that you've been "too honest" for your own good, and that others have done better than you simply by cutting corners and closing their eyes to sharp practices?

When you suggest that your children got into trouble because of "bad company" and "outside influences" that you were powerless to control?

When you call yourself an "innocent bystander" to some flagrant injustice perpetrated in your presence, and about which you decided not to protest or interfere?

When you proclaim that people are "too selfish," and thus imply that you would become less so if only the world would let you?

When you blame one, or both, of your parents for conditioning you in such a way that your defects and failures become their responsibility rather than your challenge to change or overcome?

When you cling to the "Devil theory" of human affairs — that one particular group of people, or segment of society, is to blame for most of our woes, and that if this group were eliminated, the rest of us could all be prosperous, peaceful, and happy?

When you preach "bold individualism" in your economic life, but practice absolute conformity in your social, intellectual and emotional life?

When you believe that "everybody is entitled to his opinion," but simultaneously hold that some opinions are too "dangerous" to be permitted free expression?

When you come out strongly in favor of "rights," but somehow they always happen to be the rights of people like your-self, and not the rights of people in other life situations?

When you call yourself "a victim of circumstances," even though the circumstances have been largely contrived by your past actions?

When you complain that your motives are generally "mis-understood," and fail to reflect on the possibility that they may be understood better by others than by yourself?

6

OF WORDS AND PHRASES

Antics with Semantics: 1

I AM in favor of "liberty"; you are in favor of "license"; he is in favor of "anarchy."

I go to the office on Sundays because I am "conscientious"; you go because you are "overmatched for the job"; he goes "to get away from home."

Our party arrives late at the theater because "we like a nice, leisurely, civilized dinner," but your party arrives late at the theater because you've been "guzzling martinis until curtain time."

Daddy isn't very good at math because "he doesn't have a head for figures," but Junior gets poor grades in math because "he's lazy and won't apply himself."

If I don't cotton to a person, it's enough reason for me that "I just don't like his looks," but if a person doesn't like me, I complain that "he has no reason to feel that way."

I am "diplomatic"; you are "smooth-tongued"; he is "two-faced."

I am all in favor of dissent as long as it is "responsible" —

but I want to be the one to decide what being "responsible" signifies.

I am giving the matter "judicious consideration"; you are "overly deliberate"; he is "stalling."

What parents call "a harmless prank" is what they would call "vandalism" if they read about strange children doing it.

When I am seeking mercy, I remind you that Jesus enjoined us to return good for evil; when I am seeking vengeance, I remind you that Jesus scourged the moneylenders out of the temple.

A "crisis" is any sudden development in international affairs that shows how shortsighted or pigheaded the foreign offices were; and a "resolution" of the crisis is a mutually unsatisfactory agreement by which the foreign offices gain a respite until the next crisis.

A "man of the world" is generally one whose world excludes 90 percent of what is real in human existence.

I overbid my hand at bridge because I am by nature "optimistic"; you overbid because you are "rash"; he overbid because he is "egotistic."

When you are defending what I want to change, you are just defending "the status quo"; when I am defending what you want to change, I am defending "tradition."

I don't mind my son "sowing a few wild oats," but I don't want my daughter reaping the kind of oats he sows.

I Am the Man in the Middle: 1

I AM the man in the middle; for the middle is, by my definition, where I stand.

I am "tolerant" in sexual matters; anyone more tolerant

than I is "dissolute"; anyone less tolerant than I is "prudish."

I am a "friendly" sort of person; anyone more friendly than I is "familiar"; anyone less friendly than I is "aloof."

I am an "open" person; anyone more open than I is "brutally frank"; anyone less open than I is "devious."

I am a "prudent" person; anyone more prudent than I is "timid"; anyone less prudent than I is "rash."

I am a "dignified" person; anyone more dignified than I is "pompous"; anyone less dignified than I is "brash."

I am an "even-tempered" person; anyone more even-tempered than I is "phlegmatic"; anyone less even-tempered than I is "impetuous."

I am a "determined" person; anyone more determined than I is "pigheaded"; anyone less determined than I is "indecisive."

I am an "ambitious" person; anyone more ambitious than I is an "opportunist"; anyone less ambitious than I is "shiftless."

I am a "realistic" person; anyone more realistic than I is "cynical"; anyone less realistic than I is "naive."

I am a "religious" person; anyone more religious than I is "fanatical"; anyone less religious than I is "just paying lip service to God."

I am a "responsible" person; anyone more responsible than I is a "congenital worrier"; anyone less responsible than I is "frivolous."

I am an "individualistic" sort of person; anyone more individualistic than I is a "lone wolf"; anyone less individualistic than I is a "part of the mass."

I am a "practical" person; those more practical than I "can't see the forest for the trees"; and those less practical than I "can't see the trees for the forest."

I am the man in the middle; for my position, per se, defines where the middle is.

I Am the Man in the Middle: 2

I AM the man in the middle; for where I stand determines where the middle is.

I am compassionate; those less compassionate than I are "cold," and those more compassionate than I are "sentimental."

I am steadfast; those less steadfast than I are "fickle," and those more steadfast than I are "stubborn."

I am friendly; those less friendly than I are "standoffish," and those more friendly than I are "pushy."

I am decent; those less decent than I are "disreputable," and those more decent than I are "priggish."

I am civil; those less civil than I are "rude," and those more civil than I are "obsequious."

I am dutiful; those less dutiful than I are "irresponsible," and those more dutiful than I are "subservient."

I am an individualist; those less individualistic than I are "conformists," and those more individualistic than I are "kooks."

I am brave; those less brave than I are "lily-livered," and those more brave than I are "hotheads."

I am a moderate; those less moderate than I are "extremists," and those more moderate than I are are "fence-sitters."

I am firm; those less firm than I are "softhearted," and those more firm than I are "hard-nosed."

I am competitive; those more competitive than I are "wolves," and those less competitive than I are "worms."

I am normally sexed; those less so are "repressed," and those more so are "promiscuous."

I am prudent; those less prudent are "spendthrifts," and those more prudent are "skinflints."

I am patriotic; those less patriotic are "un-American," and those more patriotic are "jingoists."

I am reasonable; those less reasonable are "too emotional," and those more reasonable are "too logical."

I am a fond parent; those less fond than I are "authoritarian," and those more fond than I are "permissive."

I am a careful driver; those less careful than I are "reckless," and those more careful than I are "slowpokes."

I am the man in the middle; for where I stand determines where the middle is.

Nipping Clichés in the Bud

I SHOULD LIKE to read or hear, just once, about an apology that is not abject, a void that is not aching, a test that is not acid, and a swoop that isn't fell.

And, just once, about beauty coming before age, the line of greatest resistance, the worse half, better never than late, colonels of industry, and unchecked careers.

And, just once, about leaps without bounds, all without sundry, bags without baggage, ways without shapes or forms, reducible minimums, and a last that was also least.

And, just once, unconsidered opinions, indiscreet silences, unblanketed snow, unnipped buds, unblissful ignorance, undue consideration, and a few ill-chosen words.

And, just once, a common without a garden variety, an introduction that is badly needed, a few that aren't also far between, a whole fist of destiny, a sublime that shuns the ridiculous, and someone who is inconspicuous by his absence.

And, just once, glee that isn't girlish, generosity that isn't faulty, a hale that isn't hearty, the depth of absurdity, and retreats that aren't ignominious.

And, just once, in this day without in this age, an unravishing beauty, underwhelming odds, a square of applause, sadder but not wiser, an unseething mass of humanity, and sleeping the sleep of the unjust.

And, just once, a softened criminal, a sum without a substance, a strong and loquacious man, an untelling effect, trials without tribulations, speculation that isn't rife, and a body falling with a healthy thud.

And, just once, people from every run of life, small hours that aren't wee, unbated breath, the short and stubby arm of coincidence, the heavy fantastic, bolts from the white or green or yellow, and people who are more sinning than sinned against.

And, just once, an unforegone conclusion, clean lucre, a badly number, a pink-eyed monster, the benign reaper, a cool argument, a reparable loss, and a labor of hate.

And, just once, an impeachable authority, chaos out of order, other things being entirely unequal, an unpronounced success, the seamless side of life, an indiscriminate few, a subhuman effort, a tale that doesn't hang, time memorial, and alloyed pleasure.

And, just once, a view without alarm, a point without pride, a smile without wreathes, an injury without insult, and a good time that was had only by some.

Antics with Semantics: 2

I WAS an "innocent victim," but you were a "dupe."

Those who work with me in a shady deal are my "associates"; those who work with you in a shady deal are your "accomplices."

When I cannot offer a clear answer, I tell you that "we must learn to tolerate ambiguity"; when you cannot offer a clear answer, I tell you that "we can't afford to be muddleheaded about this."

One of the most refreshingly semantic sales signs I've ever seen was hung on the wall of a little Wisconsin shop this summer: "We Buy Junk — We Sell Antiques."

Their army commits an "atrocity"; our army makes "a regrettable miscalculation."

In his amusing *Left-Handed Dictionary*, L. L. Levinson makes this neat distinction: "barbarism," he says, "is killing a stranger and taking his wife"; while "civilization," he contrasts, "is waiting for an acquaintance to go on a trip and then taking his wife."

When I don't want to be distracted by larger issues, I justify it by the fact that "I like to keep my eye on the ball at all times"; when you don't want to be distracted by larger issues, I accuse you of having "tunnel vision."

The recent awarding of the Nobel Prizes reminds me of the student who wrote a thumbnail sketch of Alfred Nobel: "He was the man who invented dynamite and then awarded a prize to the person who could best figure out a way not to blow ourselves up with it."

I am "portly," you are "stout," he is "obese."

We call somebody a "snob" who manifestly feels about us the way we feel about somebody else; this is how we recognize snobbishness.

The learned man with whose theories I agree is "erudite"; the learned man with whose theories I disagree is "pedantic."

"Progressive" is what both disputants call themselves, even when they are progressing in opposite directions.

A "reckless driver" is one who passes me while I'm going slower than I should; while a "slowpoke" is one who refuses to move over when I want to go faster than I should.

Our association has "a spokesman for our viewpoint in Washington"; your association has a "lobbyist."

A "rabble-rouser" is a politician who rouses the other party's rabble; the one who rouses my party's rabble is a "fighting campaigner."

A Pretty Kettle of Clichés

I SHOULD LIKE to read or hear, just once, about tacks that aren't brass, questions that aren't moot, coasts that aren't clear, fates that aren't worse than death, and a mean that isn't golden.

And, just once, a null without a void, a might without a main, a far without a wide, a six of one without a half-dozen of the other, tooth without a nail, and ways without means.

And, just once, an unfit fiddle, a warm cucumber, a young hill, a stupid owl, a hard impeachment, a black elephant, a sage's paradise, feet of gold, the pepper of the earth, an unbloated plutocrat, and a sad Lothario.

And, just once, a social caterpillar, Father Nature, the orange of one's eye, an uncracked dawn, a picture of illness, ignorance after the event, a tower of weakness, an unsure slowness, a low dryness, and a lively earnestness.

And, just once, a fair without a square, a safe without a sound, a sackcloth without ashes, a wear without a tear, a fast without a loose, a rack without a ruin, a kill without a cure, a long without a short, and a storm without a port.

And, just once, a merciless errand, an ungrieved error, an unpsychological moment, a light horse, a live certainty, an indecisive effect, an embarrassment of poverty, an eternal quadrangle, an emaciated calf, and someone who has been frightened into his wits.

And, just once, a nail that isn't hit on the head, a feather that can't knock you down, a gift that doesn't come from the gods, a bad Samaritan, a delicate exaggeration, and a pin that doesn't drop.

And, just once, an ungilded lily, good dirty fun, tepid congratulations, a wagon hitched to a meteorite, something that costs an ugly penny, someone who is gone and forgotten, and someone who would go through fire but not through water.

And, just once, a hue without a cry, a hem without a haw, a hit without a miss, a hither without a yon, a head without a shoulders, a spick without a span, a hammer without a tongs, fish on a string or a net or a pan but not in a kettle, a prophet with honor, and purely without simply.

And, just once, sweet grapes, soft facts, an unpicked bone, a tempest in a coffeepot, a ducksong or a goosesong but not a swansong, a bull that is taken by the tail, and a rhinestone in the rough.

Let's Have Varnished Truth

I SHOULD LIKE to read, or hear, just once, about a man with a deuce up his sleeve, a man who was alive and not kicking, a man who was not all things to all men, a man who was at death's window, and a man who was not Grand as well as Old.

And, just once, about a distance of 60 miles as the buzzard flies, an inauspicious occasion, a battle that is nonroyal, a plot that thins out, a straight and broad path, a tepid congratulations, a dog that is let out of the bag, a heavy fantastic, and an elephant's share.

And, just once, a lock and a stock without a barrel, a fish without a fowl, a flash in the pot, a cake that is either eaten or kept, a heart in the wrong place, cooks who improve the broth, penetrable darkness, a velvet hand in an iron glove, and a power before the throne.

And, just once, an absence that is not prolonged, a ship that does not pass in the night, a bolt that is not shot, a burden that is not shouldered, a silence that does not reign, a suspicion that is not sneaking, an atrocity that is not brutal, and an axe that is not ground.

And just once, a document that is signed and sealed but not delivered, a five-foot-pole for people only half as bad as the ones we wouldn't touch with a ten-foot-pole, and a person who is cool and calm but not collected.

And, just once, a flea or a bee instead of a fly in the ointment, a fool's inferno, a charge that is not hurled, a new car that is not unveiled, a single-dyed villain, a cup that depresses, a fully-fleshed corpse in the closet, and a tale that does not thereby hang.

And, just once, a heart that is worn on the lapel or the pocket but not on the sleeve, a welcome with closed arms, a sheep in wolf's clothing, 80 winks, food for thoughtlessness, an unlucky star, long shrift, a finger in every cake, and too little of a good thing.

And, just once, an ounce of flesh, midwinter madness, an undisguised blessing, wheels that are not within wheels, a nest that is papered or twigged but not feathered, an analysis that is penultimate, a sight for healthy eyes, a character that is only silver-plated, and time that limps or staggers or runs but does not march on.

And, just once, a hurting hand, a hook without a crook, by a different token, alligator tears, crying over spilt Burgundy, praising with faint damns, drifting together, and killing two swine with one pearl.

And, just once, the thigh of luxury, the straw that broke the llama's back, the fully-clothed truth, the forehead to the grindstone, the unscholarly gentleman, and the rank without the file.

Antics with Semantics: 3

WHEN MY side refuses to give up even against hopeless odds, it's because they have "gallant bulldog hearts"; when your side refuses against the same odds, it's because they are composed of "stubborn diehards."

My failure to laugh at your kind of off-color story indicates my "good breeding"; but your failure to laugh at my kind of off-color story indicates your "stuffiness."

When I speak of plumbing, I use the word "modern" in an approving sense; but when I speak of art, I use the word "modern" in a deprecating sense.

When the majority of people agree with me, I call them "the public"; when the majority of people disagree with me, I call them the "mass."

Poor families' daughters have "a high rate of illegitimate births"; rich families' daughters are "visiting friends in the East."

When a merchant can't think of any other adjective to describe an article that is wholly without decorative or esthetic appeal, he calls it "sturdy."

Likewise, when we can't think of any other adjective to describe a homely unmarried female relative, we call her "wholesome."

My summer attire is "casual," yours is "collegiate," his is "sloppy."

Our government's note was a "diplomatic evasion," but their government's note was a "barefaced lie."

A man who steals a parcel out of a boxcar is a "thief," but a man who steals the whole railroad is a "titan."

The same man who is attracted to a woman because she is "vivacious" is later repelled because she is "fluttery."

Every large nation prepares for the eventuality of waging what it calls a "preventive war"; but no large nation ever makes a massive effort to wage a "preventive peace," and even the phrase has never been used.

I am "hopeful," you "cling to faith," but he "lives in a fool's Paradise."

When Good Points Go Sour

SHE MARRIED HIM because he was such a "dominating man"; she divorced him because he was such a "domineering male."

He married her because she was so "fragile and petite"; he divorced her because she was so "weak and helpless."

She married him because he "danced so well"; she divorced him because he "never takes me dancing any more."

He married her because "she reminds me of my mother"; he divorced her because "she's getting more like *her* mother every day."

She married him because "he knows how to provide a good living"; she divorced him because "all he thinks about is business."

He married her because "we were childhood sweethearts"; he divorced her because "we were both just children when we got married."

She married him because he was "gay and romantic"; she divorced him because he was "shiftless and fun-loving."

He married her because she was "steady and sensible"; he divorced her because she was "boring and dull."

She married him because he was "sweet and attentive"; she divorced him because he was "spineless and indecisive."

He married her because she was "such a beauty"; he divorced her because "all she thinks of are her looks."

She married him because he was so "intelligent and witty"; she divorced him because he was so "critical and wisecracking."

He married her because "we have such a great sexual attraction for each other"; he divorced her because "we have nothing in common any more."

She married him because he was "the life of the party"; she divorced him because "he never wants to come home from a party."

He married her because "she's so neat and efficient"; he divorced her because "she thinks more of the furniture and the food than she does of me."

She married him because "we have such great talks together"; she divorced him because "he never listens when I tell him anything."

He married her because "she has such a gentle nature"; he divorced her because "she doesn't know how to discipline the children."

She married him because "he swept me off my feet"; she divorced him because "he knocked me off my feet."

He married her because "she was so crazy about me"; he divorced her because "she was so insanely jealous."

Antics with Semantics: 4

A POLITICIAN I approve of has "friends"; a politician I am doubtful of has "cronies"; a politican I dislike has "confederates" or "camp followers."

Likewise, my political party needs a stronger "organization," but your political party has too strong a "machine."

My candidate is "silver-tongued"; yours is "leather-lunged"; his is "a windbag."

My statesman is "firm"; yours is "authoritarian"; his "runs roughshod over all opposition."

What the government gives me is a "subsidy"; what it gives you is a "handout."

Our participation in Vietnam is "advisory intervention"; but the other side's participation in Vietnam is "Red domination."

I am for "individualism" in the market place, but when I run across someone who wants to express his individualism by wearing a beard, I suspect him of being "un-American."

In the political sphere, I have "principles"; you have "ideology"; he has "dogmas."

Our military makes "surprise sorties"; their military makes "terrorist raids."

We "indoctrinate" with "information"; they "brainwash" with "propaganda."

The candidate I voted for won "because of the good common sense of the people"; the candidate I voted for lost "because not enough people have good common sense."

I am for "leadership" when the mayor I supported is in office, but I am against "bossism" when the mayor I opposed is in office.

My relative is in "public service"; yours is in "politics"; his is "a payroller."

As an officeholder, I accepted a "gift"; you took a "rake-off"; he was guilty of soliciting a "kickback."

My alderman did me a "favor," but your alderman "put in the fix."

When I run for office, it is because I am "civic-minded"; when you run, it is because you "have a taste for power"; when he runs, it is because he "is out to get everything he can."

A "sincere" politician is one who sincerely wants you to believe what he says; a "hypocritical" politician is the same.

Poor Translations Can Trip Us Up

I WAS TALKIKG with a Russian who is in this country on an exchange program, and he said that one of the things that bothered him was our frequent references to Khrushchev's phrase: "We shall bury you." This, he said, was a poor translation of the idiom actually used. What the phrase meant in Russian was, "We shall leave you in the dust" in the race between the U.S. and Russia for economic supremacy.

The translation of idioms from one language to another has always posed a tricky problem. Some informed persons insist that a wrong translation was responsible for our dropping the first atomic bombs on Hiroshima and Nagasaki — the Japanese verb, "mokusatsu," meaning both "no comment" or "to kill with silence."

As Dr. Mario Pei points out in his revised edition of *The Story of Language*, the Japanese reaction to our demands for unconditional surrender was interpreted as rejecting our ultimatum as "unworthy of notice." What the Japanese premier actually said, according to the story, was that his government had decided to withhold comment until they had time to study the demand further.

The Italians have a phrase, "Traduttore — traditoire," which means "A translator is a traitor." Words and phrases take on different nuances and connotations in a different language: Balzac's *Droll Stories* are not what we mean by "droll"; the Spanish "Los Toros Bravos" does not really mean "the brave bulls"; and Dante's *Divine Comedy* is nothing like what we would be inclined to call a "comedy."

Even the same language has its own pitfalls of misunderstanding regional use. I recall a story about an Englishman, an American and a Scotsman telling their experiences in other English-speaking areas.

The Englishman recounted: "I'll never forget my feelings the first time I had breakfast in America, when the waitress leaned over my shoulder and whispered: 'Are you through with your cereal?' It was some time before I discovered she meant, 'Have you finished your porridge?' "

The American rejoined: "Well, shortly after I landed in England, a waiter came up to me at lunch and said, 'How did you find your chop, sir?' I replied, 'Oh, I looked behind the potato and there it was,' before I realized he was asking me how I liked it."

And the Scotsman weighed in with: "I was once in lodgings in a small town in the west of Ireland. When I'd finished supper, an exceedingly pretty girl came into my room and said, 'Will I strip now, sir?' I fled into my bedroom and locked the door, but learned afterwards that Irish girls always talk about 'stripping the table' when they clear dishes."

Antics with Semantics: 5

MY SENATOR is making a "probe"; your senator is on a "fishing expedition"; his senator is starting a "witch-hunt."

I am "cautious"; you are "timid"; he is "cowardly."

I believe something to be a fact because "I saw it in black and white"; but you mustn't believe something to be a fact "just because you happened to see it in print somewhere."

Our country is engaged in "security measures"; your country is engaged in an "arms race"; his country is engaged in "stockpiling weapons."

My church denomination lives by a "creed," but yours subscribes to a "dogma."

The ceremony I approve of had "dignity and grandeur"; the ceremony I disapprove of had "pomp and ostentation."

I believe in "authority"; you believe in "force"; he believes in "violence."

I am a "man of few words"; you are "taciturn"; he is "unresponsive."

My outburst was "indignation"; yours was "anger"; his was "petulance."

My crude friend is "a diamond in the rough"; yours is "a touch on the common side"; his is "a loudmouthed boor."

If she picks up men in bars, she is a "floozie"; if she picks up men at a Hollywood shindig, she is a "swinger"; if she picks up men at a fashionable garden party, she is a "femme fatale."

I am a great champion of "tolerance" — as long as you let me define the precise point at which it becomes intolerable.

My cutting remark is an "epigram"; yours is a "wisecrack"; his is a "cheap jeer."

I am a "realist" when I am doing to you that which, if you were doing it to me, I would call "ruthless."

If it was your fault, we had a "collision," but if it was my fault, we just "banged the bumpers up a little."

There are really no "juvenile gang leaders" because, according to the parents, each of the boys "just happened to get in with the wrong crowd."

I am opposed to your newfangled ideas because I believe in "the value of tradition," but you are opposed to my sensible reforms because you are "blindly clinging to the past."

Why is the female of the species called a "songstress," when the male isn't called a "songster"?

Getting "Livid" Over Semantics

A PSYCHIATRIST FRIEND, the other night, was protesting against the misuse and vulgarization of Freudian terms in ordinary speech. "I don't mind the public using jargon," he said, "but why must people invariably change the meaning so that it makes little sense?"

This, I suppose, is the way in which language is shaped. In our time, it is the Freudian vocabulary that is distorted; before then, even ordinary medical terms were wrenched out of context and made to mean what people wanted them to mean.

Consider some words we use nearly every day — words like "livid" and "hectic" and "chronic" and "allergic" and "contagious" and "infectious." Almost none of them is nowadays used in its original sense; indeed, the original sense has never been known, except to medical specialists.

"Livid," for instance, has utterly changed its color. When we say, "He got livid with anger," most of us visualize someone getting red or purple in the face; actually, "livid" means getting paler, a sort of ashy gray or bluish leaden color. What we are thinking of when we say "livid" is "apoplectic," an old-fashioned medical word that is scarcely used any more.

"I had a hectic day at the office" bears absolutely no resemblance to the medical origin of the word. It comes from the Greek "habit," and meant the kind of flush that consumptives have, as distinct from ordinary flushing and blushing. A "hectic fever" in the 19th Century was reserved to indicate tubercular patients, and that was all.

"Chronic" was originally opposed to "acute" in describing a disease or ailment; a chronic ailment was one lasting a long time. Today, however, we use chronic in the sense of "bad" or "severe" or "intense," which is a vulgar blunting of a useful term.

The latest of these medical popularizations, of course, is "allergic," which has come to fill a genuine need in the language. "I am allergic to him" is a succinct way of expressing a feeling, even though it has little to do with the dictionary definition of "sensitivity to generally harmless substances, such as foods, pollens, etc., which results in dermatological or respiratory symptoms of discomfort."

In the Freudian realm, we call people "sadists" and "masochists" who are neither; we label as "complex" what is not;

we give "repression" a meaning wholly at variance with Freud's; we speak of "fixation" and "introverts" and "trauma" with no idea of their precise meaning. And we will keep on doing so, despite the protestations of scientists and the sneers of semanticists. In language, we are all Humpty-Dumpties.

Antics with Semantics: 6

I won't modify my demands because "it's a matter of principle," but you won't modify your demands because you refuse to accept the fact that "all life is a matter of compromise."

A man who takes bold chances in a sport I admire is "gallant," but a man who takes bold chances in a sport I am indifferent to is "foolhardy."

A large, old-fashioned house is "gracious and spacious" when we are offering to sell it, but "a crumbling barn" when we are offering to buy it.

I don't allow sentiment to influence my decisions because I am "objective"; you don't because you are "calculating"; he doesn't because he is "cold-blooded."

I am willing to stand up and be counted; you are rather outspoken; he is a troublemaker who likes to shoot his mouth off.

Why aren't the people who preface their remarks with "In my humble opinion" ever humble enough not to offer their opinion?

An "inspirational writer" is one who tells you that "the best things in life are free" — and charges you $4.50 for his book in which this profound truth is enunciated.

Some words just have no character: for instance, after all these years, I still have to stop and think whether "biweekly" means twice a week or every two weeks.

The note at the foot of a clothing ad: "At better stores everywhere," really means "any store which carries this is a better store than one that doesn't."

When my senator gets us a new post office, he is working for "public improvements," but when your senator does the same, he is "dipping his hands into the pork barrel."

I have taken wise advantage of "credit facilities"; you have "extended yourself"; he is "wildly in debt."

A "crisis" is any sudden development in international affairs that was accurately predicted several years ago in a scholarly monograph that nobody bothered to read.

Squandering Strong Words

IT IS APPALLING how words cheapen and flatten and lose their power and original meaning through indiscriminate use. Over the years, there is a kind of "language inflation" in which the currency of words becomes debased and nearly worthless.

What has happened, for instance, to the *wonder* in "wonderful" now that almost everything is called "wonderful," from a bagel to a bath soap?

What has happened to the *awe* in "awful," now that almost everything is called "awful," from a cold to a musical comedy?

What has happened to the *terror* in "terrible," now that almost everything is called "terrible," from a tie to a trip?

A word such as "vital," means pertaining to life, of the essence of a living organism — but it has now been so abused that it has virtually no meaning and no impact in speech or writing.

A word such as "crucial" means ultimately decisive, and comes from the same root as "crucifix" — but our "crucial" decisions have neither the seriousness nor the finality of going to the cross.

A word such as "ironic" means a contrast between the thing said and the thing intended — but now "irony" has come to mean any disappointment or discouraging event.

We use "essential" for things that are not essential, "drastic" for actions that are not drastic, "cryptic" for secrets that are not cryptic, "creative" for innovations that are merely fanciful, "genius" for capability in trivial areas where even "talent" would be an overstatement, "edifice" for buildings that are simply structures, and "fabulous" for anything that a fabulist like Aesop would have been ashamed to mention.

Things are "adorable" that we don't really adore, "colossal" that bear no resemblance to the Colossus, "divine" that have no relationship to God's handiwork, "dreadful" that don't inspire dread, "fantastic" that have no element of fantasy, "horrible" that convey no sense of horror, "sensational" that evoke only the mildest of sensations, "stunning" that fail to stun us, "shambles" that don't resemble a place of slaughter, and so on, and so on.

Moreover, we use such fad words as "allergy" when we are not really allergic, "dilemma" when there are more than two choices, "fixation" when we are not fixated in any true sense of the Freudian term, "reaction" when most of the time we mean "response," and "rationale" when we mean "reason."

If we used our money as carelessly as we use our words — spending dollars where dimes are called for — we would soon be bankrupt. Little wonder, therefore, that our language has become so depleted.

Antics with Semantics: 7

I AM discreet; you are crafty; he is sneaky.

My friend is suffering from an "emotional disturbance"; your friend is "mentally ill"; his friend is "off his rocker."

I am "enterprising" when I am doing that which, if you were doing it, I would call "opportunistic."

Perhaps the most dangerous and delusional semantic trap of our age is the phrase "nuclear war," which assumes that the next conflict will be of the same nature as past wars, with winners and losers; when the phrase "nuclear suicide" is the proper description to use.

"Realistic" is my solution to a given problem, as opposed to your contrary solution, which is "academic," "idealistic," and "unworkable."

My school tries to "interest" athletes to come there; your school "recruits" athletes; his school "buys them on the slave market."

Our "agents" engage in "intelligence" work; their "spies" engage in "boring from within."

I was "victimized by my trusting nature"; you were "betrayed by your naivete"; he was "played for the sucker he really is."

My tall female friend is "statuesque"; yours is a "long drink of water."

At the office, I voice a "legitimate complaint"; you are "beefing"; he is a "chronic malcontent."

A "cryptogenic" ailment is one in which a specialist charges $50 for failing to find the cause of it.

My political views are based on "common sense"; yours are based on "wishful thinking"; his are based on "a wild distortion of reality."

What we mean by the "free world" is that part of the world which finds it economically and militarily more feasible to take help from us than from our enemies.

I was driving at "a good clip"; you were "exceeding the limit"; he was "speeding recklessly."

Couldn't We Say It Better?

WHY DO WE ALWAYS "take" a bus, but "jump into" a cab and "hop" a plane?

Why do city people "go to bed," but country folk "turn in"?

Why do we call it a "fashion" if we like it and a "fad" if we don't?

Why do we call our nation's spies "secret agents," and another nation's secret agents "spies"?

Why do we call any snarl-up a "big bottleneck" when properly it should be called a "little bottleneck"?

Why do we call a last-minute substitute speaker a "pinch hitter," when a pinch hitter is somebody better sent in to bat for somebody worse?

Why do signs on some roads say "Heavy Traffic Prohibited," when what is prohibited is not heavy traffic but heavily-loaded vehicles?

Why does a house in English "burn up" when it "burns down"?

Why do we "sail" when we go by steamer without sails, and "ship" goods without a ship, by rail or road?

Why do we say "literally," when most of the time we mean its opposite, "figuratively"?

Why do we call a young child two years "old"?

Why do we call someone a "front runner" just because he's in the lead, when a front runner means a fast starter who soon falls behind?

Why do we invariably leave the "toil" out of Churchill's famously misquoted "blood, sweat and tears"?

Why do we say approvingly that a man has "the Midas touch," when the whole point of the Midas fable is that his touch was a curse and not a blessing?

Why do we have "waitress," "hostess," "authoress," and others, but not "teacheress," "doctoress" or "lawyeress," to clear up the confusion and avoid the awkward "lady —— "?

Why do we say that someone who gets drunk is "tight" when he is actually "loose"?

Why do we call an escaper an "escapee," a stander a "standee," and an absenter an "absentee"?

Why do we "close up" a house, but "close down" an office?

Why do we put the unnecessary "up" in "hurry up," "cheer up," "wake up," "fill up" and "clean up"?

Why is the "aftermath" always unpleasant?

Why do we say "cheap at half the price," when we usually mean exactly the opposite?

Sobriquets That Make Me Sob

YOU'LL NEVER be a writer if you refer to boxing as "fisticuffs," to a baseball as a "horsehide," to a football as a "pigskin," to horse racing as "the sport of kings," to a bowler as a "kegler."

You'll never be a writer if you refer to a theater section as the "Rialto," to a restaurant section as the "Tenderloin," to the derelicts' section as "Skid Row," to the rich section as the "Gold Coast," to the outdoors as "God's country."

You'll never be a writer if you refer to Shakespeare as the "Bard of Avon," to Napoleon as the "Little Corporal," to Washington as the "Father of his Country," to England as "John Bull," to Joan of Arc as the "Maid of Orleans," to the devil as "Old Nick."

You'll never be a writer if you refer to Rome as the "Eternal City," to the U.S. flag as the "Stars and Stripes," to bread as the "staff of life," to the lion as the "king of beasts," to America as "Uncle Sam," to New York as "Gotham," to Chicago as the "Windy City," to Australia as "Down Under," to Japan as "Nippon," to Irishmen as "Hibernians."

You'll never be a writer if you refer to usurers as "Shylock," to lovers as "Romeo," to curmudgeons as "Scrooge," to assistants as man or girl "Friday," to female lawyers as "Portia."

You'll never be a writer if you refer to a strong effort as "Herculean," to a vulnerability as an "Achilles' heel," to a handsome man as an "Adonis," to a female sex symbol as a "Venus," to a foreordained fate as "Nemesis," to a long trip as an "Odyssey," to a destination as a "Mecca."

You'll never be a writer if you refer to an unsexual relationship as "platonic," to an adviser as a "mentor," to fun as "galore," to an event as "gala," to marriages as "nuptials," to debutantes who "bow," to proper speech as the "King's English," to madness which has "method" in it, to circles as "vicious."

You'll never be a writer if you refer to women as the "fair sex," to children as "tykes," to influential men as "moguls" or "tycoons," to managers as "pilots," to the luxurious as "swank" or "plush," to a herring as "red," to a feather as "white," to a thumb as "green."

You'll never be a writer if you refer to correct procedure as "according to Hoyle," to a stalwart woman as an "Amazon," to difficult positions as "behind the eight ball," to a person who brings ill luck as a "Jonah," to a pleasant spot as an "Eden," to a hope as "forlorn," to a defeat as a "Waterloo," to human kindness as constituted of "milk."

Antics with Semantics: 8

OUR GOVERNMENT issues "information"; your government issues "publicity"; their government issues "propaganda."

A "voluntary" confession to the police is one which no one can prove was involuntary.

The young nations which oppose our policies are "backward"; the neutral ones are "underdeveloped"; and the ones supporting us are "developing."

What a bad teacher means by a "good" pupil is one who is immobile, docile, passive, and unquestioning; what a good teacher means by a "poor" pupil is one who is immobile, docile, passive and unquestioning.

I lost the match because I was "off my form"; you lost because you were "overconfident"; he lost because he was "too cocky."

Someone we don't know who takes drugs is an "addict"; someone we know who takes drugs is a "victim."

What is called "crime" on a small scale is called "conquest" on a large scale; if Napoleon while still a corporal had seized a farm, he would have been executed; when as a general, he seized a whole country, he was crowned.

When our statesmen say what they do not really mean, they are exercising "diplomacy"; when their statesmen say what they do not really mean, they are engaging in "guile."

What we call an "unforgivable" action is one we cannot contemplate committing; if we could contemplate committing it, it would no longer be considered "unforgivable."

"History" is what we point to when we want to draw some parallel between olden times and today; and what we conveniently ignore when the parallel runs counter to our viewpoint.

Courtroom trials will remain contests of rhetoric, not of rights, as long as only the witnesses, and not the lawyers, are compelled to tell "the whole truth and nothing but the truth"; for the art of the advocate consists largely in repressing those aspects of the truth which do not serve his client's interests. (For perjury by suppression is a far more frequent occurrence than perjury by overt statement.)

A "good marriage" is one in which the initial expectations were so low that no illusions could be shattered by the reality.

Some Books NOT to Read

DEAR BOOK PUBLISHERS — if you have any forthcoming books in your spring list which fall into the following categories, please do *not* send me advance copies:

Any book with the title, *So You're Going to* —— .

Any book with the title, *I Was a* —— .

Any book with the title, *Ten Ways to* —— .

Any book with the title, *The* —— *Story*.

Any book with the title, *You Can* —— .

Any book with the title, *A Treasury of* —— .

Any book with the title, *The Immortal* —— .

Any book with the title, —— *at the Crossroads*.

Any book with the title, *The Fabulous* —— .

Any book with the title, —— *Rules for Success in* —— .

Any book with the word "Fighting" in the title.

Any book with the word "Dynamic" in the title.

Any book containing the line "as told to —— ," after the name of the putative author.

Any book with the title, *Inside* —— .

Any book in which the phrase "will power" is mentioned even once.

Any book with the title, *The Unknown* —— .

Any book with the title, *Passionate* —— .

Any book whose title contains the word "Positive," "Creative," "More," or "Better," followed by an exclamation point.

Any book with the title, *The Man Who* —— .

Any book with the title, *Twenty Years a* —— .

Any book with the title, —— *Is My Home*.

Any book with the title, *Stop* —— *and Start* —— .

Any book with the title, *Secrets of* —— .

Any book with the title, —— *; City of* —— .

Any book with the title, *Titans of* —— .

Any book with the title, —— *Can Be Yours!*

Any book with the title, —— *For All Occasions.*

Any book in which faith in God is bracketed with financial success.

Any book in which faith in God is bracketed with social popularity.

Any book about the theater containing in the title the words, "Footlights," "Greasepaint," "Curtain," or "Star."

Any book written by an actress, a rear admiral, a bull fighter, an ex-communist, a reformed dope addict, a retiring president of a woman's college, a self-made industrialist, or a famous song writer.

Any book with the title, *Whither* —— ?

Antics with Semantics: 9

THEIR FOOTBALL TEAM "plays dirty"; our football team plays "a hard-nosed game."

The man who deserted our side for theirs is a "defector"; the man who deserted their side for ours is a "convert."

My party's people in office are "public servants"; your party's people in office are "payrollers."

When acquaintances heard that my eldest daughter was at Stanford, they nodded that she must be a "good student"; now when they hear she is doing graduate work at Berkeley, they ask if she's a "beatnik"; yet it's the same girl — only the school has changed.

I had an "emotional setback"; you had a "nervous breakdown"; he "went out of his mind."

I am "average"; you are "mediocre"; he is "a dime a dozen."

I bought a sports car because it gives me "a sense of exhilaration"; you bought yours because "you want to act 20 years younger than you are."

A "consultant" is an expert who is called in when nobody wants to take the blame for what is going wrong.

When my large dog jumps on you, it's because he is "playful"; when your large dog jumps on me, it's because he is "ill-mannered."

Natives beat on drums to ward off evil spirits because they are "primitive" and "superstitious"; we lean on our automobile horns to break up traffic jams because we are "civilized" and "rational."

I'm "a little the worse for wear this morning"; you're "not up to snuff"; he's got "a frightful hangover."

When an interviewee for a household job admits that her cooking is "plain," one may be sure that she is not being modest; just as, when the interviewer admits that the room is "small," one may be sure that she is not overstating it.

Politically, as well as physically, the man who is always in "the middle of the road" gets knocked over by both sides.

My child is an "underachiever"; your child is "limited"; his child is "dull."

Our deadly weapons are "antipersonnel"; their deadly weapons are "for killing people." (And isn't "antipersonnel" the greatest and most wicked euphemism the world has ever known?)

My malicious remark was a "*mot*"; yours was a "jape"; his was a "cheap wisecrack."

7

THOUGHTS AT LARGE

The common law wisely provides that no man shall be compelled to testify against himself; but the garrulous egotist violates this protection every time he opens his mouth.

*

Naivete in a woman can be utterly charming — until we are forced to live with it, when we rapidly begin to call it by another, less endearing, name.

*

Our nation today is increasingly filled with polluted air and polluted water — yet 90 percent of the public's indignation is raised against polluted books, which have never been demonstrated to hurt anyone.

*

When a nation begins talking about its "honor," the chances are better than even that national leaders are preparing for some dishonorable action toward another country.

*

The most important thing a top executive can do is to make suitable provision for his successor; when an organization falters, it is most often because of a weak chain of command in which subordinates were chosen for their docility rather than for their aggressiveness.

*

With so many persons being labeled "accident-prone" and "sickness-prone" these days, I was pleased to hear a Hollywood friend describe a certain promiscuous actress as being "prone-prone."

*

If you're bothered by the uneasy thought that you may be a bore, take heart from the fact that the true bore never has such uneasy thoughts, and is supremely oblivious of his defect.

*

Laborsaving devices are downright dangerous to a society, unless the labor that is saved is utilized in some creative and growing way, and not just dispersed in torpitude and triviality.

*

A letter which begins, "I don't quite know how to say this . . ." is always unpleasant and usually dishonest.

*

We all know about the people who "can't stand success"; less widely recognized, but equally prevalent, are those who can't stand the closeness of love — no sooner do they achieve it than they must do all they can to jeopardize it.

*

Nobody thinks of himself as ill-bred; if one were to ask the most ill-bred person to describe his manners in a word, he would doubtless reply: "Earthy."

*

Those who most make the future are most oblivious of its direction and consequences; men of action are concerned with immediate goals, and rarely have the time, temperament or inclination to envision the new problems created by their "practical solutions" of present difficulties.

*

What is called "symbolism" in art is effective and artistic only when the artist is unaware of it himself; the conscious manipulation of symbolism in a film or a novel is utterly self-defeating, like lovers who keep verbalizing their emotions and soon find that they have been drained of content.

*

It is a mistake of immaturity to regard pain and suffering as things that "happen in" life, like so many raisins in a cake; they are, rather, the modes in which life itself is expressed, like the flour in every cake; and a person (or a people) who refuse to accept this truth may justly be called childish.

*

Woman is like a private fortress, and men who regard her like a public building are always shocked and surprised, after they have successfully surmounted the "No Entrance" sign, to find on the other side an even more implacable sign reading "No Exit."

*

The only trouble with the "Socratic dialog" is that if there are two men in the room, both of whom imagine they are Socrates, the issue is never joined.

*

An artist must be like an athlete, severely disciplined in his craft, before he can take liberties with it; and nothing is more dismaying than the artist who has "gone beyond form" before he has demonstrated that he can come up to it.

*

To succeed with a crowd, one must seem two things at once: a part of them, and yet above them; for masses of people are looking for a divine contradiction in leadership — an uncommonly common man.

*

Once a man can examine his conscience and find it "clear," there is no limit to the amount of evil he feels free to do.

*

"Everything absolute belongs to pathology," said Nietzsche — not realizing that his absolute statement is self-rejecting.

*

For the amateur in any enterprise, the danger lies in failing to see the subtle; for the expert, the danger lies in failing to see the obvious, in "thinking himself" out of blessed simplicity.

*

The "scientific approach" is nearly useless in discovering the nature of man, since science is an *objective tool* for detecting the nature of physical things, and it is only through a *subjective involvement* with human beings that we gain insight into the character of man.

*

One of the most disconcerting, and perplexing, aspects of middle age is waking up one morning and discovering that we have become more like one of our parents than we ever dreamed was possible; and, in many cases, it is not the parent we admired most.

*

A woman who can't forget she is wearing a new gown destroys its effectiveness by her very awareness — for the beauty that is in the eye of the beholder must not be marred by self-consciousness on the part of the object.

*

We delude ourselves that we want to implant "honesty" in our children; what we really want is to imbue them with our particular kind of dishonesty, with our culture's dishonesty, our class's dishonesty, our cult's dishonesty.

*

The asininity of political conventions is equalled only by the gullibility of those viewers who actually believe that such words as "freedom," "courage," and "principles" bear any relationship to the power structures in political parties.

*

There is very little *positive evil* in mankind; true wickedness is as rare as true goodness; where we fail it is through *tepidity*, the unwillingness to pay the price for what we know is right, the wistful hope that we can somehow remain passive and virtuous at the same time.

*

It must be more than a coincidence, or a mere genetic trick, that those families which have an effeminate son usually have also a masculine daughter; the reversal of roles among siblings of opposite sexes indicates strongly, to me, that the parents have somehow reversed their own emotional roles.

*

Experience can be the worst teacher as well as the best; all that experience teaches a delinquent is to grow rich and successful enough to be able to afford a top lawyer.

*

We deplore the "senseless vandalism" of delinquents, as if it would be more excusable if it made more sense; but such boys, not having learned to do what is right for its own sake, proceed to do what is wrong for its own sake — which, in a perverse way, is more "moral" than committing wrongs out of calculating greed.

*

How many of us would attend certain parties if we didn't fear that by staying away, other guests might assume we hadn't been invited?

*

A mature society would pay its policemen at least twice as much as they make today, give police work the status of a profession, divorce it utterly from politics, and put all candidates through a rigid psychological examination to weed out the psychopaths, misfits and sadists.

*

What the ordinary person means by a "miracle" is some gross distortion or suspension of the laws of nature, some vulgar and melodramatic spectacle; but life itself strikes him as commonplace, when in truth a blade of grass or a neuron in the brain is a greater miracle (to the thoughtful person) than any piece of cosmic showmanship.

*

When a child complains that there is "nothing to do," he is not bored with his environment, but with himself; and his education in resourcefulness has been defective, no matter how well he does at school.

*

It is only a beginning to say that "The proper study of mankind is man"; we must go on to focus that statement and say, "The proper study of mankind is — me."

*

I have never understood how a candidate can attack his opponent bitterly in the primary and then urge all good party members to support the scoundrel a few months later; all this does is breed cynicism and disbelief in the electorate.

*

Someday, for a refreshing change, I hope a candid club chairman will present the speaker of the evening by saying: "So-and-so is rather obscure outside of his own small circle, and therefore requires a fairly elaborate introduction." I am tired of speakers who "need no introduction" — and get a lengthy one, anyway.

*

One of the first things a husband learns about feminine semantics is that the difference between a "dress" and a "gown" is at least $50.

*

To dismiss someone else's pain by saying glibly, "It's only in the mind" is false even when true — for where is pain more real than in the mind?

*

Men are much less realistic about women than women are about themselves — as evidenced by the fact that many men envy other men's wives, but most women pity other women's husbands.

*

The only valid purpose of economy is for the sake of a wild extravagance at the right moment; economy for its own sake is debilitating to the spirit.

*

Increased leisure, without an increased cultivation of the mind and refinement of the senses, is the most dangerous enemy of what we call "progress" — for boredom, which soon hunts pleasures with a vicious intensity is the Fifth Horseman of modern life.

*

No matter how great the fear of retaliation, nations will never disarm as long as ambition pays; and even when ambition no longer pays (as in the nuclear age), nations still act blindly as if it did.

*

There is less to fear from a conscious phony than from a man who believes every word he utters; and the world's irony is that it has always been betrayed by the decent men with bad ideas, not by the scoundrels.

*

Parents who hold one child up to another as a "good example" are guilty of two crimes: encouraging priggishness on the part of the good example, and evoking resentment on the part of the other.

*

The most futile books in the world are those which give advice on "how to succeed" — it is a subject impossible to transmit, for those who have succeeded don't know how they did it, and those who require the instruction are not capable of benefiting from it.

*

Paradoxically, the only way to express a narrow view is with a broad statement.

*

Men of power often complain that they are losing their basic liberties when they are only losing their license to infringe on other people's liberties.

*

One of the chief reasons the human race makes such slow and laborious progress is that by the time a valuable idea achieves general acceptance, it has already been perverted into a shape that would shock its originator.

*

An "acquaintance" is someone who exists in that hazy middle ground between those we are proud to acknowledge we know, and those we are not yet sure we want to know.

*

"When the nose is always to the grindstone, the eyes can see little else," is an old Persian proverb I have just made up.

*

The most dangerous heresy of our time, it bears repeating, is the belief that *belief* in itself is a good thing, regardless of its content; for faith that is attached to an unworthy or inadequate object makes people less than they are, not more.

*

Any philosophy that can be put "in a nutshell" belongs there.

*

Between the arrogant artistic attitude that the public is always wrong, and the contemptible commercial attitude that the public is always right, there is a sensible middle position — which holds that the public is nearly always wrong in the short run and nearly always right in the long run; which is why the serious artist refuses to work only for the public of today, and must keep in mind the verdict of the future.

*

In the parlance of the film and novel advertisements, "Realistic!" has come to mean "with all the brutality of life left in, and all the beauty of life left out."

*

A good lecturer never puts his watch on the rostrum to remind him when to stop talking — he lets the emotional currents of the audience inform him when he is overstepping the bounds of toleration.

*

It is ironic justice that the dominating father who tries hard to make his son "rugged" more often succeeds in driving the boy into effeminacy, just as the father who pushes his son too hard to be "scholarly" will more likely than not set up a deep aversion to learning.

*

One of the main reasons for divorce (one out of two marriages in girls under 20) is the large number of girls who marry because many of the other girls who were in their class have done so; marriage, to them, has become a status symbol, rather than a vocation.

*

A woman wants to be loved for her "inner self"; yet she spends 90 percent of her time on her outer self, and then wonders why she can't hold a man long after she attracts him.

*

We have the "highest standard of living" in the world — so high, indeed, that it keeps us broke to maintain it; and a family is said to be living within its income if it doesn't have to borrow money to pay income taxes.

*

As parents, we hope our children will be superior to us; but when they grow older, if they tend to look down their noses at our tastes and inclinations, we deeply resent their "superior air."

*

As voters, most of us are proud that we vote for "the man" rather than for "the party"; but the blunt fact is that when the man gets in, he is more often the tool of his party than its leader.

*

Whenever someone proposes a reform that might pinch us in a delicate area (the pocketbook or the prejudices), we object to it on the grounds that "you can't change human nature"; yet, if we ask our children to modify their conduct, and they reply "You can't change human nature," we brush aside their objection (and rightfully so) as irrelevant, impertinent and self-serving.

*

We think the police ought to have more power to handle suspects and offenders; while at the same time, we decry the loss of "personal liberties" by government usurpation; just as we ask for "weaker government" while demanding greater military strength — and we fail to see, much less resolve, this contradiction in attitudes.

*

We reject and deny the "economic determinism" of Marx, which insists that pecuniary motives are the driving force in human history; yet, at the same time, we make this the basis of our "incentive" system, and insist with equal fervor that to limit pecuniary drives is to sabotage "the American way."

*

There are two kinds of men who fear women: one kind holds them off at a distance so that they cannot strike; the other kind clasps them so closely that they cannot strike; thus, both the misogynist and the Don Juan are displaying the same fear in directly opposite ways.

*

Has anyone ever heard of an actor writing to a newspaper complaining that the review of his performance on opening night was too favorable, and that he was really in rotten form? So long as performers object to underestimation, and never to overestimation, we cannot take their complaints seriously.

*

Hardly anything that man has created or invented in the world is greater than the concept of *law*; yet hardly anything else is so thwarted and corrupted in practice than this beautiful and noble concept — the terrible danger being that when the practice is so abused, the principle becomes rejected and despised in the eyes of most men.

*

Everything difficult can be made simple and comprehensible, if we are willing to reduce it to the lowest level — which means sacrificing those very elements which constitute its existence and meaning.

*

Some men turn to the classics to escape their contemporaries; others to understand them better; *what* we do is often not nearly so important as *why* we do it, in every field of behavior.

*

Man is the great imitator: although he has neither fins nor wings nor claws nor shells, he can imitate the fish under water and the bird in the sky and the lion on the hunt and the oyster in the bed; there is only one creature whose nature he has not comprehended and whose resources he has not learned how to utilize to the fullest: Man.

*

It is the mark of a mediocre mind that when it hears the truth, it agrees and does not agree, believes and does not believe, is aware and is not aware, assents "in principle" but finds some obstacle in practice.

*

A politician is someone who has diligently trained himself to distrust all his first impulses, because they are usually generous and uncalculating.

*

Love is a romantic island of emotion, surrounded on all sides by expenditures.

*

Most people are so easily swayed (except where their immediate self-interest is at stake) that whoever speaks last in a symposium sounds most plausible to them.

*

Nothing in art is more embarrassing than profound sincerity coupled with absence of talent.

*

A confiding husband is one who promptly tells his wife anything he feels she is bound to find out anyway.

*

Most men are welded together by a common error, not by a common truth; it is truth that liberates the person, but error that consolidates the mass.

*

Genuine thinking requires two persons within you — the one who questions and the one who answers; and if these are not sufficiently separated, then what passes for thinking is merely a kind of mental solitaire which one always wins by cheating.

*

Those who do not appreciate *play* refer to all vitality as "vulgarity"; while those who do not appreciate *propriety* refer to all formality as "stuffiness."

*

In only one respect is the pen mightier than the sword: it is easier to commit suicide with; and for every one author who has scattered his enemies, a dozen have commited *felo-de-se*.

*

When a young person learns, to his indignation and dismay, that this is not the best of all possible worlds, he often ricochets to the opposite belief that it is, therefore, the worst of all possible worlds — a cynicism just as distorted as his previous naivete, and even more dangerous in its consequences.

*

We enjoy hearing gossip, but we have little respect for those who retail it; our contempt for the purveyor enables us to accept his wares with a clear conscience.

*

Refusing to let a child read a book because he won't understand all of it is as foolish and shortsighted as refusing to let him climb the monkey-bars in a playground because he's too little to get all the way to the top.

*

A prig is one who denies the child that remains within him, while a libertine is one who is ruled by the child that remains within him; the former is a tragedy of the past being tyrannized by the present, while the latter is a tragedy of the present being tyrannized by the past.

*

The fact that we are vain is no sin, only a weakness; but the fact that we commonly go to such lengths to conceal our vanity is more of a vice than the thing we are ashamed of.

*

The man who is always as funny as he can be suffers the fate that when people stop laughing at his quips, they pay no attention to anything serious he may say.

*

Every person has a life-style best suited to his temperament; and only those who find it, and accept it, can rest comfortably within themselves, regardless of the buffetings of external circumstances.

*

Much of the confusion and disagreement in our national political views is caused by the fact that the United States was founded by "revolutionary conservatives," and the contradictions in their position are reflected and magnified in the complexities of present-day affairs.

*

To believe something, then not to believe it, and then to believe it again, is the best way to grasp a creed; for those who have never doubted, nor stood where their adversaries stand, have an incomplete hold on their own beliefs.

*

Children begin to deceive themselves only after they observe the ways in which adults deceive themselves; self-deception is not an inborn, but an acquired, trait, and there will be little meaningful progress in the human character until this chain is somehow broken, if ever it can be.

*

There are people who perpetually shortchange themselves in life; making the least of what one gets is as much a talent as making the most, and gives some personalities a morbid pleasure they could not achieve from maximizing their opportunities.

*

The pride of the Don Juan type of man might possibly be dampened if he ever reflected that if other men devoted as much time and energy to conquests as he does, they would be equally successful; for, if there is one thing that is sure, it is that the world is full of women waiting to be taken advantage of.

*

Everybody is for "competition" until he is big enough to gobble up his competitors; and everybody is against "monopoly" until he is big enough to call it "public service."

*

Few verbal habits are more irritating than giving false emphasis to a statement by ending with the word "period" — viz., "I don't care to go, period."

*

The human being is an animal so incapable of standing uncertainty that he drives himself toward a certainty that is far worse than the tension he could not bear.

*

That men are more romantic, and less realistic, than women can be seen from the fact that men expect a pretty woman to have much more than her prettiness, while women do not expect a handsome man to be anything more than handsome.

*

Telling an artist that he ought to paint "nature as it is" makes no more sense than telling a composer that he ought to write music imitative of the surf, the thunderstorm, the birds, and the lowing cows.

*

Statistics are fully reliable — *if* they are fully expressed and fully understood; our resentment and suspicion of statistics comes from those who manipulate them in a partial manner, for dishonest motives: I can prove by statistics that more children die from smallpox vaccination than from smallpox in this country — but I would be a fraud if I concluded from this fact that vaccination is bad.

*

Childless couples don't feel the lack of children after a time, for one of them commonly adopts the attitude of a parent toward the other.

*

Mistresses tell stories on their maids to other mistresses, while maids tell stories on their mistresses to other maids; it is the peculiar defect of the social organism that each class can see only the pathology of the other class, and is as unaware of its own pathology as a fish is unaware of water.

*

Perhaps the last lesson that parents learn is that to overcorrect is worse than not correcting at all.

*

What the essential difference between the wise man and the ignorant man boils down to is this: the wise man will often know without judging, while the ignorant man will judge without knowing.

*

When we no longer fear an enemy, we begin to pity him — more proof that hate is always based on some kind of fear.

*

Most people who think they disagree about "government" really disagree about "police" — their differences lie in which segment of society they feel should be most punished.

*

It is weak men, not strong men, who are cruel — for cruelty is almost always an admission of failure of character in the past, and a desperate effort to rectify by pain what should have been prevented by firmness.

*

When a mother says "I can't handle" a small refractory child, what she really means is that she can't handle her own contradictory impulses, part of which secretly sympathize with and encourage the child's revolt.

*

Success is not a "ladder," as the popular metaphor has it, but a labyrinth — not a climb upward, rung by rung, but a maze filled with false turnings and dead ends; failure does not consist in falling from the ladder, but in becoming so involved with the labyrinth that one no longer desires to reemerge into the sunlight.

*

One of the astonishing and gratifying things about correspondence is that if we refrain from opening a letter long enough, it answers itself.

*

The greatest pain is incommunicable pain; whatever can be expressed is alleviated through the expression; and what we call "madness" is simply the outer limit of incommunicable pain.

*

Both opposite statements are true: men hate what they cannot understand, and men adore what they cannot understand; that is, they hate the incomprehensible that seems to threaten their security, and they adore the incomprehensible that seems to bolster their security.

*

The whole trouble with the philosophy of "accepting the inevitable" is that soon we fall into the habit of accepting what is not inevitable, and by so doing we turn it into an inevitability.

*

Most melancholiacs are obscurely proud of the fact, and look upon their chronic depression as evidence of more spiritual profundity than their "shallow" contemporaries; they mistake their temperamental defect for an intellectual superiority.

*

To define love is to diminish it — just as to try to describe God is to delimit Him; which is why the ancient Hebrews quite sensibly banned any reproductions, any statues or portraits, of the Almighty, as a form of idolatry.

*

Evil attracts the weak by seeming to confer an aura of power upon them; but since the essence of weakness is that it cannot control itself, it cannot long control any power it assumes for itself.

*

Men will sacrifice themselves to save a nation, but no nation will sacrifice anything to save mankind; nations ask their subjects to demonstrate a nobility that they themselves would never venture — and this is what makes peace on the political level so nearly impossible.

*

The man who spends his life overcoming obstacles in order to achieve repose is customarily made restless by the very repose when he gets it; after a time, our means, if they are strenuous and habitual, become ends in themselves, and leisure turns out to be more of a burden than combat.

*

The best way to resolve an argument is to allow the other to taste the consequences of his fallacious proposal; this is also the most expensive way, and few of us are forebearing enough to pay the price.

*

Most people who are gruff are afraid to be pleasant, for something in their early background convinced them that civility would be considered as a sign of weakness by others, and they might be downgraded or taken advantage of.

*

If the true reason for the majority of divorces were given in the courts, it would be "temporary insanity at the time the marriage was contracted."

*

The best way we remember a truth is by dramatizing it in our minds; when we dramatize it, we distort it — and then it is no longer the same truth we vowed to remember.

*

There's something topsy-turvy in a society like ours, where people introduce us to others by our first names — because they haven't known us long enough to recall our last names.

*

Country dwellers often act as if "the city" were a late and perverted development in the history of mankind and suggest that we ought to return to our "natural" origins; but, actually, cities have existed as long as recorded history, and the very word "civilization" comes from the same root as "city."

*

On subjects that intensely concern us, we must not promise to be "objective" — the most we can promise is to try to be objective about our lack of objectivity.

*

Expressing emotions is generally better than repressing them; but it can also be a form of concealing them — for when we verbalize a feeling, we think we have brought it into the open, when often we have simply buried it under a layer of words.

*

There is virtually no humor in the sacred works of any religion, yet there is enormous humor in creation; and perhaps a religion that is utterly solemn is as false to the spirit of God as an attitude that is utterly frivolous.

*

To become rich means a *change* of worries, not a cessation of them; for "rich" and "poor" are not opposites, like "health" and "sickness," but, rather, complementary like "fever" and "chills."

*

A young man courting a woman should pay careful attention to her mother: not merely because she is likely to resemble her mother in 20 years, but also because a woman who has a poor relationship with her mother is badly handicapped in having a good relationship with her husband and her children.

*

Life is nine-tenths a matter of *learning to cope* — and unless this is learned, it doesn't matter how few real troubles we have, for even the most trivial worries will overwhelm us.

*

The most efficient way to think is to know what is not worth thinking about; just as the expert cardplayer knows which tricks are worth pondering over, and which should be played to without a pause.

*

The mistake of the bad person lies in convincing himself that "goodness" does not really exist; the mistake of the good person lies in believing that there is only one kind of goodness — his kind.

*

Half the trouble in the world is caused by people who are trying to run away from reality; and the other half is caused by people who are trying to force their version of reality on the rest of us.

*

The grim prospect of the 20th Century is indicated by the twin facts that while medical science is discovering new ways of keeping people alive, military science is inventing new ways of killing them — the one providing a population explosion, and the other an explosion of the population.

*

To act without impulsiveness, and to wait without anxiety, are the two surest signs of maturity; for neither of these can be done, at the proper times, by the neurotic personality.

*

Coquettishness is the dull woman's imitation of charm.

*

Anybody can walk a narrow plank suspended two inches above the ground; but hardly anybody could do the same on a plank suspended between two precipices; thus, it is "imagination" rather than "fact" that controls and influences most of the critical issues in our lives.

*

Intelligence consists largely of the ability to carry on a creative dialog with oneself; the fool is condemned to a perpetual monolog, in which his thoughts persist without reply or contradiction from another part of him.

*

Eventually, every basic belief tends to turn into its opposite: in our time, for instance, most people who believe in religion turn it into a therapy (which it can't be), and most people who believe in psychotherapy turn it into a religion (which it can't be).

*

Children must have, and should be allowed to keep, secrets from their parents; and the parent who wants to know everything the child is doing, thinking and feeling will end up knowing less than the parent who respects the child's privacy.

*

Nations' images of one another are almost always faulty — for instance, we think of the French as "romantic" when in truth they are the most realistic about sex of any people; while the French think of us as "materialistic," when in truth we are much more idealistic than they, or than most peoples.

*

Whoever can be induced to tell a lie in your behalf can also be induced to tell a lie against you; the only person to be trusted is the one who will not violate his honor even to help you.

*

Chess is not a popular game with most people, not because of its complexity or profundity, as is alleged, but because it is the only game without an element of luck — which means that nothing and no one can be blamed if one plays poorly.

*

Puritans are so sour because in their heart of hearts they cannot really forgive God for having been so crude as to make men and women with generative organs, instead of permitting us to reproduce "spiritually."

*

The whole trap of parenthood consists in the melancholy truism that by the time the third child comes along, the parents have only just learned how the first one should have been handled.

*

Take away grievances from some people and you remove their reasons for living; most of us are nourished by hope, but a considerable minority get psychic nutrition from their resentments, and would waste away purposelessly without them.

*

I'm fond of the little boy's definition of "chivalry," after studying knighthood in school: "Chivalry," he said, "is going around releasing beautiful maidens from other men's castles, and taking them to your own castle."

*

What weird faculty is it that enables a woman, a half hour after a strange couple has entered the room, to tell whether their marriage is going well?

*

When a man, in conference, tells his associates or subordinates that "we need an approach that is fresh, dynamic, and flexible," you may be sure that he doesn't know what is needed.

*

"Intuition" is a way of grasping knowledge that goes *beyond* logical thinking; but most people use the word to justify a form of mental laziness that hasn't bothered to *come up* to logical thinking.

*

A friend is one who will tell you so without later saying, "I told you so."

*

Everyone believes in "brotherhood" — if he can pick the brothers; but the whole point of the concept is that we have no choice in the matter.

*

People want to be told what they ought to think, but not told what they ought to do; the public has a great craving for intellectual direction, and an equally great resistance to changing its behavior.

*

Poverty breeds lack of self-reliance, and then the poor are blamed for having no self-reliance; which is rather like blaming an invalid for having bed-sores.

*

All revolutionists have this in common, that once entrenched in power, they are unalterably opposed to revolution; for nobody can be as rigidly conservative as the successful ex-radical.

*

Odd how words fall out of usage — that we should have a "prelude," a "postlude" even an "interlude," but no "lude" anymore.

*

Too often, a self-styled "patriot" is a man who loves his country but despises 90 percent of the people who comprise it; what he really "loves" is his private idea of a country composed solely of persons like himself.

*

The political credo of most voters (rarely expressed, but usually voted upon) is that both political parties are bad, and therefore why not support that form of badness which most nearly coincides with my own self-interest.

*

The secret of triumph is no secret at all; it is easy to grasp and hard to execute — namely, *to reorganize the obvious on behalf of the nonobvious*, as an Einstein organized those obvious ideas of time and space into the stunningly nonobvious concept of relativity.

*

The best argument against promiscuity is not a moral one, but a psychological one; as Rosenstock-Huessy tersely put it: "Sexuality throws no light upon love, but only through love can we learn to understand sexuality."

*

A man is not to be blamed if he doesn't comprehend life any better at 50 than he did at 20; he is only to be blamed if he pretends to himself, and to others, that he does.

*

The most important thing a woman has to tell her friend is not said during the two-hour visit, but while they are standing at the door saying good-bye.

*

The first thing a good teacher learns, and almost the last thing a parent learns, is when *not* to correct a child.

*

The personal tragedy of the 19th Century was the young woman forced by her family to marry against her will; the personal tragedy of our time is the young man forced by his family's position to enter a white-collar occupation against his will, temperament and aptitude.

*

Those who prescribe "back to the woodshed" as a cure for juvenile delinquency don't prescribe "back to the buckboard" as a cure for the rising fate of auto fatalities, or "back to the farm" as a cure for the increasing congestion of metropolitan areas; it is as impossible to "go back" in the treatment of personal problems as of technical and physical problems.

*

Great ideas take their revenge upon their opponents, by eventually forcing the opponents to use them, despite their conscious dislike; the basic ideas of Freud, for instance, are the unconscious assumptions today even of people who think they disagree with Freudianism.

*

Both "love" and "hate" are distortions of reality — but the former is a distortion that amplifies reality, while the latter diminishes it.

*

What we call "idiocy" is a recognized mental state, but we have not yet recognized the widespread state of "moral idiocy," which is most commonly exemplified by the man who says, "I'm just doing my job," when he knows that the job is a wicked one; Eichmann was the highest example of a man who was neither a criminal (in a legal sense) nor a lunatic (in a psychiatric sense), but a moral idiot.

*

When a parent too ardently desires a child's love, it is the very ardor that becomes the chief impediment to filial love; for it is an emotional axiom that excessive feeling provokes repulsion, not attraction.

*

The greatest mistake in life is to think that one will change; the second greatest mistake is to think that one cannot change.

*

Primitive societies have no "pornography" or "obscenity"; they are the excrescences of "civilization," just as dirty air is the price we pay for industrialism.

*

It always offends me, for some irrational reason, when a plane crash with 50 passengers gets a much larger headline than one with 10 passengers; we judge "importance" by quantity, but to each of the 10 in the smaller crash a whole universe has been extinguished, as much as in the greater crash.

*

The history of despotic nations is all the same; only the history of free peoples is different; indeed, history in a meaningful sense is possible only after despotism has been overthrown.

*

The past was an age of cruelty but only sporadic violence; the present is an age of sentimentality and widespread violence; a child was treated meanly at home, but safe on the streets; today he is indulged at home, but in peril on the streets.

*

An ideology that tries to explain too much is like an overextended military line — so thinly fortified that the enemy can break through at any one of many points; and this is why extremist regimes are so easily overturned, at last, while moderate regimes make up in stability what they lack in force.

*

Women often forgive a man who makes a move before he should, but never one who makes a move long after he should have.

*

In social periods of chaos and transition, those who say they are for "the restoration of order" are usually for the restoration of the *old* order, and not for any new order, which might be more equitable than the old.

*

Moralists are so earnest about sex that their own attitude defeats their purposes; if they could appreciate the large element of the ridiculous in sex, their humor could accomplish a thousand times more with young people than their fervor.

*

THOUGHTS AT LARGE   315

There is nothing more dangerous than a person with a good mind who begins to reason, logically and coolly, from insufficient premises: for his answers will always be valid, justified, rational — and wrong.

*

Most second marriages are either duplicates of the first, or else complete opposites; in both cases, the person has committed a second error — either that of repetition, or of assuming that the contrary of something bad is necessarily something good.

*

Being "mature" does not mean, as many mistakenly think, overcoming the childishness in us and becoming uniformly adult and rational; it means, rather, knowing how to channel and express the childishness in us so that it takes its proper (and charming) place in the spectrum of the personality and does not dominate or distort the other elements; to attempt to subdue, repress or extirpate one's childish tendencies is to become not mature but psychically constipated.

*

Every nation commits its own characteristic kind of crime against humanity; and its particular sort of weakness springs from its special sort of strength — as Britain's did from colonialism, Germany's from militarism, and America's from . . . do we know it yet?

*

The intellectual's hatred of mediocrity should be tempered by the knowledge that only through the existence of such mediocrity does he attain the status of an intellectual; to lift all men to his level is actually the last thing he wants, pretend though he may to the contrary.

*

The moment we can give a reason for loving someone, the love has been diminished and turned into a kind of calculus of emotions; for instance, a baby loved because it is "cute" faces an awful fate as its cuteness recedes.

*

Of conspicuous successes, perhaps no more than 10 percent get ahead by their own merit and industry; the other 90 percent get ahead merely by the ineptitude of others.

*

An avant-garde thinker is one who begins to reject his own ideas as soon as any considerable number of the public show signs of accepting them.

*

"Only" is the word that rules the world — the universal will-o'-the-wisp that makes each of us say to himself, "I could be contented if only . . ." and off we go again, in quest of another "only."

*

There are two kinds of lies: those that are the opposite of truths, and those that are the opposite of what we want to believe; and it takes an uncommonly sane man to be able to distinguish between the two.

*

In primitive societies, the men flourish while the women grow old fast; in industrialized societies, the women stay young forever while the men die off at an alarming rate; there must be some possible combination that would achieve parity between the sexes.

*

What most nations call "foreign policy" is not policy at all, in any rational sense of the word, but simply a construct for justifying their desires — like the little boy I once heard in a schoolyard, who said, "I hit him first in self-defense."

*

There is no limit to the interpretations people can make out of Bible stories; if one asked a booster-type person the moral in the tale of Jonah and the whale, he would probably reply, "It proves that you can't keep a good man down."

*

The smaller the mind, the more interested it is in the rare, the extraordinary, the sensational; the larger the mind, the more interested it is in studying the obvious, examining the ordinary, and investigating the commonplace.

*

You can't give anyone an education who doesn't want it — keeping children in school when they have not acquired an appetite for learning is as pointless as providing a bicycle for a legless man.

*

Conventional society has as its guiding, if unspoken, maxim the censorious attitude: "If we can't make the unconventional people act like us, the least we can do is make them miserable."

*

To be proud of having no bad habits can be a greater spiritual vice than having some of the habits.

*

The shallowest of thinkers are those who make a dichotomy between "ideals" and "reality" — forgetting that everything we call a "reality" today began as nothing else but an "ideal."

*

Ignorance breeds frustration; nothing is more painful than to have enough sense to know that a statement is wrong, and yet not enough learning to be able to disprove it, either logically or factually.

*

A most useful area of research would be discovering what happens to the fantastic power of observation in a young child as it grows older; what accounts for the diminution of this power, and what sort of training or inducement might enable us to retain it in later years.

*

Those who genuinely believe that virtue is its own reward should also believe, as a corollary, that vice is its own retribution — and should not desire to add society's revenge to nature's punishment.

*

The chief difference between a politician and a statesman is that the latter never tells a lie that he doesn't first believe himself.

*

A play must be an organic creation, like a person, or it will not be viable; when a play collapses in its third act, it is because the first act was improperly conceived — just as a person falls apart in middle age because his childhood failed to consolidate his personality.

*

It matters not how many technical problems we solve or surmount; there will be no peace and little real progress in the world until we are able to make the optimum equation between freedom and order in human society.

*

We hate what we fear, and we fear what we do not know; the ancient half-truth that "knowledge is power" should be revised to read "knowledge is acceptance of otherness."

*

In times of misfortune, we are prone to reflect that we do not deserve such unhappiness; but in times of felicity, it rarely occurs to us that we are equally undeserving of such happiness.

*

It is a mistake to believe that the feeling called "love" connotes the same thing to a man and to a woman; as one example among many differences, a woman prefers being ill-treated by a man she cares for to being indulged by a man she is indifferent to; whereas few men, whose love has more vanity and less self-abnegation, would long tolerate such a condition.

*

Fame does not satisfy its most lavish recipients, but it prevents them from ever again being satisfied with obscurity.

*

Teaching children to suppress their generous emotions is much worse than allowing them to be fleeced or victimized; they will naturally learn to guard against the latter as they get older, but once generosity has been constricted into suspicion, they remain emotional paralytics for a lifetime.

*

Everybody wants to live long, but nobody wants to be very old; our passion for longevity is equalled only by our horror of its infirmities.

*

To confess sins or transgressions to a mate is often not motivated by the "honesty" we call it, but rather by a desire for punishment, and even by an unconscious wish to hurt the person we are confessing to.

*

The "mass" is that part of the citizenry which doesn't know what it wants — until its leaders try to cram something it doesn't want down its throat.

*

The hardest thing in the world to know is whether one's demand for "justice" on behalf of oneself is not a demand (however cunningly rationalized) for injustice toward somebody else.

*

All the charming contradictions in the feminine nature can be summed up in the fact that nearly every woman wants a man who is strong enough to be leaned upon and weak enough to be controlled.

*

Premature good fortune is the worst mishap that can befall some people — for if luck seems to approve their ways, they have no incentive for correcting their faults of character, and may even come to regard them as virtues.

*

Intelligent patriotism is the rarest (and most valuable) of qualities, because it leads to an appreciation of the deep feelings other peoples have for *their* countries; undiluted patriotism, which lacks this sense of sympathy, breeds an attitude of superiority that can only lead to war.

*

The hardest fact in the world for a parent to recognize and accept is that by the time a child is 17 or 18, everything good and bad that can be done has already been done, and nothing the parent is going to say will affect the child's basic behavior.

*

In the past, some distinction might be made between "just" and "unjust" wars; but as soon as war becomes "total," as it is today, the distinction disappears, and no "just" war is even remotely possible.

*

All those profound differences between political candidates, that loom so large on election day, usually dwindle a few

months after election to the point that the candidate one supported seems barely discernible from the candidate one opposed, and the same old problems are evaded in the same old
way.

*

The beauty of "spacing" children many years apart lies in
the fact that a parent has time to learn the mistakes that were
made with the older ones — which permits us to make exactly
the opposite mistakes with the younger ones.

*

The animosity between two persons who don't like each
other and know it is negligible compared to the tension between two persons who don't like each other and won't admit
it to themselves.

*

It is one of the supreme ironies of language that the word
"semantics" has become just as misused and abused as the
words it tries to analyze.

*

When we read an author, our first obligation is to find out
what *he* means, not what *we* would have meant had we written the book.

*

In all forms of international competition, the rivals get
along beautifully and have much respect for each other —
whether it is chess, tennis, bridge or musical contests; it is only
in political competition that the rivalry is bitter and intrac-

table, which may indicate that talent is the humanizing factor in life, while power is the dehumanizing element.

*

It is one of the frustrating paradoxes of persuasion that a man who is entirely wrong can be made to change his position more easily than a man who is half right; possession of a part of the truth is often the greatest obstacle to achieving the rest of it.

*

If you can count your friends on more than the fingers of one hand, you are not counting friends any more.

*

A man who earns the reputation for working hard can loaf for a long time without anyone being aware of it, or looking askance at it; reputation builds up credit over the years just as surely as a bank account, and many men are living handsomely off the interest of that investment.

*

The most fantastic comment that still lingers on these days is that "professors can't do anything practical." Who do we think invented the atom bomb — two tire salesmen and a marketing executive?

*

The idea of simple "cause and effect" has pretty much been abandoned in physical science, and I suspect it should be abandoned in the psychological realm as well; people *interact* with each other, and it is futile to guess whether her nagging drove him to drink, or his drinking turned her into a nag.

*

It is worth remembering that boys who comprise juvenile gangs are highly moral creatures — within the gang; they practice the cardinal virtues, but only with each other; it is not that their morals are too "low," but that they are too narrow, and their area of loyalty does not extend to the rest of society.

*

Surveys which show that, say, 90 percent of Americans "believe in God" are pointless and misleading; for nothing is easier than a vague "belief" in God, and nothing is harder than acting in consonance with such a belief.

*

What begins as an "impossibility," turns into a "luxury," then into a "convenience," then into a "necessity," then into an "impossibility" to do without; this circularity is what most people mean by "progress."

*

Many people know how to work hard; many others know how to play well; but the rarest talent in the world is the ability to introduce elements of playfulness into work, and to put some constructive labor into our leisure.

*

Some people ask questions after a lecture not so much to get information from the speaker as to prove to the audience that *they* should have been up there giving the talk.

*

No other phrase from the Bible is so generally misinterpreted and misused as Jesus' saying, "I come not to send peace, but a sword," which means (in full context) almost the direct opposite of what it is commonly taken to mean.

*

Perhaps the predominant mark of maturity is the willingness *not* to accept credit for a good idea that we initiated, even with the acute provocation of seeing someone else take credit for it.

*

Much has been written about "love at first sight," but little about "hate at first sight" — which, I am convinced, is just as chemically potent, and as prevalent, though usually concealed.

*

When a theologian uses the word "God" in the pulpit, he and the congregation may be further apart in their definition of that term than he and an atheist.

*

"All men are alike" and "all men are different" are not contradictory statements, but *supplementary* ones; they must be considered together, and understood together, if we are to avoid the twin fallacies of blind collectivism and shortsighted individualism.

*

We truly possess only what we are able to renounce; otherwise, we are simply possessed by our possessions.

*

Every man, deep in his heart, secretly believes that if the leaders of the world would sit down and listen to him, and follow his advice, most of our problems could be solved; this despite the fact that another part of him recognizes that not even his own children can solve their problems by heeding his advice.

*

The therapeutic (and self-renewing) value of family life does not lie in its camaraderie and congeniality, but in the reverse — that it provides an environment in which we may be uncongenial when we like, without suffering the penalty of rejection or retribution.

*

Young people *know* less than we do, but they understand more; their perception has not yet been blunted by compromise, fatigue, rationalization, and the mistaking of mere respectability for morality.

*

Naivete can get people into trouble, but on the other hand it is probable that more people are saved from disaster by their naivete than others are saved by their sophistication.

*

When we win in any contest, we always attribute too much of our success to our skill, and not enough to our opponent's ineptness; only the real expert is aware that most contests are lost by the loser more than they are won by the winner, as in a tennis match, where the number of errors, and not the number of placements, determines victory.

*

A second-rate writer plagiarizes from others; a first-rate writer eventually begins to plagiarize from himself, merely changing the forms of his original thoughts — and, if he is not careful, ending as a pretentious parody of himself.

*

People who stare at other parties in restaurants or at the occupants of passing cars are not being merely rude — they suspect that others are enjoying themselves more and are searching for the secret, either wistfully or enviously.

*

The most essential trait for survival and equanimity in the modern world is the ability to *tolerate ambiguity*, to live comfortably with the tension generated by opposite ideas that cannot be resolved or suppressed. (A condition which all extremists, by their very nature, are unable to accept.)

*

People used to believe that insanity was a form of evil; now we believe that evil is a form of insanity; the excess of moralism has been overcompensated by an excess of psychologism.

*

What the idealist calls an "uncompromising ideal" usually appeals more to the uncompromising part of his nature; and what the practical man calls "brute fact" usually appeals more to the brute part of his nature; each uses only a portion of the truth in order to shore up the weakness of his position.

*

The worst thing about a college education that isn't seriously pursued is that it takes the student far enough to tell how little other people know, but not far enough to make him aware how little he knows.

*

When we are zealous to "liberate" others, it is often our unconscious desire to bring them out of their kind of slavery into our kind of slavery.

*

When two young people want to get married, no argument or force in the world can stop them — not necessarily because of the depth of their passion (one or the other may even feel that the marriage is a mistake), but because they are determined to make their own mistakes as the only form of freedom open to them.

*

Mankind can get accustomed to anything, except the continual need to get accustomed; it is not the *substance* of change that bothers us as much as the *process*.

*

What we know best are those things we have not consciously learned; this is why, even when they are wrong, it is so terribly difficult for us to consciously "unlearn" them.

*

"Truth" is often portrayed as a beacon, but it is really more like a fog light — it pierces through the fog, but does not disperse it.

*

If every man were given a chance to find a job he *loved* to do, and would want to do even if he weren't paid for it, most of the world's criminality and national aggression would disappear overnight.

*

A few men make counterfeit money; in many more cases, money makes counterfeit men.

*

The chief cause of illness is not any specific set of germs or viruses, but life itself; just as the chief cause of divorce is marriage.

*

People who customarily do things to "save time" customarily have no idea what they are saving time for, except to continue doing things to save more time.

*

Our current annoyance at the long hair affected by young men is both trivial and parochial; what matters is the amount of substance *inside* the head, not outside.

*

When we say of antiwar demonstrators, "They wouldn't be allowed to do that in China or Russia," we are expressing precisely the point they are making — for if we banned their freedom to demonstrate, how then would we differ basically from China and Russia?

*

There is a difference between the "contradiction" that comes from confusion, and that which comes from profundity; the former is the result of not seeing clearly enough,

while the latter is the result of seeing all too clearly the paradoxes sometimes inherent in the very nature of things.

*

One of the knottiest psychological problems in police work
is that if a policeman isn't a suspicious person, he can't do his
job well; and if he is a suspicious person, his attitude alienates
many ordinary citizens and thus also makes it harder for him
to do his job well.

*

The most truly lonesome people are those who have not
been able to make themselves necessary to somebody.

*

Revolution results from a collision between that immovable
object, an institution unwilling to change, and that irresistible
force, an idea that must change everything in its path — at the
conclusion of which, the institution is in ruins and the idea
turns into an immovable object.

*

Children's first cynicism about language begins when they
learn that the parental phrase, "We'll see" actually means
"Let's wait until I can find some plausible reason for denying
what you want."

*

Parents today seem to be divided into those who blame
themselves too much for what isn't their fault, and those who
don't blame themselves enough for what is their fault.

*

What we do usually shows what we are most afraid of — the man who habitually sneers is most of all terrified of being sneered at; this explains why the hypercritical are the most thin-skinned about criticism directed against themselves.

*

Just as the poor are pursued by the threat of indigence, the rich are pursued by the threat of boredom; their excessive entertaining and traveling are not so much symbols of affluence as symptoms of ennui.

*

When a child's murderer turns out to be a quiet, affable, ordinary-seeming kind of man, people are always amazed and disbelieving; but the headline phrase, "sex fiend," is a reversal of the truth — for the so-called "sex fiend" is nothing like a fiend and is deficient in sexuality.

*

It is one of the paradoxes of maturation that women who resent their mothers become very much like them as they grow older; only those who have had good relationships are free to become who they are.

*

Almost all our technical, strategical and industrial decisions are made on the basis of scientific thinking; but almost all our decisions in international affairs are made on the basis of prescientific thinking — much as if a surgeon used the latest and most efficient instruments, but operated on the wrong patient because he didn't like the looks of the one he was supposed to operate on.

*

The desire to please, if it is to succeed, must be tempered by a certain fatalism; for it is the overanxious host who is most likely to fail at making his guests comfortable, precisely because he cannot face the possibility of not pleasing them.

*

Bitterness in men goes to the eyes; in women, to the mouth.

*

Gradualness is the only means that truly conquers — all sudden changes and revolutions, when the excitement dies down are forced to retreat and retrace their path through gradualness in order to consolidate their gains, or they perish.

*

That state which aims at "defense" slides imperceptibly, but inevitably, into war; that state which aims at "peace" slides just as surely into acquiescence and slavery; only that state which aims at justice toward other states as well as itself can tread the narrow ridge between war and slavery — and history has not yet seen such a state, and perhaps never will, because of the very nature of national sovereignty.

*

It's always the semi-cad who is the most careful to be proper about the little amenities, for he wants to preserve his reputation by concealing his character; it's only the man who is sure of his decent instincts who can afford to dispense with the amenities when necessary.

*

Praying to "succeed" or to "win" is profoundly irreligious; praying that if we fail we bear that failure manfully is the only kind of supplication that can give us any help.

*

Sleepwalkers, no matter how old, are still looking for their parents' bed.

*

It is true, as Huxley said, that every great advance in knowledge has involved the absolute rejection of authority; but it is equally true that such an advance, when established, then sets *itself* up as an absolute authority.

*

The underdog who condemns the behavior of the overdog rarely stops to consider whether his attitude would be any different if destiny had consigned him to the role of overdog.

*

The trouble with the theological idea of "sin" is that it presumes more freedom than the individual really has — most people are not psychically free enough to be "bad," in any voluntary sense; they are merely slaves to the deficiencies in their early upbringing.

*

If a doctor doesn't prescribe medication, the patient thinks he is not being adequately treated; so, in many cases, the doctor prescribes medication not as therapy but as a symbol of *concern*.

*

When two persons meet for the first time, knowing that they are expected to like each other, their very awareness of this expectation sets up a resistance that is hard to overcome.

*

It is psychologically naive to expect a criminal to feel guilt after committing a crime; in such characters, the sense of guilt *precedes* the crime, and it is precisely to get rid of the feeling that he commits it, and then unconsciously hopes to get caught and punished.

*

Celibacy may be outmoded for the priesthood, but not for the commonly given reason that a celibate can't understand the problems of a married woman — how many husbands can understand them?

*

The reactionary wants us to return to the ways of our ancestors; but those ancestors we most admire are the ones who violently broke away from the ways of *their* ancestors.

*

Children play at being soldiers, and the ones who never grow up tend to become generals.

*

It takes a long time in life to learn that sometimes our prayers are best answered when they go unanswered; if I had got what I thought I wanted at 20, I would have been miserable at 40.

*

How much we enjoy our animosity was brought home to me vividly last month, when a TV program I despised was cancelled — and, rather than rejoicing, I resented the fact that I could no longer stride over to the set and forcefully turn off the program the moment it showed its face!

*

The silliest thing big cities are doing, prompted by civic vanity, is putting up large and expensive buildings to house the arts, and then casting around desperately for enough "culture" to stuff them with.

*

What is there about us that makes it less unpleasant to endure our own disappointments than to see someone else's hopes gratified?

*

A sound historical case could be made out for the assertion that World War I is not yet finished; the Armistice ended nothing, and the surrenders in World War II ended nothing; today's fighting is merely a resumption of nationalistic rivalries, having little to do with the ideologies of "democracy" or "communism."

*

To my mind, the ten most overworked adjectives in the modern American vocabulary are: "glamorous," "fabulous," "fantastic," "intriguing," "great," "immortal," "divine," "challenging," "ultimate," and "creative."

*

The most neglected child in the whole educational system is not the backward child, but the gifted one who is bored with a mediocre milieu — and it is a depressing fact that among the upper 20 percent of mental ability, fewer than half ever enter college.

*

Almost all choices in life are between "lesser evils" and "greater evils"; and the tragedy of the human situation consists in the realization, when it is too late, that the "lesser evil" was not as much "lesser" as we had thought.

*

A religion which says "You *have* to do this" to its communicants, without at the same time motivating them to *want* to do it, is dead in spirit, no matter how large in numbers and influence it seems to be; loyalty out of fear or submission has no real strength in a crisis.

*

Perhaps women aren't great creative writers, in a literary sense, but what man could do half as well as a woman in writing a vibrant thank-you note for a present he hasn't the slightest use for and intends to exchange at the earliest possible moment?

*

Inspirational orators who praise "will power" as a paramount virtue tend to forget that the most determined, patient, persistent, ingenious and relentless man in society is the bank robber.

*

We call those who try to live above themselves "upstarts"; why don't we call those many more who live beneath themselves "downstarts"?

*

People who have to ask the same question two or three times ("Is this the bus to downtown?") before they believe the answer, must have been lied to consistently by their parents when they were young.

*

The soundest financial advice I've ever heard was handed me on a card the other day: one side proclaimed, "How to Become a Millionaire in Less Than One Year!" The other side gave the answer: "Deposit $20,000 in the bank every week. In 50 weeks, you will be a millionaire."

*

Almost no one is foolish enough to imagine that he automatically deserves great success in any field of activity; yet almost everyone believes that he automatically deserves success in marriage.

*

The history of all institutions goes through three stages — they are created by need, then sanctified by law, then they try to become a law unto themselves, in order to prevent the rise of rival institutions.

*

Misery is endurable only when it is widespread enough; it is intolerable when we seem specifically to have been picked out by fate; this is why whole communities bear great burdens more equably than individuals bear lighter ones.

*

Why do so many people who "love to travel" feel comfortable only when they can immediately transform their foreign environment into one as closely as possible resembling their native environment?

*

An intellectual is one who customarily has much compassion for the physically and economically deprived, but much scorn for the mentally limited — for the imperialism of intellect does not permit him to see that a man whose mind is stunted deserves at least as much consideration as one whose body is crippled or whose heritage is meager.

*

Western civilization has not yet learned the lesson that the energy we expend in "getting things done" is less important than the moral strength it takes to decide what is worth doing and what is right to do.

*

It is not what men do at their worst that makes tragedy, but what men do at their best, with good intentions, or what men find they must do in spite of their intentions, that creates the most misfortune in the world.

*

A fanatical man who believes the world is flat has more impressive arguments than a sensible man who knows it is spherical; and the reason that fanaticism so often triumphs over sense is that those who hold a position passionately are the only ones who take the trouble to arm themselves with persuasive arguments, however wrong they may be.

*

Many fewer minds are chained by the taboos and restrictions imposed from the outside than are paralyzed by the fears and prejudices imposed by oneself; external freedom is meaningless so long as we remain the prisoners of our own psychic infancy.

*

The physical laws of perspective are strangely reversed in the psychological world — to the eyes, what is close seems large and what is far seems small; but to the mind, what we have at hand seems small and what we crave from afar seems large. We are aware of the illusion of sight; few are aware of the illusion of desire.

*

When good luck strikes us, it is helpful to remember the maxim that "fortune is fickle," in order to avoid becoming smug or complacent; but, likewise, when bad luck strikes us, it is equally helpful to keep the same maxim in mind, in order to avoid self-pity or despair.

*

Hair, to women, must have some deeply symbolic or sexual meaning far beyond the mere physical appearance, for nothing else explains the vast amount of time, money and energy devoted to care of the hair; nor is this merely a modern obsession — in Biblical times, the Book of Timothy warns women against excess in attention to the dressing of the hair.

*

Some wine turns sour with age, and some wine improves with age; so it is with wisdom — and when an elder takes it upon himself to offer advice to a young man, he should first make sure that it is the kind of wisdom that time has improved and not turned sour.

*

A good teacher will not only make his pupils aware of the half-truths and beguiling fallacies dangled before them by propagandists, but he will go further and guard the pupils against his own, the teacher's, prejudices and preconceptions. (This is perhaps the hardest task in teaching a "live" subject.)

*

If Clemenceau's famous remark that "War is too important a matter to be left to the generals" is true, is it not equally true that peace is too important a matter to be left to the diplomatists?

*

The character of a man consists of three elements: what he believes, what he does, and how he reconciles what he does with what he believes — and it is in the last operation that the ultimate assessment of character must be made.

*

People are friendlier in the country, but freer in the city; and the price one pays for having a neighbor who will take a kindly interest in you when you need him, is having a neighbor who will take an officious interest in you when you don't want him to.

*

The meanly ambitious man can be distinguished from the decently ambitious man by the fact that the former has no moderation of posture — he is either groveling before his superiors or strutting before his subordinates, but is incapable of standing easily erect for any sustained period.

*

We are naively disappointed when justice does not arise out of law, but it was never supposed to be that way — laws are meant to arise out of justice, and if the community does not provide the proper soil, then the laws that shoot up will merely reflect the rankness of the soil.

*

Marriages are more apt to founder because of little flaws than because of any major discordance, for the same reason that it is easier to bear a pain than an itch.

*

What highly verbal people often forget is that what can be expressed is never quite true, and that what even the greatest creative writer puts into words is not exactly what he meant, for the deepest feelings are incommunicable by words — which is no doubt why music was invented.

*

Simple and open egotism is a harmless enough foible; it becomes dangerous only when it disguises itself as philanthropy.

*

To live successfully requires a fusion of opposites, of which few of us are capable — that is, to engage in large matters as though we were going to live forever, and to take care of small matters as though we were going to die tomorrow.

*

All unacted desires turn poisonous in time; they must either be acted upon or drained off by reflection, else they will suppurate.

*

How can we ever have much more than an uneasy truce among peoples when, for instance, in England about the most contemptuous thing you can call a man is "clever," while in France it is considered a high compliment?

*

The worst tactical command a parent can make is to issue a command he or she is not sure will be obeyed.

*

Why is it that the good things people say about us never give us as much permanent pleasure as the bad things they say about us give us enduring pain; and that the glow of praise quickly dims and must be continually replenished, while the barbs of dispraise rankle for an unconscionably long time?

*

A striking demonstration of the irrational power of words is the fact that almost everyone wants to be "normal," while no one wants to be considered "mediocre" — but mediocrity is simply a middling quality between the high and the low, which is all that normality stands for, too.

*

People who are proud of their "energy" usually use it in behalf of their self-assertiveness; they seem unaware that as much energy (and some might say a superior kind) is involved in exercising self-restraint.

*

There is a law of diminishing returns in pleasure as well as in profits — the rich who may gamble for shockingly high stakes eventually don't find as much pleasure in winning a thousand dollars as their chauffeurs do in winning five dollars.

*

Every system has a natural tendency to convert its means into ends: the business system, for instance, is a means to enable man to devote more of himself to higher attainments, but it has become largely an end in itself; whereas, at the other end of the spectrum, scholarship is a means to achieve more relevant knowledge, but it has degenerated mostly into academic nit-picking as an end in itself.

*

The current "God is dead" controversy is the healthiest thing that's happened to theology in the last 50 years, for whether or not God is dead, the word "God" has been drained of content by popularizers, preachers and politicians, and requires serious reexamination at the deepest level of meaning.

*

Most young people mistakenly believe that to be "free" is to be able to do what you want to do; when, in truth, to be free is to be able to do what is best for yourself — and learning what is best for yourself is the only way to get rid of the slavery of self-indulgence.

*

When the angry man says he wants "justice," what he really wants is vengeance; and when the guilty man says he wants "justice," what he really wants is forgiveness.

*

The best test of a democracy consists in the range and variety of things it is safe to laugh at; for the one tendency that all totalitarian societies have in common, whether left or right, is a constantly diminishing sense of humor, and a corresponding aversion to satire.

*

The seeking after a status symbol is futile and endless — for as soon as enough people have attained it, it is no longer a status symbol; true status is achieved only by those secure enough to live by substance and spirit, not by symbols.

*

"Statesmanship" seems to be largely the art of leading the people into such an *impasse* that only another kind of statesmanship can lead them out, and so on ad infinitum.

*

The worst effect of the rise of communism in the 20th Century is that its evils are so obvious that they make us hug our own evils closer to our breast, rather than reexamining and reforming them, as we should.

*

Wisdom has never been combined with power for more than a short time in any period of human history, and then wisdom soon became subservient to power; and the contemporary version of wisdom, which we call "science," seems to be faring no better than its ancient counterpart.

*

That popular phrase, "the naked truth," is a misnomer, for every truth comes to us clothed in some kind of emotional preconception — even the mathematical equation $10 + 10 = 20$ reveals a hidden bias in favor of the decimal system.

*

It's odd that many of the same people who believe that "you can't legislate morality" by passing laws forcing people to respect others' civil rights, at the same time seem to believe that you *can* legislate loyalty by passing laws forcing people to take loyalty oaths.

*

To be "normal" in a highly abnormal age is a shocking sign of abnormality; our goal cannot be to be "normal," but to recognize when our personal abnormality is out of proportion to the stimulus of the age.

*

It is cheap cynicism to think that mostly dishonest men are attracted to political office, for just as many honest men covet it; the tragedy lies in what happens to the honest men after they get in, and the ways in which they compromise their principles to stay in.

*

Nations are never killed by conquest from the outside; from this, they always can recover, even to the extent of overcoming their conquerors; when a nation is permanently killed, it is nearly always by suicide.

*

We prosecute those who cause injury to others by their actions, but we who cause sometimes even greater injury to many others by our inaction congratulate ourselves on our decency, our respectability, and our good feelings.

*

Most of what passes for "thinking" is *calculation* and not *meditation;* we spend hours calculating the consequences of an act, but scarcely a moment in meditating on its value.

*

It is a gross mistake to believe that a mirror tells us how we look to others; all it can do is tell us how we look to ourselves, which is always a distortion of the external reality; for the expression we adopt while looking in the mirror is not the expression by which the world catches us unawares.

*

Much of what we call our "modesty" is a sense of shame at how much pride we privately take in some accomplishment for which we are praised.

*

The "stature" of a person is not necessarily commensurate with his "position" — for a man is no bigger than the things that annoy him.

*

"Why should one child turn out badly when they were all treated the same way?" asks the distrait parent, never realizing that to treat dissimilar children the same way is not fairness but blindness.

*

Executive ability consists largely in making decisions to be carried out by others who, when the decisions turn out badly, can be blamed for not understanding how you wanted things done.

*

The wages of sin is not death, for that is the wages of everything; the particular wages of sin is to keep on sinning compulsively, long after any pleasure has gone out of it — and surely this, psychologically, is the meaning of Hell.

*

It is hard to believe that man, as he is presently constituted, is the final step in the evolutionary process; it may be
true that we were created in God's image — but an image may
be only a dim approximation of the substance it reflects.

*

What two men would strike a bargain if they knew that
both would be losers; yet this is what nations do when they
strike a war, only they are not longsighted enough to perceive
their mutual loss.

*

The conservative believes that an old error is made sacred
by its antiquity, while the liberal believes that an ancient truth
is rendered obsolete merely by its age; both are seduced by
Time, in opposite directions.

*

The human race perpetually oscillates between two tendencies — to build up an ordinary man into heroic proportions, and to cut a hero "down to size"; we are not content unless our public men are either larger or smaller than life.

*

For every one person that hate kills, a thousand are anni-
hilated by indifference.

*

In any art or craft, the chief difference in motivation between the amateur and the professional is that the amateur
desires the applause of the public, while the professional is
mainly concerned with the respect of his professional colleagues.

*

Everybody tries to make a virtue out of his particular vice: the compulsive Don Juan no doubt believes that men less preoccupied with women than he is are "undersexed."

*

People who serve the world without despising it soon become the world's slaves; and those who despise the world without serving it soon become slaves to their own egos; the hardest and most useful attitude is a delicate blend of affection and contempt.

*

The indubitable fact that "a leopard can't change his spots" is used by many people simply as an excuse for skinning him.

*

The best way to win an argument is to concede as much as can possibly be conceded to your opponent's view without sacrificing anything essential to your own; success in argument is a direct opposite to success in bargaining.

*

The best reason for offering our opinions tentatively, rather than dogmatically, is that we then remain free to be able to change them without losing face; for most stubbornness in argument springs out of vanity rather than conviction.

*

A teacher is someone employed by the community to prove to their children that being educated doesn't pay very much.

*

People who like us too quickly don't usually become our fast friends — for when they are disenchanted, they blame it on our faults rather than on their impetuosity.

*

People laugh at the fact that geniuses like Einstein tend to be terribly absentminded; but how could a man with a tremendously retentive memory be an original thinker?

*

Speaking of geniuses, the men who make the most significant advances are those whose glittering self-confidence is mottled with self-distrust, so that they are neither frustrated by their failures nor infatuated by their seeming successes.

*

The founder of every creed, from Jesus Christ to Karl Marx, would be appalled to return to earth and see what has been made of that creed, not by its enemies, but by its most devoted adherents.

*

The upper classes deplore the lower classes' "lack of respect for law and order"; but why should they respect law and order when they constantly hear the upper classes referring to "government" in a deprecatory way, as if it were some alien force inimical to their interests, instead of the instrument through which they act?

*

Old people gain a reputation for wisdom when they succeed in outliving all those who could recall how foolish they were in younger years.

*

Low wages are not cheap wages; what the individual employer withholds, the whole society must pay for, many times over.

*

When we draft young men for a war, we reject the physically unfit, the mentally inferior, and the morally deficient — leaving them home to reproduce the race, while we send out the finest stock to be killed off; this is what each country calls "defending the future of the nation."

*

When any group is denied equality long enough, it no longer seeks equality — it seeks superiority: hence, the tragedy of Black Muslims.

*

The paradox of lawlessness in our society is that the public is most tolerant of gambling and most resentful toward syndicate "gangland" operations — yet it is organized gambling that provides the bulk of the bankroll for syndicate operations and influence everywhere.

*

Whoever divided sheep and goats and put himself among the goats?

*

Even though education is our largest industry ($39 billion a year), while business spends about ten percent of revenues on research and development, we allocate less than one-tenth of one percent of our educational expenditures to research, and thus still don't know the best ways to teach children.

*

One of the chief paradoxes of human society is that the greater the social evil, the less effective against it is the coercion of law; the law can prevent or prosecute many little infringements, but the biggest obstacle to a just society — the perversion of law for partial interests — is a moral, not a legal or juridical, matter.

*

The trouble with talking about "underdeveloped countries" is that we tend to forget they are underdeveloped *economically*, and we begin to believe they are also underdeveloped intellectually, ethically, and spiritually — which does not necessarily follow in many cases.

*

Women seem to talk more than men, not so much because their total verbiage is greater, but because psychologically most women cannot tolerate a lull in the conversation, and will rush in to fill the void, no matter how irrelevant or needless their comment.

*

The biggest crybabies in our society are the police forces, who seem to believe that everybody should implicitly obey the law, except themselves when the law hampers them in twisting or trapping a confession out of a suspect.

*

What most parents — and almost all trustees — fail to understand is that the function of a college is to encourage dissent and disagreement, to offer choices, and let the students think out problems for themselves; and if such freedom had been offered in the past, the kind of dissent now being practiced would not be so violent and irrational.

*

The motive for a deed is never the same before, during and after its performance; for the very act itself changes the motive, unearthing deeper aspects we were unaware of.

*

The worst drawback to wealth is the accompanying fear of losing it; and it is this fear, rather than all the political rationalizing, that makes the privileged class in every society so rigidly (and often so self-defeatingly) conservative.

*

Watching otters frolic ceaselessly in a pool, one wonders if it is not possible to be *condemned* to pleasure.

*

Lovers rarely talk: they sigh and stroke and nuzzle, perhaps subconsciously realizing that if they spoke, fully and frankly and at length, they might be lovers no longer.

*

It is the sentimentalist, not the realist, who believes that the more terrible the instruments of war become, the more reluctant will mankind be to use them; and the archsentimentalist was Nobel, who actually declared that his invention of dynamite was so fearsome that nations could no longer war against each other.

*

Eventually, the patient knows more about the disease than the doctor does; but by then it is too late to change either one of them.

*

It is narrow to think that only individuals become insane: whole cultures can be deranged, whole strata of society, or geographical areas, can be mentally sick; and the treatment of social psychopathology may become in the future one of the most rewarding fields of study.

*

All criminals (by which I do not mean merely those who break the law), however diverse their other traits, have this one thing in common: they do not truly believe that other people exist.

*

You don't really know yourself unless you are capable of changing those aspects you know about and don't like; self-knowledge as an intellectual exercise can go on for a lifetime, like a chimpanzee scratching the same place, but never getting rid of the flea.

*

The best combination of parents consists of a father who is gentle beneath his firmness, and a mother who is firm beneath her gentleness.

*

Those who continually equate size and number with quality have no true conception of what quality is; they are among the multitude who foolishly imagine that two vitamin pills a day make them twice as "healthy" as one.

*

One of the real problems with teen-agers today is that most communities do not make enough provision for recreation — and when they do, the teen-agers stay away because they don't like adult-supervised activities.

*

While knowledge *of* sex has increased enormously in this generation, knowledge *about* sex is still sparse, confused and contradictory; the technical and biological aspects have been given the widest currency, but the psychological, social and marital aspects have not been clarified or codified to anyone's satisfaction.

*

Speaking of young people, one of their favorite phrases is that somebody "has it made" — what they need to learn is that nobody has it made, that keeping it is harder than getting it, that continuing to enjoy it is hardest of all.

*

What we need now is to apply the power of advertising and public opinion to making the cities as ashamed of their collective odor as we have been successful in making persons sensitive to the possibility of their personal odors.

*

It's difficult for adults to imagine how children visualize the things that are told to them; the other day I overheard my six-year-old explaining to a playmate that "when you die, your body is put in the ground — but your head goes to heaven."

*

The first lesson a child should be taught is how to laugh at itself easily; without this ability, all manners are a mockery, and politeness hardens into mere priggishness.

*

To feel the temperament of a city, you have to see it late at night; but to know the character of a city, you have to smell it early in the morning — Paris, for instance, smells of freshly baked bread, New York of stale tobacco.

*

My favorite sign of the month, handwritten over a display table in a neighborhood drugstore: "Junk for Reducing." We realize how rare such commercial honesty is only when we unexpectedly run across such delights.

*

A family I don't care to know better is one in which the daughter is called "Sis."

*

Speaking of families, it is a sentimental myth that a "good son" will make a good husband; in most cases, a dutiful son's excessive — if unconscious — attachment to his mother is a major factor in marital conflicts.

*

Isn't it richly ironic that the two most important facets of human life — politics and parenthood — are the only ones for

which no special training is provided, or even thought necessary?

*

Those of us who are inordinately proud that we don't rape
truth by falsehood, like to forget how we suffocate it by silence.

*

The only way a society can work for any length of time is
to make self-interest coincide with the common good; communism has failed because of a false idolization of the common good; if capitalism fails, it will be because of a false idolization of self-interest.

*

How foolish of us to accept violence in the great world,
and deplore it in our neighborhoods; to condone physical
conflict as a means of resolving international disputes, and at
the same time to profess shock at the rise of physical conflict
in the conduct of local disputes. This is as absurdly illogical as saying that elephants have a right to fight, but mice
don't.

*

It is ironic that many of the people who are so passionately
concerned with permitting prayers in the public schools have
little conception of the purpose of prayer — they look upon
it as a vague passport toward getting into heaven when its real
purpose is to draw strength to make us more human and
more humane toward one another.

*

For decades, we have ignored the growing cancer of slums in American cities; now that the symptoms are erupting, painfully and frighteningly, we tend to blame the patients for not dying decently and quietly.

*

Asking governments to renounce militarism and to settle differences by law is to ask them to voluntarily abandon their power, which no government will ever do; if peace ever comes to the human race, it will come through the efforts of people, not through governments.

*

An invariable sign of a special pleader who is posing as a "historian" is that he attributes the decline of Roman civilization to a single major cause which happens to fit his own prejudice about the decline of modern civilization.

*

The God that most people think they believe in deserves to be "dead"; only in this way can the God of the prophets be resurrected.

*

One way of dividing people is into those who want to *enjoy* life and those who merely *endure* life — the trouble being that those who want to enjoy it don't know how to endure it when things are bad, and those who endure it don't know how to enjoy it when things are good.

*

The state is not founded upon individuals, but upon couples and family groups; if we dared to practice the "individualism" we preach, the fabric of society would be torn apart in a single day.

*

The way we interpret the world makes it become more that way, for us — the suspicious man makes the world more suspicious, the greedy man makes the world more greedy, the belligerent man makes the world more belligerent; for every distortion of reality becomes, in the end, a self-fulfilling prophecy.

*

Women talk to their women friends about their husbands in a way that no man talks to his man friends about his wife; to a woman, marriage is a collective experience that is naturally shared with her sex, while to a man marriage is a personal enigma he will not reveal to anyone, even if he could.

*

Why are so few American women capable of accepting a compliment gracefully?

*

Why do mayors look alike the world over?

*

Why is it that no one ever includes himself when he speaks of "the mass"?

*

Why don't most people with the courage of their convictions try to get some better convictions?

*

If the best things in life really *are* free, why does it cost us so much to learn and accept this simple fact?

*

Why do we say "I wasn't myself" when we are provoked by anger or vanity or greed into disclosing what we really are?

*

When will the man who is forever trying to prove he *is* a man ever realize that his efforts only succeed in giving the impression that he feels like a boy who doesn't quite believe he is a man?

*

Can't that dreadful phrase, "mental hygiene," be replaced with something more human-sounding and less like a smug chapter heading in a social worker's casebook?

*

Why is it that the American male, who is obsessed with pictures and statistics of bosoms, is invariably shocked or repelled if a foreign woman begins breast-feeding her child in a public place? (Could this mean that our culture is fantastically pro-breast — except when it is being used for the purpose nature intended?)

*

Wouldn't it be nice to have an "Operation Cessation" to stop all this verbal nonsense of calling every project "Operation This" and "Operation That"?

*

In historical perspective, we can see that the people who were said to be "ahead of their time in their thinking" were actually the only ones who understood their own time and what was needed to plan for the future; this is because only the man "ahead of his time" can grasp the present, while most of us think in terms a generation behind our times.

*

Unless we can comprehend both these opposites — "Human nature doesn't change," and "Human nature is always changing" — then we can't begin to cope realistically with society's problems, for both terms must be held in equilibrium, and neither must dominate our thinking.

*

Nobody's attitude can make you feel inferior unless you secretly believed it yourself before.

*

Ninety precent of what we *believe* has nothing to do with the process of *thought*, but comes instead from the four sources of *family inheritance, individual temperament, national culture,* and *economic self-interest;* and while we cannot wholly cast off these shackles, we should at least recognize their cramping and distorting influence upon the free process of thought.

*

The social organism, like all nature, abhors a vacuum; and what the power structure in any society rarely learns until too late is that if the legitimate needs of the people are not met in a human way by the community, they will be filled in an official way by the state.

*

It is not "logic" that keeps people sane, but a sense of reality; insane people think much more logically than most of us do, but their rigorous train of thought is based on an utterly false premise about the nature of reality.

*

The greatest mystery of modern times is how so many people manage to live as well as they do on what we suspect they make.

*

It is not divorce itself that does damage to the children of marriage, but the emotional conflict *leading up to* the divorce; and recent studies indicate that adolescents from unbroken unhappy homes are more troubled and delinquent than those from broken homes, at least in middle-class environments.

*

"Integrated education" is meaningless in itself, unless we can raise the *quality* of education generally; and it is a dangerous and hopeless illusion to expect the schools to do what society will not do.

*

Perhaps the most precise definition of a small town, regardless of population, is a place where people with money have to go away to spend it the way they like to.

*

It's hard to accept the fact that a "poor" picture of us really looks more like us than a "good" one — the "good picture" is an artificial distortion displaying our best points in repose, but the "poor picture" shows how we look in action 90 percent of the time.

*

Not to drink liquor on principle is as absurd as to drink liquor on principle; some people, I am convinced, are born a couple of drinks under par and need a little liquor medicinally just to make them more human; some are born a couple of drinks over par, and liquor makes them subhuman; our job is to know who we are, and the rest takes care of itself.

*

The chief advantage of the exquisite courtesy in tennis is that by shouting "Great shot!" to your opponent when he hits a ball you can't get, you are not only complimenting his prowess but excusing your own ineffectuality.

*

Citizens who agree perfectly with their own police are ripe for a police state, whether they know it or not, want it or not.

*

"Atomic war is inevitable," says the pessimist; "Atomic war is impossible," says the optimist; "Atomic war is inevitable unless we make it impossible," says the realist.

*

Attempts at disarmament only relieve the symptoms of the war disease, without cleaning out the basic infection; and if we could learn to look upon war as the most serious pandemic disease of mankind as a species, we might then begin to focus as much energy, time and funds on research for peace as we now do for a host of lesser diseases.

*

It is the old fallacy of *post hoc, ergo propter hoc* ("after this, therefore caused by this") that makes us believe that a higher level of education leads to higher earning power; college graduates make more not because they are better educated (except in a few specialized cases), but because they come from a social and economic milieu that brings them in contact with richer opportunities.

*

It is entirely possible that by the year 2000 we shall be living in a world without work, as it is understood today; but the liberty of leisure will become a hell, rather than a heaven, unless we train ourselves to find new and proper objects for our energies, aggressions and satisfactions.

*

The greatest danger for both liberals and conservatives does not lie in their opponents, but in the extremists within their own ranks — for the liberals are constantly being seduced by their most illiberal elements, while the conservatives are pulled by the reactionaries in their camp; both sides have more to fear from their "friends" than from each other.

*

Why do grandparents and grandchildren get along so well together? Perhaps the best answer is the one I heard from a psychiatrist recently: "Because they have a common enemy — the parents."

*

In physics, a neutrino can move from point A to point B without a path, which is ridiculous and impossible, although true; modern man has no difficulty in accepting (if not understanding) this scientific paradox, but balks at accepting any religious paradoxes which are not as incredible — not because he has *less* faith, but because the *object* of his faith has shifted from the theological to the scientific field.

*

When will we be grown up enough to abolish the double standard of demanding "punishment" for those offenders we do not know, and imploring "understanding" of those offenders we do know?

*

Isn't it true that all of what we call "anxiety" consists simply of different forms of fearing one's self?

*

The most brilliant, witty and intellectual man in the world still finds it difficult to make talk with his own relatives; for, usually, we have the most to say to those we have the least to do with.

*

When a man cannot choose between two women, or a woman between two men, they should choose neither — for love is not a scale or a slide rule to be balanced or calculated, and the very act of choosing between two indicates that neither is right.

*

Speaking of this delicate and treacherous subject, it is surely one of nature's mischievous ironies that the qualities that attract us to a person are often the most superficial ones, and not the deeper ones — thus, the reasons couples *stay* married have little to do with the reasons they *got* married.

*

No man should consider himself a philosopher until he knows how to get along with a fool — which most self-styled philosophers don't.

*

The one "moral" lesson that little children should be taught, perhaps more than any other, is that cruelty is a form of weakness, not of strength, and that only a person who is growing into strength and self-confidence can afford to drop cruelty as excess emotional baggage of childhood; this one lesson, I am convinced, could do more good than all the parental sermons and strictures on "ethical" matters.

*

Little girls want to be princesses, but little boys don't want to be princes — and from those two different starting points come all the confusions, contradictions and cross-purposes of courtship and marriage.

*

A "civilized" person is one who thinks it was horribly barbarous to burn people at the stake, but finds it acceptable if electricity is used.

*

We can justify anything by turning it in a different light; after all, the sadist can point out that he is really being kind to the masochist, by providing what he wants and needs.

*

A philosopher is generally a man who takes his own temperament as a model for the world, and creates a system of thought that is more a projection of his temperament than it is a product of his intellect.

*

Husbands want novelty, and wives want security; but wives, when they are bored with security, look for novelty; and husbands, when they are bored with novelty, return to security.

*

In the calculus of human existence, it seems to me that life is 30 percent what is handed to you at birth, 30 percent what you are, and 30 percent what you make yourself . . . the final, and often determining, 10 percent, is sheer luck.

*

Has it occurred to anyone that the real reason for the Biblical myth of Adam — that is, *one* created man instead of a multiplicity of men created all together — is to stress the common parenthood of everyone on earth, so that no one could point to "superior" lineage if he goes back far enough?

*

Everyone is in favor of laws which he cannot imagine *himself* breaking; the laws we object to are those which penalize misdeeds we feel ourselves capable of.

*

There is no record in history of a nation building up a large store of arms and not using them; if the arms are available, they will be used, one way or another, under one pretext or another.

*

It is a shallow definition to say, as Harry Truman did, that "politics is the art of government" — politics is the art of circumventing government on behalf of partisan goals that are cunningly disguised as public needs.

*

I'd like to "initialize" the extinction of the man who "finalizes" a decision.

*

The word "freedom" should be, but rarely is, divided into its two components of "inner freedom" and "outer freedom"; this might clarify the point that without the inner freedom to think, outer freedom is meaningless; and without the outer freedom to act on our judgments, inner freedom is irrelevant.

*

Many mistakenly believe that "ideas are dangerous," but they are not; only feelings are dangerous, and most dangerous of all are precisely those feelings which masquerade as "ideas."

*

The mediocre man who is bored with his environment seeks to find other diversions and only sinks further into boredom; the extraordinary man who is bored seeks to alter his environment, and succeeds in providing himself and others with social and cultural advance.

*

The only time for a father to be a "pal" to his son is before the boy is old enough to find pals elsewhere: after that, it is too late.

*

A person of cold rectitude is usually unaware that character is no substitute for charm; and a person of engaging personality is often just as unaware that charm is no substitute for character; for we cannot make one trait do the work of others without impairing the machinery of the self.

*

What a thing costs is not the price one pays for it, but the price one must *go on paying* for it, either in monetary or psychic terms; and, thus regarded, many desiderata come far too high.

*

A woman nags her husband not because she wants to dominate him, but because he has been unsuccessful in dominating her; nagging is almost always an expression of the woman's unsatisfied need to be dependent.

*

The nations of the world sometimes remind me of patients in a mental institution, each insisting that he alone doesn't belong there, and each agreeing that all the others are quite mad.

*

The supreme art of giving presents is not to give someone what he wanted (which he could get for himself), but to give someone what he didn't know he wanted until he got it, which adds delight to gratitude.

*

People don't give up their pretensions because they would feel naked without them; but how much better to face the world naked than cumbersomely clothed in a "counterfeit" costume.

*

If you can't joke about your religion, you're not steadfast in your piety — you're simply afflicted with the disease of "religiosity."

*

No economy is more false than economizing on luxuries; to approach a luxury in a niggardly, calculating fashion is already to miss the whole spirit of the thing.

*

It is foolish and futile to tell children not to lie; being small and defenseless, they *will* lie, and the most of morality we can instill in them is getting them to guard against *lying to themselves*, hoping they will outgrow lying to others, while self-deception is a deadly and lifelong disease.

*

"Patriotism corrupts history," observed Goethe, nearly two centuries ago; today an excess of patriotism is more likely to *end* history.

*

Every inanimate object in the world seems to reach out and rub up against an injured finger; and so it is with an injured psyche, which cannot see that the sensitivity resides within itself, not in the objects it encounters.

*

Most men regard their wives the same way they regard their religion: they know which church they belong to, but sometimes wonder wistfully whether some other denomination might not be less demanding.

*

Because intelligent people generally take a minority viewpoint, some pretentious nitwits adopt a minority viewpoint in the hope of being mistaken for members of the intelligentsia — and this is what gives minority viewpoints such a bad reputation among the majority.

*

The *ideas* we believe in may depend upon our thought processes; but the ways in which we implement such ideas depend far more upon our temperament.

*

To a mother, a son is never a fully grown man; and a son is never a fully grown man until he understands and accepts this about his mother.

*

Success that comes too soon makes one cocky, and success that comes too late makes one bitter; even in the realm of good fortune, timing is all.

*

It would take a hundred clerks working for a hundred years to make one mistake as monumental as a computer can make in a thousandth of a second.

*

The man who dismisses something by saying, "That's only symbolic," has just dismissed the principal element that distinguishes mankind from the whole rest of creation.

*

The scientific point of view, which looks upon man as simply a special kind of *animal*, misses the whole unique quality of humanhood; while the "spiritual" point of view, which dismisses or depreciates man's material and physical aspects, is equally guilty of ignoring and distorting the essence of our creatureliness.

*

For every one quarrel that goes to the roots of the disagreement, a dozen quarrels are engaged in over the mere *symptoms* of the disagreement; and if we really knew, and could admit, what we were quarreling about, disagreements could be resolved twice as fast with half the woe.

*

I have always felt there was something cheap about the popular wartime phrase, "There are no atheists in foxholes"; if a man has to get into a foxhole to be converted, the odds are high that he is just taking out "God-insurance" which will lapse when he returns to safety.

*

With some exceptions, it is generally true that beautiful women have no sense of humor — possibly because they fear that laugh lines will mar their pulchritude.

*

Half the world hasn't learned the meaning of "duty," and the other half has learned it too well.

*

To teen-agers, the Depression might as well have happened during the days of Buffalo Bill, and even the Second World War and Hitlerism are as remote to their minds and imaginations as the Punic War and Hannibal; and what is distressing is that those who took part in either are incapable of transmitting the emotional core of these experiences to the young.

*

Mistrust anyone who has a "formula for living"; for you may be sure that he will twist life to fit his formula, rather than changing his formula to fit life.

*

What makes us ridiculous is not our failures, but our pretensions; not our inability to cut a fine figure, but our deluded vanity that we are impressing others when we pretend to be better than we are.

*

Half the people in the world spend their time in making simple things much more complex than they need to be; while the other half spend their time in trying to persuade us that complex things are much more simple than they really are.

*

One of the most hypocritical phrases in modern usage is "premarital sex" — for most of what we call "premarital" sex is actually "nonmarital," and often "antimarital."

*

It is a paradox of nature too little understood by most people that "normal" is often the rarest case in any group of phenomena; it is "normal" for the human organism not to have a cold, but not one person in a thousand is this normal for even one year.

*

A painter who paints only what everyone sees is a hack, talented though he may be; a painter who paints only what he sees is a narcissist without hope of immortality, talented though he may be; a great painter paints what everyone *ought* to see, but, doesn't, until he makes it manifest.

*

Children want to cut what they cannot untie; and adults too often try to undo by force what they cannot straighten out by patient persuasion — war being the most glaring and widespread example of this infantile residue in the human race.

*

The most intolerable old people are those who are keeping themselves alive out of sheer habit and sense of survival; the most engaging are those who want to keep alive in order to find out what is going to happen in the world next week.

*

The most dangerous man in the world is he who believes he is acting without prejudice, for nobody acts without prejudice — and the most we can do is admit that we harbor this subclinical infection of the soul, and make allowances for its inevitable influence on our judgments, as a scientist weighs the "personal equation" in his laboratory activities.

*

The deepest and rarest kind of courage has nothing to do with feats or obstacles in the outside world; and, indeed, has nothing to do with the outside world — it is the courage to be who you are.

*

It is commonly easier to make a man mad by impugning his taste than by attacking his ideas, for he considers his ideas as cultural accretions, while he (wrongly) imagines that his taste is inborn.

*

We use our beliefs to shape our experiences, and then we offer our experiences as evidence of the rightness of our beliefs; given this circular process, it is little wonder that we almost always fail to convert others to our beliefs.

*

To accomplish great things, we first have to know what greatness consists of — for if we lack this concept, we run the strong risk of monumentally achieving what was not worth doing in the first place.

*

Starting and stopping are the most dangerous parts of any venture, and not the going itself; most ships are wrecked near shore, and most airplanes crash near airports.

*

Once a year, I like to quote the prayer of Goethe, which to me makes more psychological sense than any other I have heard: Help us, God, and give us light so that we don't stand in our own way; let us do from morning to night what should be done; and give us clear ideas of the consequences of our actions.

*

Character is not so much *what* we do as *why* we do it — the world is full of busy people doing the right things for the wrong reasons, and wondering wistfully why the world isn't a better place than it is.

*

Many people think that "a sense of humor" consists in the ability to laugh at jokes, but that is only its lowest and crudest form; a genuine sense of humor consists in seeing the joke in things that most people ordinarily take with the utmost seriousness, and, conversely, in detecting the profound seriousness at the bottom of every good joke.

*

The poor in the past were better off than they are today; then, they had nothing, and owed nothing; today, they have a little, but they owe much more.

*

There are men proud to be fighting for lost causes, who would be horrified and struck with impotence if they thought the causes had any chance of winning.

*

Skepticism is the best mode of inquiry, but the worst philosophy of life; when skepticism ceases to be a *means* and becomes an *end*, it neutralizes its own moral force.

*

When a man finds it hard to sleep, it is generally because he is worrying about tomorrow; when a woman finds it hard to sleep, it is generally because she is worrying about yesterday.

*

The greatest resister to a movement is the man who started the movement and then learns that his followers are taking it farther than he ever contemplated. (An interesting modern example is Supreme Court Justice Black, in his recent civil rights decisions.)

*

All governments, all police forces, all authoritarian organizations, no matter what they preach in public, privately believe that the end justifies the means — and this deeply held belief is responsible for more mischief in the world than all individual wrongdoing.

*

People who hate, act their hate; but people who love, rarely act their love; thus the basic human problem is — how can we activate love so that it becomes something more than merely a diffuse sentiment?

*

The chief folly of intelligent people is to believe that the world is more rational than it is; because of this, they make miscalculations of judgment that less intelligent people don't make.

*

When we try to imitate successful men, in order to learn the secret of their fortune, we quickly learn that the main secret is that they had no need to try to imitate anybody else.

*

Fichte was only superficially right when he remarked that "The root of all morality is self-control"; the root of all genuine morality is self-respect.

*

If we have to *will* ourselves to relax, as a release from tension, it becomes as futile as *willing* ourselves to be happy when we are anxious; the mind-body complex cannot be commanded, it can only be invited to respond if it pleases.

*

The temptation to be well thought of by those around us can lead us into greater sins against the spirit than any of the classical temptations, such as lust, greed, or love of power.

*

The true course of world history — properly understood — doesn't consist of *events*, but of *motives;* the events are only symptoms, but we mistakenly take them for causes.

*

The current rage for spy novels and spy films and spy TV shows is our way of having our aggressive cake and eating it, too — for a spy, by definition, is a man who can lie, steal and kill, and still stay unpunished and "within the law" of the country he is working for.

*

The same beauty that initially attracts a man eventually repels him if there is no strength of character beneath it; and the same strength that initially attracts a woman eventually repels her if there is no tenderness of character beneath it.

*

Those pins some college students wear, "Make Love, Not War," embody a deep psychological truth: that an exaggerated power drive is a perversion and a thwarting of the erotic instinct in man, and aggressors from Alexander the Great to Hitler have always been deficient in the erotic area.

*

Try though we may to keep it out, vanity creeps in through all the little interstices of character: for instance, it is certainly a virtue to concede a point, but how many of us can do so without a tremor of pride at our magnanimity?

*

Only a man we have persuaded can be trusted; a man we have subdued must always be watched — and this is the practical advantage of reason over force, which conquering nations never understand.

*

We look to others for sympathy at our bad luck, yet we resent it if others are envious of our good luck; but why should we expect the one and not the other?

*

Perhaps nothing is as characteristic of a woman as the way she behaves toward hired help when no one else is around.

*

Whenever I hear a scientist speak with a great air of authority, I know he isn't a scientist, for his attitude contradicts the whole meaning of his vocation.

*

A "patriot" is too often a man who loves all the symbols of his country and very few of the people who comprise it.

*

A good storyteller is not as rare as a good nonstoryteller; that is, the man who can look in your eye, discern that you *have* heard it before — and stop.

*

I have never heard a truly intelligent person ever describe anyone else as a "cynic" — it is a word which fuzzy-minded people use to dismiss anyone whose views they find uncomfortable.

*

When a writer says, "to put it more simply," he should have done so in the first place.

*

Autobiographies by public figures always conceal more than they disclose; for the whole life of a public figure is one huge concealment, or distortion, of his inner self; and when this is most successful, the inner self gradually withers away, and only the public husk remains.

*

Infants should be picked up and fondled and fed when they cry and demand it; there is no danger of "spoiling" them, but failing to do so runs a fair risk that they will grow up feeling a fearful discrepancy between their deepest needs and the outside world's response.

*

One proof, among many, that men are more vain than women, is the fact that women often fear they are boring, while men, in their male conceit, are often quite boring to women without the slightest realization of it.

*

Speaking of women, when two female friends are on the telephone, they keep talking until they find something to say.

*

There may be some biological sense in the fact that there are so many more older widows than widowers; old men are more helpless and lonely than old women, less able to cope with the present or warm themselves with memories of the past.

*

The structure of authority is so precariously balanced that almost no ruler, or man in power, will publicly and voluntarily admit he has made a mistake; and most governmental crises are compounded not so much by malice or greed as by the felt necessity for defending and camouflaging past mistakes.

*

We know that knowledge today is rapidly becoming obsolete, and we must continually renew our education to keep up with new developments; why then do both liberals and conservatives cling to the naive notion that their past ideas of how society should be run are still practical, relevant, and valuable to the new generation?

*

The person who does nothing at all about a problem is not as morally culpable as the person who does less than his best; we realize we can expect nothing from the former, but the latter betrays us by assuming a responsibility he does not intend to fulfill.

*

When the implied motto of an executive is "Don't make waves," it is generally because he feels that any motion will knock him overboard.

*

Being busy may be better, for many people, than being idle — but, in the end, it is no substitute for having purpose.

*

There are no "superior" or "inferior" nations; there are only nations whose time has passed, whose time is here, or whose time is yet to come.

*

The law must always change, it cannot be static, it must develop in response to new conditions; yet the paradox is that unless it changes around a permanent axis, it does not deserve to have the legitimacy of what we mean by "law."

*

There is an art in complaining as well as in anything else — and some people's complaints about poor service or other defects go unheeded because they complain so querulously that they put themselves in the wrong even when they are in the right.

*

The double duty of friendship consists in helping a friend get rid of those illusions which are retarding to his progress while at the same time helping to sustain those illusions which are necessary for his self-esteem.

*

A baby, of necessity, is all take and no give; and growing into adulthood means redressing this balance by eventually giving to the world more than you take from it, or it means nothing.

*

There are people who are incapable of making deep, permanent and authentic contact with another single human being — and yet they imagine that they can make contact with God, and indeed often think of themselves as "religious."

*

It is extremely difficult to be a statesman of a high order, because such a person must do two things at once — to think like a man of action (which comes naturally to him), but also to act like a man of thought (which goes against the temperamental grain of most politicians).

*

The greatest punishment of laziness is witnessing the success of others who are far less talented, but more industrious.

*

The only way a man can get a woman to tell him a secret is to pretend no interest in it; this so infuriates her congenital sense of curiosity that she is forced to assail him with the secret.

*

The trouble with courtships is that they consist more of dinners than of breakfasts; anybody can be pleasant and endearing at dinnertime, but breakfasttime is the true test of character and comradeship.

*

The chief difference between a scholarly book and a popular one is that in the scholarly book the most interesting material is often to be found in the footnotes.

*

To understand a foreign country, it is not enough merely to live in it a long time, as many persons believe; it is also necessary to *think* in that country's way, or else one remains a perpetual stranger.

*

The cost is always too high for "keeping up appearances" at the expense of reality; not necessarily the financial cost, but the psychic cost in a loss of a genuine sense of identity.

*

Those who insist that something "can't happen here" have yet to learn that anything that has happened to mankind anywhere can also happen here, for our similarities to the rest of the human race are far greater than our differences.

*

When anyone remarks to me, "You can say that again," it makes me feel sorry I said it in the first place.

*

Trouble is like a voracious infant, and the more one feeds it with worry, the larger it grows; it can only be starved to death by judicious neglect, but few are resolute enough to adopt this firm regimen.

*

On the conscious level, Santayana was correct in saying that "Those who cannot remember the past are condemned to repeat it"; but on the unconscious level, it is truer to say that those who cannot *forget* the past are condemned to repeat it, and keep making the same old mistakes over again until they die.

*

There is practically no difference at all among reducing diets: all are equally effective or equally futile; the whole difference is in the dieters, in the *will* and not in the *way*.

*

The future of mankind belongs to those who are willing to take truth wherever it is to be found, and not to those who select only those truths they find palatable to their beliefs, customs and position; this, ultimately, is what separates the redeemable sheep from the irreclaimable goats.

*

What should teach us tolerance in personal relations is that all of us have dear friends who have other friends we cannot stand; nor must we expect all our friends to like all our other friends — for a bond between individuals is based on unconscious factors bearing little relation to reality.

*

The paradox of sudden failure amid success springs from the fact that often the very quality which lifts a person to the peak is the same quality responsible for his abrupt fall — for example, the aggressiveness that drives a man to the top can also drive him to self-destruction when he has reached the top and has nowhere to go but down.

*

Observers at the front are the last ones to know what is going on in a war, just as a chessman is incapable of realizing what is happening on the board.

*

We believe that everyone should practice what he preaches; but when we hear beatniks and the like preaching what they practice, we become unaccountably upset, for we really prefer hypocrisy to unconventionality.

*

Forcing young people to study who lack the desire to study is as absurd and futile as forcing someone to eat who has no appetite — and, ultimately, is just as regurgitative.

*

It requires a secure sense of maturity to accept the fact that what people say about us is always true — not *our* truth, perhaps, but *theirs*, and equally valid in the final equation of the personality.

*

Everyone has a right to discuss the turmoil in civil society today, but, likewise, everyone has an obligation to define for himself, as clearly as he can, the distinctions among "violence," "force," and "power."

*

When a reform succeeds, the sheer energy and power it required to attain its goal usually carries it beyond its goal, and eventually it becomes necessary to reform the reform.

*

The worst kind of remorse is not that we have done what we have done — but that we have become what we have become; remorse over misdeeds can be creative and regenerative, but remorse over lost character is inconsolable.

*

There are no perfectly straight lines in Nature, no perfect circles, no perfect organisms or specimens of anything; the whole idea of "perfection" is a human concept, and is to be found nowhere in Nature; whence, therefore, did it come, if not from Nature?

*

It is an absolute libel on childhood to say that children resist being taught; children *love* to be taught, and when they resist it is because something has already gone wrong with the child or with the system of teaching.

*

It always irks me when I am forced to complain about some merchandise and the clerk replies smugly, "We've never had a complaint on this before," which may only mean that most customers are too timid, too lazy, too busy, or too disgusted to pursue the fruitless matter.

*

How can we call someone "successful" when he has failed to realize his personal life, his social life, his spiritual life, his esthetic life — when he has, indeed, sacrificed all these sustaining elements for the sole purpose of succeeding in his acquisitive, or public, life?

*

It is a delusion that those engaged couples who know each other for a long time increase their chances for a happy marriage; for no matter whom you marry on Saturday, you wake up on Sunday married to somebody else.

*

The sense of morality can be defeated only by engaging in some activity that projects far beyond one's own time and

place; and it is ironic that those who have the greatest aversion
to death are precisely those who have least known what to do
with their lives.

*

"He preached a good sermon today" generally means
"one that applies more to the people around me than to me."

*

It is a *non sequitur* to think that because a teacher is "good
with little children" she would therefore be good with her
own, if she had any; for it is easy to be "good" with children
who are ultimately someone else's responsibility.

*

The main reason that social progress is so slow and painful
is that we are (quite properly) committed to majority rule as
the safest form of government, and yet history discloses that
it is the minorities of each age who most often turn out to have
been right — for instance, the majority of American colonists
opposed our bid for independence.

*

The shrewd man looks ahead; the simple man looks up; the
resigned man looks down; the frightened man looks behind;
only the wise man looks within.

*

In the complexity of modern society, a successful executive
is often one who is wasting time when he seems to be engaging
in business, and engaging in business when he seems to be wasting time; for in our tangled relationships, the cocktail hour is
often more productive than the conference table.

*

Although not classified as such in the medical dictionaries, the most common, widespread and deeply rooted form of mental disease is bigotry — and the only mental disease that is infectious within the family from childhood on.

*

The man who makes use of his good traits in order to further the cause of his bad traits is simply embezzling from his own account.

*

Genuine maturity is so hard to achieve because it consists of two opposite processes: Developing a sophisticated mind, while retaining a naive heart, believing little but trusting much.

*

Many a man can govern an empire who cannot govern his own son — for it is much easier to manipulate huge impersonal forces than to move one personality who knows you well.

*

It is not true that women want a great deal; a woman is quite content with very little, if that very little is precisely what she wants; if not, then nothing is enough.

*

Conservatives delude themselves by imagining that if we withdrew welfare from the poor they would become more industrious and self-reliant; liberals delude themselves by imagining that if we expand welfare to the poor they will become more productive and self-sufficient; neither policy is capable of healing the badly damaged psyche and self-image that the long-time poor have of themselves.

*

If you can't also love, in some funny way, the unattractive parts of your work, then you can never love the attractive part of it as much as you should. (And might not the same be said of loving our mates?)

*

We forget kindnesses far more easily than we forget injuries; for we unconsciously regard a kindness as something that is our due, while we regard an injury as utterly undeserved, even when it is not.

*

It is harder to dislike someone you know well than someone you know slightly; even a murderer, to those near him must seem almost as much victim as culprit.

*

Half the people miss the fruit for lack of energy in shaking the tree; while the other half sacrifice next season's crop by shaking so hard they tear the tree down.

*

Talking baby talk to a baby is absurd, for the baby isn't talking baby talk at all, but is expressing himself at the fullest capacity of his verbal powers, and should be respected as such.

*

You're not really educated until you can clearly express the differences among *education, learning, schooling,* and *infor-*

mation; and many persons who possess the latter three have little grasp of the first.

*

Most people who labor to obtain the approval of others do so because they believe that in this way they will win self-approval; but there is no necessary relationship between the two, and a million people exclaiming that you are good do not add up to one small voice within, for one's unconscious self-evaluation is impervious to the outside world.

*

When you begin to notice how well you feel — that is a sure sign of age.

*

Most of us would like to get rich not for unworthy motives but so that we could be more benevolent; yet the virtue of benevolence lies in being that way *before* one can afford it.

*

Our carelessness with words amounts almost to an anarchic contempt for meaning: In a college paper recently, I ran across the phrase "a new tradition on the campus."

*

To the employer who complains (and with justice), "We can't find good workers who care about anything except more pay," one is tempted to reply, "How many employers do you know who set an example by caring about anything except more profits?"

*

Even the idea of a "generation" has been accelerated in our time; it used to be considered 30 years, but the rate of growth has been so speeded up that about seven years is now the effective span of a generation, in psychological and social terms today.

*

Speaking of age, it used to be said that "the good die young"; now it is hard for the young to die good.

*

A woman in love tends to worry that the man doesn't love her back enough; and the irony in such matters is that her very concern tends to diminish his fund of spontaneous affection.

*

A man who can resist any form of bribery can nevertheless be swayed by flattery; and a man who can resist any other form of flattery can be swayed by the award of a plaque in his honor; only saints and utter misanthropes have the will to turn down an award, no matter how trivial it is.

*

In contemporary industrial society, the architect is subordinate to the builder — which is as ludicrous a situation as if the physician were subordinate to the hospital administrator in treating patients.

*

It is shallow to condemn the younger generation for "losing their standards," when in reality many of them have simply found *our* standards unacceptable in terms of their self-realization, and are seeking desperately for their own, because they don't like what ours have done to us.

*

Speaking of standards, both the hips and the squares could learn from one another, if each were not deaf to the other's values; but, in flatly rejecting each other, both have thrown out the clean baby with the dirty bath water.

*

Perhaps no other factor is more important in understanding a problem than that of "perspective" — half the time we can't comprehend a situation because we stand too far from it, and the other half because we stand too close to it.

*

Most philanthropy sustains the disease by making the symptoms more bearable.

*

It is a curious irony that the same person who thinks more of himself than he should also underrates his real value; a display of vanity almost invariably indicates ignorance of one's good points along with the false glorification of points that are not so good.

*

The whole psychological difference between our modern economy and the economy of the past is that in the past people lived *within their incomes,* and now they live *up to their expectations;* and who is to say that the latter is less realistic than the former?

*

Superiority of the body — as with athletes — makes us respectful; but superiority of the mind — as with intellectuals — makes us resentful; possibly this is because athletes don't try to tell us what to do, while intellectuals want to make us over in their own image.

*

A man without a *job* is merely unemployed; but a man without a *vocation* is scarcely alive, no matter how good or continuous a job he may hold.

*

For every one person ruled by thought, a hundred are ruled by appetite; for every hundred ruled by appetite, a thousand are ruled by custom, fear, and inertia.

*

One can always tell when a nation is preparing to violate justice against its neighbors — for then the ruler assembles great congresses and assumes all the formalities of law, in order to invest the transgression with the proper trappings of legality, hoping that the pomp will create a cover for the piracy.

*

We are grateful for narrow escapes in the course of life, but hardly anyone considers how narrowly he escaped not being born at all.

*

Note on Changing Times: A 40-year-old man I know recently shaved off his beard; when I asked him why, he replied, "Because I had the feeling it made me look too *young*."

*

We can improve ourselves only in the direction of our natural bent, and not against the grain; and most campaigns of self-reform fail because they take too much account of rules and not enough of temperament.

*

Women become expert in concealing love, men in concealing hate; but hardly anyone has enough skill in dissimulation to conceal indifference.

*

Revolutions are never begun by men of action, but by men of thought; thus, the first task of despotism is to exile the thinkers.

*

The hawks are half right in insisting that there is no victory in peace; what they cannot see is that there is no peace in victory, never has been, and never can be for very long.

*

The way a people *spend* their money is much more indicative of national character than the way they *make* their money; the latter is usually necessitated by natural resources and economic considerations, while the former is a free gesture expressing their basic drives.

*

The poorest prophet is the man who did well in different times.

*

Looking for direct "cause and effect" in history is a vain and fruitless pursuit — for every "cause" is itself the "effect" of some previous cause, and so we go backward *ad infinitum*.

*

By the time parents know enough to give sound advice, it is usually too late to make much difference one way or the other.

*

The personal dilemma of so many celebrities is that they are irritated by hangers-on and by public attention, yet they can't stand being alone.

*

Politics is the art of pretending that *everybody* will be better off if the politician's party is in power, whereas it is perfectly plain that no matter which party is in power, some elements will be better off and some will be worse off.

*

Human nature, as a whole, is somewhat manic-depressive: for things are never quite as good nor quite as bad as we think they are.

*

Hitting a child is always a sign of weakness; if an adult can't control a child merely with a look, his own character betrays a lack of authority that should be rectified before the child is blamed.

*

Silence and egotism go together more commonly than we suspect; the chatterbox merely hopes to be liked for what he expresses; the taciturn demands to be respected for what he contains.

*

We all like to learn, but we do not like being taught; therefore, the best teacher is he who seems to do the least teaching and makes us feel that we are learning for ourselves.

*

For every one person who is genuinely "broadened" by travel, a hundred are merely confirmed in their preconceptions and prejudices.

*

When a statement scandalizes you, when it seems utterly wrongheaded from beginning to end — that is the time to examine it most carefully, for it may contain a truth you have long suppressed, out of fear or embarrassment or rigid self-interest.

*

Attending church began, in the early days, as a *symbol* of religion; when did it become a *substitute* for it?

*

A clever man avoids all the little blunders that a stupid man stumbles into — and then falls into the most enormous pit that even a child would know enough to circumvent.

*

No one can get to "know himself" better through introspection, but only through action; *doing* is our best clue to *being*, and it is how we relate to the world (and not what we think about it) that determines our character.

*

We complain about the "apathy" of the people — but if people were less apathetic, might they not be more likely to respond to wild emotional appeals than to rational doctrines, and might the "apathy" of the public not be an unconscious guard against being aroused to primitive instincts by the witch doctors?

*

The ignorance of the unlearned is called simply "ignorance"; but the ignorance of the learned is dignified by the term "scholarship."

*

Almost nobody today gets "fired" from a job in the old-fashioned sense; those who are dismissed have put their heads on the chopping blocks and smoothly prepared the way for their own execution.

*

To "thank God" that your family was saved from a tornado, while the family across the street was blown to bits, is really to blaspheme against the true God.

*

Some problems present a vicious circle that cannot be broken within their own context: For example, as pollution gets worse, we have to drive farther to find clean air — and the farther we drive, the more we pollute the atmosphere.

*

Every weekend, the squares troop down to the neighborhood of the beatniks, to gawk and gape and giggle; but (along with a sense of superiority) there is also in them an envy and a wistfulness that they would be unwilling to admit, for the lost part of their nature.

*

The invariable sign of a bad writer is the use of strong adjectives and weak verbs; this is especially true in fiction, where poor writers are fond of "describing" what is happening, rather than *making* it happen.

*

A man finds it easy to be a friend to another man only if they share common goals; but a woman does not take to another woman unless they have different goals — this is why a woman very interested in men always picks as her best friend another woman who will serve as a confidante but never as a competitor.

*

Perhaps the principal difference between a "woman" and a "lady" is that a woman wants to be admired, while a lady wants to be admirable — which is a much harder and higher goal.

*

What the world most needs is a flexible fusion of the doctrine of the West — that action is paramount — and the doctrine of the East — that action is futile — so that we are neither infatuated with mere motion, nor immobilized by a sense of passivity.

*

One thing we try to teach children is to refrain from laughing at the infirmities of other individuals; yet, as adults, we can scarcely keep from snickering at the idiosyncrasies of other nations.

*

It may be the greatest and most dangerous fallacy committed by our popular fiction and films that marriages are divided into two classes, the "bad" and the "good"; for marriage is indeed divided into two classes, the "bad" and the "hard" — and conjugal wisdom consists in learning that one is lucky to have merely a "hard" one.

*

Those congressmen who said they would like to suspend the First Amendment to the Constitution — relating to free speech — in order to punish the more ardent war protesters, are, in my opinion, more "un-American" than any so-called subversives who have been dragged up before the House Un-American Activities Committee.

*

We are all aware of optical illusions in space; but few are aware of optical illusions in time, as it were, for we foolishly imagine when young that the second half of our life will be as long as the first half, and it never is, for time has an increasingly telescopic quality as we grow older.

*

A "well-adjusted" person nowadays is one who is reconciled to his lack of adjustment to the world, and neither mourns it nor fights it; to be obliviously adjusted to this world is to be insane along the same grain.

*

The weak hate because it makes them feel strong; only the strong know that hate makes them weaker.

*

One of the silliest and most-abused metaphors that people use to justify violence or retaliation is that "you must fight fire with fire"; but when fire is used to fight fire, it is for the purpose of *isolating* the uncontrolled fire — if the new fire were simply *joined* in battle with the old fire, it would only make a larger conflagration.

*

People who become easily outraged at long hair on young men or short skirts on young women are incapable of treating serious matters with suitable attention, since they expend so much moral energy on trivialities and social ephemera.

*

Only *natural growth* contains possibilities for permanence and value; things sudden and violent defy the natural process, and thus in the end do more harm than good.

*

A man said to me at lunch today, "I divorced my wife after 20 years, and I couldn't have cared less what happened to her; now that we've been apart for many years, I'm concerned when I hear she is ill — funny how it often takes time and distance to make us aware of intimacy."

*

Religion and nationalism are absolutely incompatible concepts, unless the latter is subordinated to the former; and when religion fails to preach and practice universal tenets, then nationalism becomes the true religion of the people.

*

Standing water soon becomes poisonous; and so do standing thoughts which are not fed regularly from fresh sources.

*

Passivity is never at a loss to justify itself; even a stopped clock, looking around at the ticking timepieces which are either too fast or too slow, must pride itself on the fact that it, at least, is absolutely right twice a day.

*

It is easier to fool those we work for than those who work for us.

*

Parents are largely incapable of recognizing the absurdity in spending the first two years of a child's life in persuading it to talk, and all the subsequent years in persuading it to keep quiet.

*

If I wished to punish a country, I would have it governed by those who considered themselves the only true patriots in it.

*

Beware of all those religious sects whose God has absolutely no sense of humor.

*

A man makes an effort to learn things about women, but still doesn't know them; a woman seems to know things about men without ever having learned them; and this is possibly because men use reason, and women use radar.

*

Speaking of women, what happens to all those girls who love to walk bareheaded in the rain — after they become wives?

*

The next time you are on the verge of making a sententious or facetious remark upon meeting a celebrity, pause and consider how many times he must have heard the same remark before, and how hard it is for him to summon up a sincere, spontaneous and polite reply — and don't say it.

*

Money doesn't change people; it merely acts like a kind of litmus paper, bringing out what was invisible but already there.

*

The paradox of age is that it brings wisdom only to those who have retained the capacity to see as a child sees; when the mind's eye hardens along with the arteries, age brings only petulance and prejudice.

*

Mentioning children brings to mind the common mistake made by parents, of wanting a child to be a credit to *them*; a child should be a credit to *itself*, and then the other will follow naturally.

*

There are no true synonyms in the language — the difference, for example, between "vision" and "sight" is the same woman in the evening and in the morning.

*

The greatest mistake you can make in life is to assume that you can see others more clearly than they can see you.

*

Livy's *History of Rome*, written 2,000 years ago, explains in a brief phrase the basic problem that confronts every thriving civilization, including ours: *"Nec vitia nostra nec remedia pati possumus."* ("We can endure neither our vices nor the remedies for them.")

*

We have a desperate need to label everyone; and when we run across someone who defies labeling, we label him a "maverick."

*

For every one bad person who lies in order to *cause* trouble, there are a hundred weak persons who lie in order to *avoid* trouble, and by so doing cause more trouble than the bad persons.

*

Children want to do as they like, and want to do as they're told; and unless given enough scope to do as they like, they cannot easily submit to doing as they're told.

*

A husband generally is satisfied if he feels his wife is "content"; a wife, on the other hand, does not find it sufficient if her husband is content — she must be sure it arises out of appreciation and not merely out of habit or inertia.

*

The aging process consists largely of redefining "pleasure" as the absence of pain.

*

The world will get better only when we stop *blaming*, for blaming is always a paranoid projection of our own feelings of inadequacy, and allows us to be as bad as we want to be, while pointing the finger elsewhere.

*

We can stand a great man only from a distance; when we get too close, he beckons us to imitate his character, and that is so frightful a chore that we must either run away or knock him down to our level.

*

It is impossible to have faith without patience; this is why quick minds generally tend to be skeptical.

*

We are more ourselves when playing than when doing anything we deem "serious"; for the way in which we play reveals a deeper stratum of our personality than the careful postures of our adult activities.

*

It's just our minor problems that can be "solved"; our major ones can only be outgrown.

*

In a tornado one must open the doors and windows, rather than shut them, for it is the disparity between outer and inner pressure that demolishes houses; and so it is in the drive for social equality, where closing our doors makes for destruction, and not for safety.

*

Despite the Protestant ethic to the contrary, *work* itself is a neutral activity, having no intrinsic virtue: That work is good which permits a man to enlarge his abilities and come to terms with his identity; and that work is bad or useless which encourages a man to shrink his abilities and disguise or run away from his identity.

*

When we wish to be younger, it is usually for a shallow reason.

*

Speaking of age, a charming woman is one who makes a youth feel mature, an old man youthful, and a middle-aged man just at the peak of ripeness.

*

The compulsive gambler is one who will take no real risks — he gambles on the throw of the dice or the luck of a horse, because he is afraid to gamble on himself, to wager his character against the monumental indifference of the world.

*

Beautiful girls don't win beauty contests, because beautiful girls don't enter them — for a truly beautiful woman would not submit to such commercialized vulgarity.

*

Watching the U.N. representatives on television, it occurred to me that the one characteristic all of them have in common is an intense humorlessness — and that the same single-minded dullness that propels them into statesmanship also makes it impossible for them to see the absurdity of proclaiming that their country is always right.

*

When a parent confesses he or she "can't handle" a child of 16, it is a safe conclusion that the child was mishandled at the age of six.

*

It takes a significant action to make a friend, but a trivial word can make an enemy.

*

Something may have been "good enough for our fathers" because they didn't know anything better; does anyone imagine that Washington would choose wooden false teeth if he were alive today?

*

The moralist fails to understand what wise women have long known — that the best antidote for lust is not indignation, but laughter.

*

When we are young, we would like to write a burning satire about mankind; as we get older, we realize such a book would have to be largely autobiographical in nature, for we ourselves have done as little to rectify the world's folly as those we scorned in our youth.

*

A fanatic is someone who believes that man's best friend is his dogma.

*

Marital conversations are usually ungratifying to the wife, simply because a woman can listen so much faster than a man can talk.

*

One of our unconscious superstitions is that hard luck is catching — which is why we uneasily avoid those who seem to be losers.

*

If you cannot endure to be thought in the wrong, you will begin to do terrible things to make the wrong appear right.

*

Alone of all creatures on earth, man and the shark share this one dubious distinction: They are their own worst enemies, and the only creatures more threatened by their own kind than by other species.

*

We try to make our children become more like us, instead of trying to become more like them — with the result that we pick up none of their good traits, and they pick up most of our bad ones.

*

Real evils can be either cured or endured; it is only imaginary evils that make people anxiety-ridden for a lifetime.

*

Nobody would even try to play the piano without study and patient preparation, but everyone thinks he is equipped to discourse on the most profound and complicated subjects without having made any serious attempt to master even their rudiments.

*

The man who thinks he is relying on "pure reason" is exhibiting as much blind faith in his reason as those he accuses of relying on blind faith.

*

If we took a picture of the molecules comprising a chair, it would look very much like "modern art"; therefore, what is the "reality" of the chair — the object we grossly see with our eyes, or the object revealed by the penetration of the microsope?

*

The best reason for implementing the U.N. in international disputes was given many years ago by Whitehead, when he observed: "The only justification in the use of force is to reduce the amount of force necessary to be used."

*

In life, unlike theater, there are no villains: there are only heroes who mistake their goals.

*

The people most eager for "new experiences" are generally those who haven't even known how to utilize the old ones.

*

Everything that is in the world is also in your head, and everything that is in your head is also in the world; until we learn to abolish the artificial (and crippling) distinction between "inner" and "outer," the human race will not begin to understand itself.

*

There's something unconsciously ironic in the slogan of the Birchers and other right-wingers: "Support Your Local Police," when at the same time these elements are doing their utmost to destroy confidence in the Supreme Court, which sets the law of the land.

*

The busy executive who boasts that he hasn't had a real vacation in five years often has no idea how fervently his subordinates may wish he would take one — for the benefit of the business.

*

When two persons profess their love, they ask each other, "How much?" which is a meaningless question; the real question, "How?" is rarely asked, and if it were, could not be answered in words.

*

About 90 percent of low-income patients in state hospitals are still incarcerated ten years after admission; and one wonders if their long incarceration has more to do with being poor than with being mentally disturbed.

*

The more successful one becomes, the more difficult one finds it to deviate from the formula and methods that made one successful — thus, when conditions change drastically, it is the newcomers who are most adapted to wrest success from the hands of the incumbents.

*

Speaking of change, students who shrug off academic subjects that "won't help you make a living" ought to realize that even the subjects that help you make a living will be obsolete a half-dozen years from now.

*

The underdog demands "equality" and the upperdog demands "liberty"; and neither can see that unless these two concepts are held in a just equilibrium, both are capable of wrecking the social fabric.

*

Children can accept the wickedness of giants and demons and dragons; what they find hard to accept is the wickedness of humans — which is why the violence in so many TV shows is far more upsetting to them than the goriness of ancient fairy tales.

*

When we see most clearly what we should be and do, that momentary glimpse is so painful that we voluntarily blind ourselves — and that blinding we call "reality."

*

People who are forever feeling themselves "insulted" are not only looking for it, but are actually encouraging it — unconsciously but purposefully — by setting up situations in which their self-esteem is bound to be bruised.

*

There is hardly a minority, no matter how wrong for its own time, that has not been right for some future time, and whose doctrines have not proved valuable generations hence; therefore, all minorities must be allowed free expression, not merely as a moral right, but because all doors must be left open to the future.

*

As long as there are human beings, there will be the idea of brotherhood — and the almost total inability to practice it.

*

Few things are more disconcerting than being utterly agreed with by a person whose general views one finds revolting.

*

It used to be truer that "knowledge is power" — but in a technological age, power simply *buys* knowledge, and harnesses it for its own ends.

*

A systematic philospher likes to think that his theory is as wide as reality — but, in most cases, his perception of reality tends to be as narrow as his theory.

*

Until modern times — say, the last 300 years — all previous civilizations looked backward to a Golden Era that might be restored; only in modern times have we had a looking *forward* into a Golden Era that might be attained; and is it not possible that our vision of the future is as much a delusion (of infantile wishing) as their vision of the past?

*

"The world must be made safe for democracy," said Woodrow Wilson in his War Address to Congress in 1917; now, exactly 50 years and two World Wars later, there is less democracy in the world than there was then — and we are still trying to make it "safe" by increasing armaments every year.